About the Author

Joe Varley is a Yorkshireman, cricketer, quiz writer and novelist.

His name can be seen on the wall of *Pog Mahones* in Queenstown, New Zealand, as one of the original members of the 100 Pint Guinness Club. He regrets not drinking 200 pints.

To Angela,

Happy reading!

Hard Up
Down Under

A Working Holiday in
New Zealand

JOE VARLEY

Fisher King Publishing

Hard Up Down Under

Published by
Fisher King Publishing
The Studio
Arthington Lane
Pool-in-Wharfedale
LS21 1JZ
UK

www.fisherkingpublishing.co.uk

Acknowledgements

The author would like to thank the people of New Zealand: passionate, down-to-earth and honest. Special thanks to Crispin Middleton, Graham Bailey (G-Man), Chris Whitaker and Alexis Middleton. A particular shout-out to Patrick Lahood.

An approving nod to all players and members of Ilkley Cricket Club – one of the best amateur clubs in Yorkshire, and therefore in the UK. You know who you are.

Thank you to Elsa Witty and Francesca Lambert for their advice and creativity with the title of this book. Thanks to my family, and especially Mum and Dad. To all who attended Aberystwyth University from 1996-1999: massive respect and thanks. Again, you know who you are.

Lastly, thanks to Singapore Airlines for getting me to New Zealand... and back again. It was worth it.

HOMER: Listen to me, Mr Bigshot! If you're looking for the kind of employee who takes abuse and never sticks up for himself, I'M YOUR MAN! You can treat me like dirt and I'll *still* kiss your butt and call it ice cream. And if *you* don't like it, *I* can change!

MR BURNS: I like your attitude – feisty yet spineless!... Welcome aboard, son!

Jeff Martin, 'I Married Marge',
The Simpsons, Fox TV, 1991

'He'll be giving it everything, but he hasn't got everything to give.'
Ian St. John

'Yes, boss. Anything you say.'
Joe Varley

PART 1

North Island

Chapter One

In *The Rum Diary*, Hunter S. Thompson observed: 'Arriving half-drunk in a foreign place is hard on the nerves. You have a feeling that something is wrong, that you can't get a grip.'

No shit, Hunter.

I was half-drunk when we landed in Singapore. More accurately, I was a wreck - a red-eyed, befuddled wreck. Damn those air stewardesses. Damn their eye-catching uniforms, faultless make-up, and their shapely figures. I tried to stop the Oriental minxes serving me drinks - I really did - but they were quite persuasive. Several beer-and-whiskey combinations came my way, each one sweeter than the last. I told them I was a sensible traveller looking for adventure, and hadn't flown long distance just to get tanked up on alcohol. I summoned a stewardess and launched into a polite tirade explaining that passengers shouldn't be *encouraged* to imbibe so much booze at 30,000 feet. She smiled bashfully and produced another bottle.

'Relax, Sir, you're flying Singapore Airlines. Another beer?'

Arriving half-drunk in a foreign place *was* hard on

the nerves. I *did* have a feeling that something was wrong and I *couldn't* get a grip. Bright lights scorched my eyes. Walking in a fashion akin to a mentally sane person was impossible. Changi Airport became a blurred playground. I staggered like a chimp on ether, my apish gait terrifying fellow travellers. I also smelt like a wheelie bin, and my stubble sent a small child running for cover.

The six-hour wait before re-boarding was tediously long. Long, but it wasn't hell. Changi was cool, garnished with tropical plants, and exceptionally clean. It was an antibacterial advert: 'For sparkling clean floors, Singapore recommends Cif.' So strict are the litter laws that if you drop anything - be it chocolate wrappers, chewing gum or bullet casings - the security guards hit you with a hefty fine. Or just hit you. Or hit you and imprison you for 58 years. I daren't buy food lest a stray wrapper found its way to the authorities; I couldn't face being fined or punched, and the prospect of jail-time thrilled me less. Never had six hours felt so long.

It was Crispin's fault.

I'd graduated in zoology a few weeks ago from The University of Wales, Aberystwyth. My tutor was the exceptionally-named Dr Fish, an academic committed to the delights of marine biology. Dr Fish's enthusiasm for aquatic arthropods was unrivalled in the greater

Aberystwyth area, and perhaps still is. He delivered his lectures with uncompromising flair, often quoting from his critically-acclaimed work, *A student's guide to the seashore*. Word spread around the campus it was the most indispensable textbook on the market. Sadly, it was only effective if opened and read.

For the first two years I bombed. Though the highlight was undoubtedly my second-year thesis *The Morphology of British Moulds and other Fungi,* the problem was the content of the course. Zoology - it evoked studying remarkable animals, weird genetic mutations, and dissecting frogs doused in chloroform. Instead, we got fruit flies, fungal forays ('We put the fun in fungi!'), and green seaweed. It's hard to get excited about green seaweed.

In my third year, Dr Fish ordered me to write a one-off essay. It was do-or-die. If the end product met with his satisfaction I'd graduate. If I failed I'd be shelf-stacking at Tesco's. Both options could be a problem.

The obstacle was the subject of the essay, which was chosen by Dr Fish - who else? After possibly two minutes into his coffee break he informed me to write 2,000 words on barnacles, the most lacklustre of crustaceans - and possibly of all animals. But at least it wasn't green seaweed.

My essay was uninspiring, naturally. According to a dictionary, a barnacle is 'a marine shellfish that lives attached to rocks, ship bottoms, etc'. What a bum deal. No wonder my essay lacked inspiration. Barnacles don't do anything; they just *cling* to things. Their one noteworthy feature is the length of penis, the longest in the animal kingdom in proportion to body length. So in a whirlwind three hours cranked on caffeine, I wrote six pages on barnacle penises. It wasn't enjoyable, and it wasn't action-packed reading. In fact, I barely remembered writing it at all.

Miraculously, the barnacles flattered me; I passed. Dr Fish shook my hand and wished me the best of luck. When asked to provide job references, he deliberated awkwardly and said, "Well, errrr... no." He was more eloquent in his lectures.

Still, I was a graduate and rightly euphoric. So much so I met Crispin in a pub to relay the good news. I'd met him "in halls" and we clicked instantly. Crispin is a gangly Yorkshireman with frizzy blonde hair, a connoisseur of the natural world. He graduated with a "first" in marine biology and has irrefutable memory, his forte remembering Latin names of cephalopods just as football fans recall past FA Cup glories (though recalling species of squid remains an unproductive chat-up line). Crispin's knowledge of fish verges on the obsessive. It's scary. Knowing that sticklebacks belong to the family *Gasterosteidae* is plainly useless, but he enjoys informing everyone of this precise fact.

He's permanently suntanned and a keen traveller with an exotic taste, having potholed in Java, abseiled in Malaysia, scuba dived in Belize, and snorkelled the Great Barrier Reef. I'd been paddling in Wales.

'So... Dr F passed you with an essay on barnacles?' Crispin said, handing me a pint. 'What the hell?'

'It's true.'

'You graduated with an essay about copulating barnacles?'

I shrugged. 'Well, it was really about their sexual organs.'

'And you called it *Big Dick*?'

'Yup.'

'Joe, you're an idiot.'

'An idiot with a degree,' I said.

'*Big Dick*? Why would you call an essay... I mean who would... what the - ?'

'OK, what would *you* have called it?'

Crispin sipped his cider, possibly for effect. 'Anything but *Big Dick*?'

It was a good point. At that moment the past three years flashed by in appalling reality. Had Dr Fish sent me a subliminal message when he ordered me to write about barnacles? Surely it wasn't a coincidence.

And then it struck me.

'Joe,' said Crispin. 'You still with me?'

Could it be that barnacles and I had similar qualities?

Barnacles are largely useless, and immobile to boot, stuck in the same place whilst the world carries on regardless. These crustaceans are as unmotivated as any organism can be. The more I thought about it, the more apparent it became: Dr Fish had played a cruel trick and suggested my ambition was comparable with a tiny invertebrate that clings to rocks. And ship bottoms. Suddenly I felt my life had zero significance.

'... Joe?'

'Sorry, mate. I was thinking. Barnacles are useless, aren't they?'

'Pretty much.'

'What would happen if, say, they were all wiped out today?'

'To be honest, no one would notice.'

'Just what I thought.' Crispin's words hit me hard: *no one would notice*.

'Listen mate, you think Dr F took pity on me?'

Crispin emitted a low snort. 'No, of course not. He passed you because you're an expert in barnacles!'

If he'd any shred of remorse Crispin would've contemplated why he was berating a fellow science graduate and best pal. Instead he said something of far more consequence.

'Enough of barnacles. I'm off to New Zealand in three weeks.'

Crispin had always been impulsive; it's in his nature

to be adventurous. One minute he'd be insulting you, the next he'd be jetting off halfway around the world. Still, this was a bombshell by his own zany standards.

'You're going where?'

'New Zealand.'

'But that's... what... about ten thousand miles away?'

'Eleven thousand two hundred and seventy five, to be precise.'

'It's a bloody long way.'

'That it is.'

'So I won't see you again for... ' My voice trailed off as I realised my friend was sailing off into the sunset, leaving me to sort out my life and wondering why I had called my university essay *Big Dick*.

'Depends. My visa's just come through, so I'll be there for a year... maybe more.'

'Doing what?' I sounded confused, and a little frantic.

'I've landed a job with a marine research company. Called NIWA. It's part of a working holiday. Cool, huh?'

'Suppose '

Crispin chuckled, certainly knowing I was as happy for him as I was feeling sorry for myself.

'Joe, why don't you join me?'

'You *what*?'

'You heard.'

'I'm skint. How would I get there... and get a job?'

My friend gesticulated as if swotting away a fly. 'Beg,

borrow, steal. I'm not loaded myself; my aunt bought my plane ticket. As for working - you'll get a job. There are loads going over there.'

Crispin had lost the plot. Working halfway around the world for a year was a terrifying prospect. It wouldn't be a gap year; I'd *already* been to university. This was bonkers. I'd never been farther than Normandy.

I took a glug of lager, my cranial neurones immediately ignited. Maybe the idea wasn't beyond my capability. It could be the spark I was yearning for. After all, as far as I was aware New Zealand was a safe country devoid of war, famine, and pestilence. Perhaps my fishy friend wasn't as loopy as I thought. More lager... and the clogs of doubt ticked in my brain. I became wary. Who went on holiday to *work*? A 'working holiday' was a ridiculous contradiction, surely, like Cliff Richard's *Greatest Hits*.

'It's not a good idea.'

'*Trust* me,' said Crispin. 'Have I ever let you down?'

'No, but - '

'I know you'll come, Joe.'

'Really, and why's that?'

'You're a graduate. You're scared of the real world. Besides, you've got nothing better to do.'

It was true: I didn't have anything better to do. I felt doomed - unless a barnacle farmer required someone with a specific knowledge of crustacean breeding. A menial job was feasible, but I needed a spark; a goal to shake me from the shackles of apathy... otherwise I'd be that barnacle *clinging* to things.

My pint disappeared swiftly. 'Okay,' I told Crispin. 'You're on!'

We clicked our glasses, and Crispin wandered to the bar for more drinks, muttering, '*Big Dick*? Jesus Christ...'

And just like that, my fate was sealed.

To his credit Crispin is usually the voice of reason - an experienced Yoda to my immature Skywalker. He really hadn't let me down yet. Maybe I could add value to my life, if only for a year.

But my knowledge of New Zealand was limited. So limited, in fact, that I only knew it was 11,275 miles away. I vaguely recalled speaking to a Kiwi last year who came to Yorkshire to play rugby. Leighton enlightened me about his country folk. Apparently New Zealanders were devoted to animal-related activities like milking cattle, shearing sheep and culling deer with spear rifles. Kiwis were hard; the men were "men's men" and the women didn't back down when challenged to an arm wrestle. New Zealanders, Leighton told me, relished the great outdoors and excelled in backbreaking farm work. They grappled feral pigs - and enjoyed it. Local magazines included *NZ Pig Hunter*, *Hooked on Boars* and *More-Pork*. Leighton could've been pulling my leg with the last one, or possibly all three.

Most stereotypes are inaccurate, but Leighton revealed Kiwis *were* independent "hard cases" obsessed with sport. Rugby in New Zealand was not a pastime; it was a religion. It was something to respect and to alter the mood. That the All Blacks won was expected. When they lost, the nation descended into a collective melancholy. Curtains were drawn and telephones switched off. Thousands of working hours were lost when rugby disciples stayed in bed, unable to face the outside world. After a rare Kiwi defeat, the All Blacks caused a National Blues. Seldom does one sports team influence a country's spirits, and so spectacularly.

New Zealanders were also resourceful. Nothing pleased them more than rolling around in animal muck assembling farm machinery from three sheets of corrugated iron, a handful of bolts and a large rubber band. They revelled in a hard day's graft, and their social life comprised drinking and provoking the Aussies. This sounded grand, but I needed to find a job out there.

Such was my ignorance I did a little light reading. It soon became clear the real problem with a working holiday was that you had to work: you actually had to get your hands dirty. Fruit picking and heavy-duty labour were all the rage amongst those living the NZ dream, but that didn't appeal to me. I'd be content working in an office where pretty girls brought me cappuccinos all day long. Surely that wasn't too much to ask?

A month later, as the plan evolved, my question was answered by Crispin's first e-mail from Auckland, New Zealand's largest city:

From: fishyfiend99
Subject: COMPOST

Joe my boy!!

How's it going? All's good over here. The job's going well and I've just been out on the high seas on a boat looking for lobsters. Life doesn't get much better than this baby! ☺

Summer's just started and the weather's great. Everyone's friendly and the girls are awesome!! Honk honk!

Listen, I've got some news for you. Forget about looking for a job when you get here - you can work at my brother's garden centre. Remember Alexander? He's the manager and he owes me a favour. He'll pay you minimum wage to carry compost around!! (C'mon... it's not as bad as it sounds!) BTW, have you got your work visa yet?

You can do all sorts of stuff over here. It's incredible: paragliding, abseiling, bungy jumping, skiing, heli-skiing, zorbing, mountain biking, surfing, windsurfing, snowboarding, diving, snorkelling, sailing, white-water rafting, kayaking, hiking, tramping, skydiving...

My heart sank. I'd gone from high-flying Business Executive to Compost Carrier. I would be a drudge, a lackey... a dogsbody. But I had to look on the bright side: I'd scored a job without even looking. You had to grab these opportunities with two hands, and it seemed my two hands would be grabbing bags of decomposed organic matter.

'Nice work,' I replied. 'But have you found a decent pub yet? And what the fuck is zorbing?'

Like most Britons who don't carry mosquito repellent, I'm a bit naïve when it comes to foreign travel. The truth was, I knew practically nothing. My one experience of air travel was as a nine-year-old flying a kite in my local park. I thought New Jersey was something you received at Christmas. I assumed Guadeloupe was a type of melon, and that Yemen was a Caribbean greeting. Only recently it was explained that Sierra Leone wasn't a model of car.

This gullibility led me to the library, and to more research. In an atlas it was forgivable to assume New Zealand was a short 'hop, skip and a jump' away from its larger cousin, Australia. It's not. The distance from Sydney to Auckland is comparable with that from Manchester to Moscow. I read several books, all of which indicated a clear difference between the two nations. Both despised being mistaken for each other.

Australia was in-your-face, the brooding older brother with leather jacket, hair slick with gel and a girl on each arm. New Zealand was unassuming, the pimply public schoolboy who'd had his tuck-box stolen.

New Zealand lacked prominent opera houses and famous zoos and large red rocks in a giant sandpit. They couldn't care less. Kiwis were happy living hundreds of miles from anywhere and being fiercely proud of their identity. In fact, nothing riled a Kiwi more than being asked, 'Mate, where in Australia are you from?'

Life in New Zealand was fresh air, spectacular walks, and quaint gardens where locals talked about stuff that happened 50 years ago. New Zealand also scored points for lacking places called Humpybong, Buckleboo, or Humpty Doo. What the Kiwis did have were magical glaciers and prehistoric forests, secluded white-sand beaches and towering national parks, as well as unpronounceable towns like Pukekohe, Paraparaumu and Whangaparaoa. The climate sounded spot on - a bit warmer than the British summer - and the alcohol was cheaper. It received a doubled thumbs-up. New Zealand sounded like a remarkable country marooned in the South Pacific quite content living a few years behind the times whilst sticking two fingers up at the rest of the world. And you really couldn't fault her for that.

I spent more time researching New Zealand than I did on my barnacles (a whole nation trumps a crustacean every time). In 1840, the Treaty of Waitangi guaranteed the Maori full possession of their land in exchange for their recognition of British sovereignty. Then in 1893 New Zealand became the first country to give women the green light to vote. A few years later it became an independent dominion. New Zealand then sent troops into World War I and II, helped Britain in the Boer War, and mucked in when needed in Korea. For a country with a small population, New Zealand has done a lot of mucking in.

80% of New Zealand's 4.5 million people live in cities. Population density is low; South Island is about as big as England with the population of Birmingham. There are more females than males, and birth rate doubles death rate. New Zealand grows at a rate of one person every 23 minutes and 31 seconds. Life expectancy is a shade under 80. There is 99% literacy. Three quarters of the population are NZ European, a tenth are Maori, a few are Pacific Islanders, with the rest labelled "miscellaneous".

My research was enlightening, and one name cropped up regularly. He was a pioneer and a gentleman, and his name was Captain James Cook. Born in Yorkshire, Cook became the first European to map New Zealand's shores in his ship, the *Endeavour*. His three major voyages required courage and resolve, qualities that I needed on my adventure. Cook prospered on the high seas and made friends with the native Maori, whilst analysing New Zealand's coastline and conducting scientific experiments. Cook was an eighteenth century all-rounder, a true superstar. He took all plaudits and held his head high... until the natives of Hawaii chopped it off in 1779.

Captain Cook and I didn't have much in common. For a start he's dead. He knew his port from his starboard. The only thing going for us was that we were both Yorkshiremen. That said, after rigorous research, I felt like I knew him, and I felt I should at least try to emulate some of his achievements during my stay in New Zealand. For that reason I devised a football-style scoring system to compare my progress with the Captain. It wasn't very precise - even juvenile - but served to give me a fair self-assessment of my headway abroad. Here's how it worked: at the end of each chapter I awarded a point to either myself or Captain Cook depending on my successes or failures. For instance, if a chapter involved earning lots of money, scoring a date or experiencing a new activity, I gave myself a rather smug point. Alternatively, if I embarrassed myself in any way, a well-deserved point went to the Captain. If it was too close to call, a draw was declared. The pendulum of bias swung in my direction but, by God, I needed all the help I could get.

Before I set off, Crispin sent me a final e-mail:

From: fishyfiend99
Subject: CHRIS AND G-MAN

Joe!

Hope you make it to Auckland in one piece...

Remember that your luggage goes DIRECTLY TO NEW ZEALAND so don't try finding it in Singapore. I know what you're like!

Guess what? I've bought a Toyota! I picked it up from a Maori who tried to sell me drugs. Alexander reckons it looks like shit but don't let that put you off.

More news: Graham is coming over soon, and Chris should be here nearer Christmas. I've rented all of us a flat in a suburb called Kingsland – I'll send the address later. Your room is a bit small and smells like wet towels, but the rent is cheap. It'll just be like uni again!

I've just got a bank account with ANZ so we'll get you set up when you arrive. How much money are you bringing? Beer is 5 dollars if that's any help! Kiwis call boozing "drinking piss"!

Listen – about the garden centre. Alexander says you'd better not be a lazy sod when you work for him. He's keeping the compost warm for you! See you in the City of Sails baby!

Your friend,

Crispin.

P.S. Don't get too drunk on the plane.

The first noticeable thing about Auckland - the northern gateway to 'The Land of the Long White Cloud' - was the heat. It wasn't hazy or muggy, but a 'clean' warmth that penetrated the soul. Though tolerable, it was as clear as my festering armpit sweat. I had obviously underestimated the heat; it was September (their spring), and I was wearing two pairs of pants and a woolly hat.

The taxi was comfortable - if a little soggy - and I felt a wave of serenity one would expect after a 30-hour journey. My driver, Tamati, was a chatty soul, but strangely didn't ask for a destination, instead simply driving off in what I assumed was the correct direction. Tamati was a talker all right. He'd spent his whole life in Auckland and was the son of a retired ship builder who worked by the harbour for 30 years. His mother had passed away (car accident in Pakurunga Heights) and he had three brothers and two sisters. Five tattoos adorned his left arm and he cherished the Auckland Blues rugby team as much as his family.

All this I knew in the short time I'd been in his company. It was becoming apparent that Kiwis were friendly folk, eager to share their interests and family life with total strangers, but when I told Tamati about my 12-month plan he looked genuinely sceptical.

'Let me get this straight, young fella. You flown all

around the world coz you got nuthin' better to do, and now you gonna be workin' in a garden centre liftin' bags of *compost*?' Tamati whistled in awe, but he knew I was deadly serious. Then a peculiar grin danced across his face. 'Damn, boy, you're bloody crazy!'

Quite. Then, without reason or provocation, Tamati developed a dangerous taste for overtaking. He became a maniac. He wove in and out, regardless of other vehicles. Wing mirrors were redundant. After rugby, it seemed overtaking was New Zealand's favourite pastime. Maybe Kiwis had a talent for doing something without thinking, then shrugging their shoulders when they didn't pull it off. Their motto was: 'If at first you don't succeed, carry on until someone gets hurt.'

Low-slung wooden houses either side of the South-Western Motorway whizzed past at alarming speed. We tore onto a bridge suspended over pristine water. Tamati narrowly missed an oncoming truck, quipped, 'That was close, eh!' and then poked an elbow into my ribcage. 'Hey, you wanna know somethin', Bro?' This was a mild shock as no one had ever referred to me before as 'Bro'. Was it derogatory Kiwi lingo for 'English dog'?

'Guess how many times I've crashed? Twice. Not bad, eh?'

'Depends how long you've been driving I suppose.'

'Dunno, Bro. Three?'

I nodded approvingly. 'Two crashes in three years

really isn't... HEEEEYYYY*!* Watch that car!'

Tamaki veered wildly into his permitted lane. 'Sorry, Bro. One of these days I'll have a *serious* crash. You were sayin'?'

I caught breath. 'I was saying two crashes in three years isn't that bad. Well, not really.' If I played to his ego we'd reach Kingsland in one piece. My friend Leighton mentioned his fellowmen were poor drivers. If there was one thing omitted in the guidebooks, it was New Zealand's atrocious road-death rate (an "L" plate on a Kiwi car means "*LOOK!* NO HANDS!").

'You're funny, Bro! Nah, I've crashed twice in three *months.*' Tamati punched the steering wheel and whooped with delight. Then he said, 'And I'm gonna git me licence soon, eh!'

Fan-bloody-tastic. Though I couldn't help wondering if Tamati had fabricated his story just to scare me, I spent the rest of the journey grasping the armrest and making damn sure my seat-belt was secure. Another thing I quickly caught on to: Kiwis are far too honest and had a warped sense of humour - sadistically so.

Kingsland is a sleepy community of 4,000 nestled between the suburbs of blissful-sounding Mt Eden and dull-sounding Mt Albert. For 'sleepy' read 'comatose'. Kingsland had apparently swallowed a packet of Diazepam washed down with Horlicks. The area was developed a century ago - and most of the locals may have been at the opening ceremony. Suddenly I was aware of a stifled murmur, which could have been the taxi's mechanics or the chirping of crickets... or 4,000 people snoring.

We waddled onto New North Road, took a sharp right, and slowed down on Third Avenue. The engine hiccuped twice, then died to a slow hiss. At this exact point I realised that my journey from a small Yorkshire town to an Auckland suburb had reached its conclusion. Captain Cook himself couldn't have made better progress.

'Here we are, Bro,' Tamati said, delighted by arriving without major incident. His tattooed biceps swelled like balloons as he helped with my suitcase. Tamati was a dreadful driver, but the big man had manners.

Thin, symmetrical trees lined the road on both sides. Sunlight burned the dark tarmac as a wrinkly lady carried her shopping. Across the road an old Pacific Islander sat forlornly on the pavement swigging from a tattered brown paper bag. Behind a jagged city skyline the marine horizon was peppered with spooky-looking islands. It was all supremely foreign, but hardly the depiction of a city enjoying a weekend to the max.

'Bro, what's the number?'

'Forty-three A.'

'Forty-three, ay?'

'Er, no... forty-three... *A*.'

Tamati laughed. 'Follow me.'

He led me down rickety wooden steps onto a veranda. He dropped my bag outside the front window and stepped back to admire his work. I peered through a blind but maybe Crispin wasn't home.

'Thirty bucks, Bro. Hey, maybe I'll see ya in town? I can recommend *Mermaids*. Best strip club in town.' Tamati let out a lecherous cackle, and then disappeared with a friendly wave. Bad driver, impeccable etiquette... and a genuinely nice guy.

Chapter scorecard: A nice start for the boy Varley, but perhaps too early to achieve the first point. Captain Cook would be content with a draw, as they'll be plenty more chances for them both.

Chapter 2

Approximately 40 hours ago I'd been standing in the rain waiting for Dodgy John to take me to Manchester Airport. I'd drunk three coffees prior to checking-in, smoked five cigarettes, and read *The Daily Mail* twice from cover-to-cover (they were still apologising for slander). I'd boarded successfully, got drunk, avoided trouble in Singapore, arrived in Auckland without a hangover, and was now in a small suburb with all my luggage intact. It was progress. On his first voyage, Captain Cook spent seven weeks repairing damages after crashing into the Great Barrier Reef (hardly an inconspicuous obstacle).

I charged through the door with a little too much fervour, dropping my luggage and yelling, 'Cooo-eee! I'm here!'

To my left, a shadow danced on black-and-white kitchen tiles. I opened both arms theatrically to receive Crispin's embrace. 'Give us a hug, you frizzy-haired fish fucker!'

A large head edged through the kitchen opening. It was debatable whether this man had an unnatural fondness for fish, but his lack of frizzy hair was clearly evident. In fact, his head was completely bald.

'Take anything you want!' the man pleaded. 'Anything! Please, just take what you want and go!'

I was baffled. Did Kiwi tradition dictate they invited newcomers into their homes and stake claim to their household possessions?

'Is Crispin in?'

'Please, just - '

'Is this number forty-three?' I asked.

'It's forty-one!'

'Ah... I'm looking for forty-three.'

'It's next door. Please, just... '

'My mistake. Sorry for calling you a fish fucker. By the way, I'm your new next-door neighbour.'

I back-tracked with apologetic steps. Moving quickly I ventured back to Third Avenue, a grimace forming on my perspiring mouth. I knocked on number 43 and tiptoed inside.

Crispin jumped from the sofa as if expecting me. He was healthy and tanned (of course), his curly blonde hair boasting a sun-drenched candyfloss texture. My friend leapt forward to give me a rib-crushing hug. 'Joeeeeeeeeeey, you *made* it!'

Crispin twirled me around like a ballerina, my feet skimming the floor.

'Hi mate! Got a beer?'

Weird. That's the only word I could think of. The

packing and the long-haul flight and the six-hour stopover in Singapore were a distant dream. I forced myself to remember where I was: a country I'd seen only in books and on TV; a country as far from home as possible; a country in which I couldn't afford any serious cock-ups for the next 12 months.

Crispin put me down, surprised. 'You really want a beer?'

'Yeah mate! Why not?'

'It's two in the afternoon, Joe.'

'And... ?'

Crispin clapped my shoulders and laughed. 'I'm not working tomorrow so sod it. Let's get hammered!'

He grabbed my suitcase and underarmed it casually through an open door. Within seconds he thrust a cold can of VB into my hand. I slumped into the weary-looking sofa and shook out a Lucky Strike.

Crispin threw me a lighter. 'I'll give you the guided tour in a minute. It'll take... uh, about a minute.'

'No probs. By the way, I called our next-door neighbour a fish fucker.'

'Old Man McMillan? Nice one Joe, that'll hold you in good stead.'

I drained my beer and threw the crushed can into an opened bin liner. 'Next!'

On the veranda we sipped numerous VBs and huffed cigarettes under an indigo sky. A muffled buzz of insects interrupted what was an otherwise gentle serenity. In the distance the Sky Tower, Auckland's most prominent landmark, gleamed bright red and purple. It was a flashing alien structure – an immense concrete needle with Christmas lights. Built in 1997 the Sky Tower stands over 300 metres, making it the tallest free-standing structure in the southern hemisphere. I later learnt that it exerted an attraction over a new tourist, like a fierce magnetic pull. It's hardly ever out of view, whether you're ten miles from town or stuck in traffic in the city centre; a phenomenon probably echoed in Kuala Lumpur by The Petronas Towers and by Toronto's CN Tower. If ever you become disorientated in Auckland you simply spin around 360 degrees and there is the Sky Tower staring smugly back at you thinking, 'Lost again, you Pommie fool?'

Despite suffering from the exhausting flight I was itching to go out. Fresh alcohol seeped through my veins, planning a new party. Captain Cook would surely have had similar feelings upon his arrival to pastures new. Staying home on your first night in a new town, I reflected, is like flying to Italy to see Michelangelo's *David* only to complain of a headache. So after more beers we called for a taxi to take us to our first antipodean drinking experience.

We started on Karangahape Road, a bustling area so infamous it's simply known as "K Road". Auckland's nucleus of late-night entertainment is a stretch of concrete sleaze jam-packed with neon-lit nightclubs, bohemian music bars and bawdy sex shops. All this and more! K Road is also the city's red-light district, where women take out their teeth before offering nookie at 30 bucks a go. Booze shops like Liquor Land, Liquor Centre and Liquor 4 Pleasure tempt customers with placards that read "Buy 12 bottles of grog, throw up, and if you're *still* not satisfied, go someplace else". One porn shop advertised a "genuine lifelike gimp costume". Crispin swore he'd never been to it.

The first bar on Crispin's hit-list was half-dark and deathly quiet. Drinkers acknowledged our entrance with nods but made no further attempts at interaction. A small group of hardened drinkers sat in a corner, eyeing us with murderous intent. My affable smile wasn't reciprocated. One beer was one too many. I tugged at Crispin's sleeve as would a child to a parent. It was time to leave.

There was a 24-hour joint next door. It was a 'spit-and-sawdust' place: the sawdust undetectable, the spit unavoidable. Approaching the bar, I chin-nodded in the direction of the nearest barmaid. She looked like Ken Dodd in a house of mirrors. 'What's a nice girl like her,' Crispin whispered, 'doing with a face like that?'

Leather-clad drinkers packed the bar with BO and attitude. I'd never seen so many tattoos. Maoris loved them. To the Maori, tattoos are not a loving memorial of their first childhood romance or a dedication to their favourite football team. Tattoos aren't a symbol of masculinity purely undertaken to impress college girls. Tattoos are symbols of pride. Each tattoo is deeply personal – a statement of history, a devotion to their ancestry. Tattoo parlours in New Zealand are big business, and the Maori show off their work like peacocks. Elaborate facial tattoos, called *mokos*, are particularly common. Not wanting to feel ostracised, Crispin rolled up a sleeve and showed me his. He'd asked it to be done last week when drunk. Beneath a white rose was the word 'YORKSHITE'.

Crispin shrugged. 'I guess spelling's not their forte.'

Our poison of choice was the local brew, Lion Red. It was tepid, flat, and tasted like motor oil. Another survey of the bar revealed we were way out of our depth; Crispin and I were both clean-shaven, observed the merit of showers and had no interest in Harley Davidsons. Additionally we weren't wearing black leather or cheap gold earrings, or brandishing pool cues with the intention of doing anything other than playing pool. Perhaps the locals were light-hearted raconteurs with a penchant for the joie de vivre, but they all gave the impression they'd sooner ditch the amiable chit-chat and hack your balls off with a broken beer bottle. The men were just as intimidating.

We made our way to the pool table. A leering drunk

enquired to a portly woman, 'Can I buy you a drink, Big Tits?'

She glared in disgust. 'I've already got an arsehole in my pants, I don't need another.'

This was Harlem, Kiwi-style, and we were self-conscious Brits with floral shirts and misspelled tattoos. Crispin necked his beer and tottered to the toilet, leaving me in the company of a scrawny Maori who correctly identified me as a solitary foreigner indulging in his first NZ Drinking Session. He had shrew-like eyes. His globular nose resembled a miniature cauliflower. The left side of his face was covered entirely with fern-like tattoos. This guy was hardcore, and he displayed no shame in hiding the fact. For a moment he watched me warily, his suspicion giving way to belligerence. 'Fuck *you* want, bro?'

'Excuse me?'

His eyes narrowed. 'Seen-once-were-warriors.'

'Sorry?'

'I said, *boy*, seen the film *Once Were Warriors*?'

I had indeed. Directed by Lee Tamahori, *Once Were Warriors* details the life of the Heke family as they 'strive to survive' in south Auckland. The film is a major Kiwi export, and centres on gang culture and domestic violence. A UK newspaper wrote an article about New Zealand's gang culture – the two most feared gangs being The Mongrel Mob and Black Power – and it made for harsh reading. Kiwi women suffered the highest rate of domestic violence in the developed world, with gang members "using the iron fist instead of talking." New Zealand also had one of the worst child murder rates. Initiation tests set by gangs included fighting three people simultaneously, committing rape, or drinking urine and excrement from a gumboot. It wasn't exactly the Boy Scouts.

My mouth became dry. 'I've seen it, yes.'

The tattooed local slammed his glass on the table with a vicious *crack*. When Crispin returned to the bar half the pub had stopped talking.

The local started to sway. He looked around to grab the attention of anyone who'd listen, as well as the nearest railing. 'Listen up! This boy seen *Once Were Warriors*. Let's ask 'im what he rickons. Well, boy, what *did* ya rickon?'

I'd never seen myself as a young Barry Norman, but it was clear this inebriated Maori valued my opinion. 'It was a splendid film, but one thing puzzled me.'

'Yeah?'

'You see, I couldn't decide if Tamahori's portrayal of the Hekes was strictly accurate, or whether it was so dysfunctional solely for the benefit of the viewer.' I popped a cigarette from my jacket. 'I mean, their bleak urban existence may have enhanced the film's authenticity, but at the same time Tamahori gave the viewer a faint glimmer of optimism.'

My interrogator stubbed out his cigarette. 'You takin' the piss?'

Forget violence, the best way to avoid trouble is to bullshit your way out of it. The second best policy is to leave, which Crispin and I achieved with a phenomenal turn of speed.

Stepping out into the cool Kiwi air we sighed with relief, thankful to have escaped that hellhole still breathing and wearing the same clothes as those with which we entered. Crispin patted me on the back. 'Well done, that showed him.'

'It showed him I can talk a load of bullshit.'

'True, Joey. Very true.'

Crispin assured me paying for a taxi to Queen Street would be too flash (and a tad lazy) so we braved the walk along K Road amidst broken glass and syringes bobbing away in puddles of piss. This was gritty urban living. I liked K Road, though. It had charisma, a sort of shabby allure. Across the road, behind a sex shop, I heard a scream...

If K Road is notorious, Queen Street is much revered as Auckland's main thoroughfare, loaded with souvenir shops, bookstores and shopping malls, with enough dairies, cafés and takeaways to satisfy Houston Thanksgiving Day. Queen Street's problem is that it's too damn long. At three kilometres it slices right through the heart of downtown Auckland, from the corner of K Road down the hill to the harbour. Queen Street takes about 40 minutes to conquer – 25 if you're sober – with some seriously steep sections that play havoc with your lungs. Consequently the walk down to the harbour is bizarrely satisfying, but the return leg is strictly for the athletic.

Conveniently The Temple was near the top of Queen Street. It was a swanky bar catering to the arty type, possibly jazz musicians, poets or songwriters. Crispin and I didn't fit that bill, but we were thirsty. My friend fetched cold bottles of Speights, a NZ favourite brewed in Dunedin that was more agreeable than Lion Red. Drinking deeply, I began to relax as the 'Three Star Pride of the South' ale worked its magic. K Road had been a mini adventure, but Queen Street felt safer.

Mingling amongst Auckland's cultural glitterati, Crispin updated me on what to expect from the working life at Alexander's garden centre. Kings Plant Barn was a multi-chain company and the most profitable in the country. I'd be based at the St Luke's branch, half a mile from our Kingsland bachelor pad.

'Gardening is huge,' Crispin said. 'Compost is always on offer so it's a big seller. The bags weigh a ton, too.' He jabbed a finger into my deflated bicep. 'You'll build up your muscles in no time.'

Cranked on booze, I was eager to talk to a girl. Any

girl would do. However, compost is not a stimulating subject for conversation – and I knew this from personal experience. Many years ago, during the school holidays, I worked at a garden centre near Leeds. The chores were gruelling for a scrawny fifteen-year-old, but they were made bearable by one of the till girls, Claire, with whom I had a palpable crush. She wore her dirty blonde hair over speckled shoulders and an ample cleavage – like a younger Erika Eleniak from *Baywatch*. Claire was friendly, but I had neither the confidence nor the verbal ammunition to initiate witty and playful dialogue. Every so often, during those sticky summer months, I stopped sweeping the greenhouse to wander to the shop area and stare in admiration at her breasts. Usually this behaviour warranted a ticking-off or an appearance on *Crimewatch*, but Claire was too preoccupied with the customers to notice saliva dribbling from my mouth onto the houseplants. After several weeks I bit the bullet and asked her out for a drink. My opening line was, 'So... do you like McClarry's Irish Moss Peat?' Claire ignored me, and wisely never spoke to me again.

So compost was off the chatting-up radar. Indeed, as the bar consisted entirely of would-be male poets, chatting-up was off the chatting-up radar. But just as I was wondering if there was any radar at all that might detect playful repartee, the door opened to reveal a group of gorgeous girls. All of them were... gorgeous.

There were about a dozen, and for a second, time stood still. The barman even dropped a glass.

Once more the sight of girls initiated dribbling. The girls were undoubtedly the main event, hip-strutting towards the bar like models on a carpeted catwalk. It was difficult for them to behaviour naturally, but they did remarkably well considering 100 pairs of eyes were gawping at them. Crispin diverted his attention long enough to notice my slobbering. He threw me a napkin, whispering, 'Be cool, baby, be cool.'

Men dutifully stepped aside to allow the girls bar access. It was a wonderful sight, like the parting of the waves. The beauties ranged from Amazonian, stiletto-wearing blondes to petite, fair-skinned redheads. The fittest one percent of Auckland's pedigree had descended into The Temple. It was like the human equivalent of Crufts.

'Stay cool, baby, stay cool.'

'Shut up, Crispin, *please* shut up.'

'You're dribbling.'

'Thank you, I know.'

In a flash a tray of gin and tonics appeared. These girls were pulling the strings; every male their puppets. When the girls dispersed into smaller groups, I was drawn towards a chestnut-skinned brunette. She was a stunner, the "Best in Show". I needed to talk to her. I needed to know her name. I wanted to know what she did for a living, and if her tan was real. A few topics of discourse fizzed around my head: What's the best town in New Zealand? Where are the best beaches? What's your opinion on McClarry's Irish Moss Peat?

The brunette hesitated as to her next move. She was wearing minimal make-up and had flawless kissable lips - lips that I wanted to get to know in an intimate capacity. Those lips were... perfect. As I was gawking at those flawless, kissable lips, she plumped for a seat not far from where I was trying to act like Dean Martin.

We exchanged a fleeting glance. I smiled. I thought she smiled back. I extracted a cigarette and lobbed it coolly to my lips. It sailed past my mouth and landed in someone's beer.

She had terrific shoulder-length hair and twinkling green eyes. Her figure suggested she was no stranger to exercise. My heart rapped my ribcage, my mouth was like sandpaper. I wanted more of her. She was a gift from Cupid, armed with a G&T. If she had an obsession in restocking fridges with beer and an IQ over 120 (give or take), I'd fall to one knee and propose.

But she just sat there. I could look at her all night, but she was waiting for me to make the first move, waiting for me to *say* something. Crispin necked his beer and took my empty bottle, wiggling his eyebrows playfully. Before joining the queue at the bar he turned and mouthed the words "Do it." Then he shooed me towards the brunette with a quick flick of his hands. When I hesitated, Crispin frowned and yelled, "Go on my son!"

Faint heart never won fair kissable lips. After examining her from head to toe in my least lecherous way, I offered her a Lucky Strike and then said something far from intelligent: 'Nice stockings.'

'Thanks,' she said warmly, 'They're my mum's.'

Correctly assessing her mother's undergarments were unorthodox for flirtatious banter, I changed the subject and commented on her accent. She was definitely a Kiwi, pronouncing 'thanks' as 'thinks'. Further probing revealed she was from Christchurch doing a spot of travelling. My luck was in; she'd travelled 1,000 kilometres and had found her way to me by sheer coincidence. Her girlfriends were all university friends celebrating a twentieth birthday.

I probed further. Her favourite colour was red ('Mine, too!' I blurted out, which was twaddle), her food of choice was Italian ('Mine, too!' I said, which was barefaced drivel), and she favoured plain black dresses and heels ('Me, too!' I exclaimed a little too quickly, and felt my cheeks turn a shade of her favourite colour).

Two fresh beers appeared. I assumed they'd been delivered by Crispin, but he was untraceable in the crowd. I wanted him by my side, an aide to combat an uncomfortable silence. But I was all alone with the girl who had bowled me over.

I didn't know how long we'd been talking. Minutes, hours... it seemed I had nothing left to give. So when all avenues of charm were exhausted I asked for her phone number. I wanted to abort the mission before getting too drunk and ruining the hard work. To my surprise she obliged, and wrote her details on the back of a beer mat. My eyes widened and I clenched a fist. Then she extended her hand as a sign that she was rejoining her friends. I grasped it. It felt like silk.

'It was a pleasure to meet you, Joe.'

'You, too. Really, it was... I mean, you are - '

She pushed the bar mat across the table. '*Call* me.'

She glided into the crowd. I stared at the beer mat. Had she made up the phone number just to get rid of me? I couldn't be sure. Did "call me" mean she really did want me to do just that? Or was it a flimsy excuse to cut the conversation so she'd never again be harassed by a semi-drunk Brit with a liking for dresses and high heels? I reverted to the bar mat. Her name was such a scribble it was practically illegible, but next to the inky scrawl was a row of impeccably formed digits.

Crispin's mouth was agape. He ushered me outside. Though his initial encouragement had been genuine, he was near speechless. He shook his head in bemusement as if to say, 'How the hell did you manage *that?*'

I took him by the elbow, a wobble developing. 'Damned if I know, mate. Beginner's luck?'

'Here, gimme that.' Crispin swiped the beer mat from my hand. He targeted in on the handwriting, beer goggles clouding his judgement. 'What's her name? Jeff? It says Jeff! Joey, you've pulled a bloke called Jeff!'

But I didn't listen. I felt like Charlie Bucket finding Willy Wonka's Golden Ticket. I couldn't stop thinking about the girl that had just made my working holiday an instant success. In fact, my first day in New Zealand really couldn't have gone any better.

Chapter scorecard: Captain Cook never pulled on his first day in New Zealand. Varley is up and running.

Chapter 3

Two days later I heard details of my garden centre job. I was lounging on the sofa, drinking a bottle of Flame lager. I was thinking about the brunette with the flawless, kissable lips when Crispin threw me his mobile.

'Hello, is that Joe?' the voice asked.

'Speaking.'

'It's Alexander.'

Alexander - Crispin's older brother and my soon-to-be boss. Though I'd met him before in Sheffield, it was wise to give the right impression. After all Alexander was an Englishman who'd climbed the gruelling rungs of the Kiwi career ladder. He'd become the branch manager of the largest garden centre in New Zealand. Profits were second-to-none and Kings Plant Barn had a solid reputation built on exceptional customer service. It was quite an achievement. That Alexander demanded my attention and commanded respect was indisputable. I had to sound eager, professional and brimming with self-confidence.

'Hello Al -'

Shit. I'd accidentally pressed the OFF button.

Crispin cackled and cracked open another beer. 'You

really have to get the hang of these things,' he said, a little too haughtily for my liking. 'Let me dial him again.'

Alexander answered instantly. He sounded a trifle irritated. 'Yeah?'

'Alexander, hi. It's Joe again. Sorry about that, I cut you off.'

'Fine. Good flight?'

'Yes thanks. Well, Singapore was a bit - '

'Sweet. Okay, about the job. I want you to - '

I'd done it again. This time Crispin roared with laughter. He was genuinely taking pleasure in the fact I couldn't handle a mobile phone. When he offered to call his brother again to explain the confusion I refused blankly. Alexander must surely think I was a twat.

Crispin eventually explained that the deal had already been sealed. Apparently I was to start work on the following Monday, 8.30AM prompt, just for a trial day. My first full week would be the week after; Alexander had called merely to confirm the time.

I hurled the phone at Crispin's head, which bounced off his spongy curls leaving him unscathed. 'So why the hell didn't you tell me that in the first place?'

'Relax, *Bro*.'

I'd quickly realised five things about New Zealand:

1) Kiwis love water. Even the dogs own yachts. If you mention that you don't swim, sail, go fishing or even

like water, New Zealanders will assign a look usually reserved for serial killers or circus freaks.

2) New Zealanders will happily admit they're poor drivers. Mention their driving is the worst you've seen and they'll shrug and offer you a drink – after they've signalled, of course.

3) Never refuse a beer or a smoke in New Zealand. It's disrespectful, like farting in a lift.

4) Kiwis take their work very seriously. They don't take too kindly to pasty-skinned Brits flying thousands of miles to steal their jobs. Better to get a suntan, *then* steal their jobs.

5) New Zealand airport officials hate the name Graham.

G looked precisely as one should after a long-haul flight from Heathrow to Auckland: crumpled clothes, unshaven and jetlagged. A musty stench followed him around like a shadow – a telltale sign he hadn't showered for at least 24 hours. G was a tramp with a passport, and a pissed off one at that.

'Bloody do-gooders,' he muttered.

'Nice to see you, too.'

G dished out high-fives and hugs before explaining frantically that he'd been accosted by the airport staff for possessing a tangerine in the bottom of his rucksack. Although merely a "yellow card" offence, G was fuming.

'Why would I smuggle in a tangerine?' he moaned. 'The guy in front of me was called Graham, too, and they got the bugger for bringing in a packet of *seeds.*'

Whilst it was possible the officials had an inexplicable prejudice towards the name Graham, it was more plausible that G simply hadn't read the warnings printed on travel cards prior to arriving in places like New Zealand. Under no circumstances is it permitted to import fruit, seeds or vegetables for fear of messing up the ecological system. Regulations are exceedingly strict, and rightly so. Foreigners smuggling illicit goods risk a severe ticking-off lest the country suddenly becomes engulfed by curious strains of weird looking vegetation. Criminals are rumbled in Miami with pythons wrapped around their armpits, and bootleggers come a cropper at Gatwick carrying South American fauna in their luggage, but in Auckland smuggling is less exotic. The authorities may turn a blind eye to firearms and crack cocaine, but tangerines are a definite no-no. I admired G with affection and imagined his mugshot on the FBI's *Most Wanted* list as the ring leader of a global contraband citrus fruit operation.

The Kiwis are very protective of their ecosystem, no doubt due to the exclusive wildlife. Indeed, a high level of endemic species prevails throughout. Though the species are intriguing, the animals are largely innocuous. If you tremble in fear by the very mention nakes, New Zealand is a safe bet. Whilst Australia harbours a menacing medley of these slithery critters – taipans, tiger snakes, king browns, death adders and the like, all of which are among the deadliest in the world – in New Zealand there are no snakes. Arachnophobes will be euphoric to learn there are only two potentially dangerous spiders, the katipo and the redback, but both are as intimidating as the *Andrex* puppy.

There are no crocodiles, and dangerous jellyfish are rare. Even disease-carrying insects are scarce. Sand flies are undeniably irksome, but their bite is little more than a nasty nip. There are frogs that can't croak and parrots that can't fly, and New Zealand has the most diverse species of penguin anywhere else on Earth.

The national symbol, of course, is the kiwi – a shy, flightless bird with an unfeasibly long bill that resembles a geriatric gerbil drinking through a straw. Whales and dolphins are aplenty (but only in the sea) and the famous 'living dinosaur' tuatara is a scientific marvel simply because it hasn't died out yet - a true coffin-dodger of the animal world.

Generally the fauna of New Zealand is unique - except for the sheep. There are 41,986,432 of them (to be entirely inaccurate), but the ovine situation in New Zealand is no different to that in Argentina, Australia or Wales: they chew grass and look stupid just like every other sheep on the planet. Nice lamb, though.

The tangerine fiasco now forgotten, G's arrival brought us a fresh impetus. Crispin was anxious to take us both to the Coromandel Peninsula in his muddy-grey/silver/shit-coloured Toyota. I was equally eager to escape the city before I started work, and the thought of exploring a more tranquil area sounded perfect. The Coromandel was idyllic, having been told by a local it was 'choice, bro'.

Before we left, G showered to erase the grime and pong he'd accumulated from his flight. Then we bundled back into the car, where my two friends spent precisely 11 minutes (by my watch) discussing the Toyota in every conceivable detail. My knowledge of cars mimics that of what I know about the mechanics of a nuclear submarine. To me, a car is a metallic wheeled machine that transports people from point A to point B - ideally via a pub for a pint.

'What's the Big T's engine alignment?' G-Man asked Crispin.

'I'm glad you asked, my friend. Transverse, I think.'

'And its unitary capacity?'

''Bout Four-Sixty cc.'

'Top speed?'

'Dunno... One thirty?'

'Double wishbones?'

'Absolutely.'

'Semi-elliptic leaf springs?'

'But of course.'

I couldn't take much more of this. 'Inter-galactic laser pods with plutonium spoof brackets?'

Crispin and G-Man both cut a look of distain. 'Tch. Joe, you're such a philistine.'

Putting foot to the pedal, Crispin steered the "Big T" in the direction of the nearest shop, where we bought much needed supplies: salt and vinegar flavoured Eta crisps; three packets of Moro bars; two bottles of warm Mountain Dew and a tube of factor 30 sun cream that smelt of sick.

We continued east, leaving behind the big city. It felt a lot more alien. With every kilometre we covered and every road sign we passed, the more exciting it became. Crispin seemed to know where he was going, which was another positive, and he relished his role as tourist guide.

'Wow! There's a long-tailed cuckoo! See it? Can you *see* it?'

The two-hour drive was exhilarating. Though it wasn't quite what Aucklanders would call summer, the weather was exceptional: sapphire skies, faint wisps of cloud, moderate humidity, and balmy sunshine.

People-watching was a dull activity; the Coromandel is a low-density area with highly dense people. I'd only seen four locals and each appeared stoned. When we stopped to ask a hippy the direction of the nearest shop he looked at us as if we were Martians and the

Toyota our spaceship. To him we were 'far out, man.'
The Coromandel is beatnik beach country. The uniform
was knee-length shorts, baggy T-shirts and sandals.
Apparently there was plenty of dope in the area, and
the locals clearly enjoyed it. Whilst Auckland boasted
skyscrapers, sensible haircuts, and Thai cuisine, the
good people of the Coromandel settled for beach shacks,
ponytails, and chilled nettle soup. It was a wonderful
place, but the people were cerebrally challenged. But,
like, in a nice way, man.

Rich, volcanic soil generated secluded tropical forest.
The most common tree was the ponga (silver fern) – a
tall, spindly plant with palmate fronds that drooped like
an exhausted octopus. As we ascended steep dirt tracks,
vast clumps grew together so tightly they looked like
acres of broccoli. For me it was new territory, and proved
a prehistoric experience. I half expected an *Allosaurus* to
charge from the trees and tear off our wing mirror.

Other plants included the common nikau palm –
an instantly recognised gregarious tree with coarse,
shuttlecock branches – piupiu crown ferns, and the
majestic rimu, an endemic pine that towered over lesser
vegetation. The dipping valleys and lack of paved roads
made the journey that much more gripping – certainly
more gripping than the Toyota's tyres. Descending deeper
into the heart of the Coromandel felt like a professional
rally race; steep corners laden with chocolate-coloured

grit resulted in a drive fraught with incident, the rear wheels barely clinging to continuous curves of loose shingle. Frequently I feared for my life.

'For God's sake, use the semi-elliptic leaf springs!'

As a self-confessed petrol-head G was thrilled, but he wasn't gripping the seat with white knuckles.

A few kilometres in and the tropical forest gave way to well-established secondary forest, the endless mess of green vegetation merging into natural mosaics. As a passenger, I had the privilege of taking all this in. Crispin, on the other hand, was too busy keeping his car under control. '*Yeeeeeeehaaaaaaa!*' he bellowed at the wheel, dodging blood-stained possums.

Crispin headed the car south of Mercury Bay, an area that Captain Cook named after the Transit of Mercury. It was here that Cook and his faithful chums found an abundance of food: sumptuous oysters, vitamin-laden greens and fresh fish. After an initial dispute, Cook's crew found the Maori amiable, although the natives described the gang of British sailors as *tupua* – strange 'goblins'. Happy to let that go, Cook sailed to the Auckland area satisfied with his progress.

He was lucky. Abel Tasman, the Dutch explorer who sighted New Zealand back in 1642, encountered the locals and immediately caused a ruckus. When half of his crew went for a coastal stroll the Maori sprung an ambush. Tasman's men were thrown into cauldrons crammed with salted kumara and rosemary, and served up for the biggest feast of the year. It was like *Ready, Steady, Cook* with Jeffrey Dahmer. Being a fellow of sound judgement, Tasman retreated with the rest of his gang, never to look back. Clearly Cook had better "people skills".

We returned to tarmac, cruising along highway 25A, which skirted below the Coromandel State Forest Park. Mellow fingers of sunlight peeked out from the nikau palms. The place was deserted. It was our *own* country. This was what New Zealand was all about: the great outdoors, fresh air, exploration, new experiences, deliciously chewy Moro bars, and smelly sun cream lotion.

Below Mercury Bay was the famous Hot Water Beach and Cathedral Cove, the two main attractions in the area. Hot Water Beach's fame needed no explanation.

'It's true,' Crispin nodded. 'The water beneath the sands is *boiling*. It's all the thermal activity.'

'Twaddle.'

'You think I'm talking tripe, huh?'

'Crispin, I salute you for your knowledge of fish – that I have no qualms about. But if you're telling me that the water will be boiling hot then yes, you're not only talking tripe, but also large piles of crap.'

Crispin shrugged. 'Okay, Barnacle Boy, see for yourself.'

The scene at Hot Water Beach was peculiar. Stretched along the sands, about 50 visitors dug frantically with small plastic spades. Sand was thrown over shoulders, into faces, into picnics. There was sand everywhere. Children hopped incessantly in what appeared to be pools of steaming water, whimpering as if forced to dance in some kind of satanic ritual.

I fell to my knees, burrowing with cupped hands. The sand was soft, the texture fine. Five minutes later I'd made a precise symmetrical hole 18 inches deep. A small amount of water lay at the bottom.

'Let me get this straight. You're telling me this water will be boiling?'

Crispin smiled. 'Well, okay, it's not actually *boiling*. Just tepid, really.'

'Gigantic piles of crap.'

I took off my shoes and jumped in two-footed.

When you boil a kettle and let it stand for a few minutes, and then spill it over yourself because co-ordination deserts you first thing in the morning, there's a very short delay before a sharp pain jolts straight through you, causing your limbs to spasm in agony. Standing in my pool was exactly like that: it was torture. Crispin and G just giggled.

"*Eeeeaaaoo... fucking... aawwwwwwww!*" I yelped, hopping on the sand to shake off the excess water.

'Like I said, Joey – quite warm!'

Some of the kids farther down the beach laughed in our direction. Even the parents looked over and joined in the heckling. No doubt they'd been here before and knew what to expect.

'Don't take any notice,' Crispin said. 'They're not laughing at you being a wimp.'

'Agreed,' G chipped in. 'They're laughing at how white your legs are.'

'And you look like Barbara Cartland with that sun cream on,' Crispin added.

I'd had enough. Being scalded was one thing, but scalded whilst being mocked for not having a suntan was too much. I couldn't understand that G had just flown in from London, yet his skin was as brown as a roast chicken. I was jealous as sin, but there was no need for insults. Marching back to the car, I heard laughter ringing in my ears.

We continued The Coromandel Tour. Up the road from Hot Water Beach was Cathedral Cove, a popular tourist attraction east of Cook's Beach near the village of Hahei. This sheltered white-sand bay had been featured a number of times in travel brochures. Being a cynical blotched-skinned Englishman, I assumed they had superimposed the image to make the sands appear whiter than white, like teeth in toothpaste adverts. Credit to the photographers, though, because the beach was identical to the brochure images: it was absolutely sublime, and arguably one of the finest beaches in New Zealand. Lightweight pieces of driftwood cluttered fine sand, and pohutukawa trees added contrast with their scarlet foliage. Chunks of chalky, white rock stood among the gently lapping waves. It was a scruffy paradise.

Crispin whipped out his camera, giving me a sharp shove. 'C'mon,' he enthused. 'Wade out to sea and I'll take a picture.'

'But it'll be cold!'

'First it's too hot, now it's too cold!' G-Man cackled. He put fire to a Marlboro Light. 'Make up your mind, Josephine!'

G goaded me to swim around the largest white rock, but my lack of courage stopped me in my tracks. Surely there were sharks around here! Instead I stood precariously in the waist high water, allowing the boys to photograph how much of a coward I was being.

Crispin summoned me out of the sea to walk through an arch in the rock. I hadn't seen it before, which was strange because its size was striking. In fact, the arch was the 'cathedral', about 20 metres wide. It was eerie striding through the arch; it felt like a cave and the sand was damp and cold to the touch.

'Beautiful,' said Crispin, snapping away fervently. 'I'll have them done in black and white. They'll look more artistic.'

Satisfied with his work, Crispin handed out warm

Mountain Dew as we lounged under the lazy afternoon sun. My face was warming up and my skin hardened, prompting Crispin to prod away with intruding fingers.

'You're looking more like a Kiwi now,' he said.

I paused to detect any traces of sarcasm. 'Really?'

'I shit you not. You've got a sun-line where your hair meets your forehead.'

'So I'm getting a suntan?'

'Well, sort of.'

I grinned with satisfaction. Hopefully my legs would follow suit, and then I'd complement the rest of Auckland's beautiful people. Without a suntan in New Zealand you feel like a white chocolate button in a barrel of coffee beans.

We'd spent six hours in the Coromandel. Driving back to Auckland at dusk was inspiring. Skyscrapers sparkled like gems under the flashing lights of the Sky Tower, the city's waterfront illuminated to perfection. There was a real sense of adventure leaving behind a semi-prehistoric wilderness for the concrete jungle.

I felt cemented in Kiwi culture, and I liked it enormously. Then it dawned on me: I had just survived my first real New Zealand experience without any notable disaster. Sure, I'd scalded my feet and been the butt of a few jokes, but I could handle that. I hadn't been sick, hadn't been involved in a car crash, nor misplaced my swimming shorts. And the girl with the flawless, kissable lips was constantly on my mind. I was on a roll. Captain Cook must be green with envy.

Chapter scorecard: The boy Varley comes away unscathed after a mini adventure outside the Big City, so is entitled to feel satisfied for this very reason. The Captain had many early successes in his career – he observed the Transit of Venus in 1769 and headed to New Zealand himself soon after – so it would be churlish for Varley to claim a point here. A draw seems fair.

VARLEY 1   COOK 0

Chapter 4

Monday, 7.15AM. Kings Plant Barn looming.

Breakfast was as disappointing as it was unnutritious: two Lucky Strikes and capful of mouthwash.

TV weather forecast: 'A high prissure front will ciscade through the cintral Auckland eria, risulting in warm wither for the nixt few hours, ay.'

My plan for this week: To make Alexander proud with my hard graft and intense work ethic, and to spend all weekend on the beach... then stroll into work next Monday showing off my bronzed pins. Girls will flock in admiration as I throw into cars heavy bags of compost. They'll gently caress my suntanned legs with slow, deliberate strokes, patting my muscled brown thighs with...

Dogsbody reporting for duty. 8.15 AM.

'Congratulations, Joe, you're on time.'

Alexander was in his office when I strolled through the sliding doors. So much for, 'Joe, my boy! Great to *see* you! Do come in and have a coffee, then I'll introduce you to all the *wonderful* staff who will make you feel welcome and laugh at all your jokes.'

'Hi, Alexander.'

'Find the place okay?'

'Yes, thanks. It was quite easy, really. I just walked up Third Avenue and along Western - '

'No, no, no, no, *NO!*'

'What?'

Alexander pointed and flapped and developed a redness in the face. He was far from happy.

'What do you think you're wearing?' he bellowed. 'Christ, Joe, look at the state of you!'

Alexander was furious. Maybe he wasn't a 'Monday person'. But honestly - what did he expect me to have done? Hired a personal tailor and gone shopping at the nearest Kings Plant Barn R Us? Well, really.

Following his verbal assault, my boss hurled at me a bundle of blue and yellow with such speed it merged into green.

'Here, put these on,' Alexander snapped. 'There's a toilet around the corner, opposite the frangipanis.'

I held the first article for inspection - a pair of baggy, navy blue shorts. The label said, 'Canterbury of New Zealand'. Excellent quality, thick and durable, like rugby shorts.

'And look after them,' Alexander added, not looking up from his paperwork. 'They cost sixty bucks.'

'Opposite the frangipanis?'

'Yup.' Alexander tapped his watch. 'And get a move on. I need you to do some sweeping before we open.'

So with my new uniform tucked underneath my arm I headed for the toilet. I walked past numerous familiar items: hoses, gardening gloves, watering cans, wooden stakes, green netting, spades, gardening forks, bags of fertilizer, rolls of fencing... but no frangipanis. I turned a corner. No frangipanis. Left, right. No frangipanis. Everywhere I looked there was a distinct lack of frangipanis. Then it occurred to me the reason I couldn't find the bloody frangipanis was I didn't know what frangipanis looked like.

I couldn't return to the office because of Alexander's foul mood... and I'd look more of an idiot. The rest of the staff hadn't arrived yet, so there was no one to ask for directions to the toilet or to give me the fundamental aesthetic qualities of the mysterious frangipani plant. I was lost in a garden centre. Being early had its downside.

With no option I decided to risk it. I pulled down my trousers, exposing my milk-white skin to Mother Nature, the early morning sun acting as a rather pleasant radiator against my buttocks. Unfortunately my bare backside was now exposed to a middle-aged woman who observed me with dread.

She had grey hair and thick leathery skin; a human pachyderm. Her eyes pierced through thin spectacles - eyes that were focusing on my arse and a pair of bollocks. Instantly I recalled the saying, 'You don't have a second chance to make a first impression.'

'Sweet Mary Mother of Jesus!' she exclaimed.

I swung round, snagging one leg in my shorts, and toppled over a tube of plastic fencing. Trying to recover some dignity I offered my hand in a peace offering, only to knock over a small cherry tree.

'What on *earth* do you think you're doing?'

'I'm trying to find the frangipanis,' I replied feebly. 'I must have forgotten to put my pants on this morning... as you can see. Do you know what frangipanis look like?'

Now a second woman had arrived to see what all the commotion was about (where had all these women *come* from?). All she received by way of an answer was an albino English boy with no underwear sprawled over a roll of fencing and spilt potting mix. She left the crime scene almost immediately.

Now Alexander himself had joined in the fun. The look on his face suggested he was appalled, but far from surprised.

'Joe, this is Sandra, the assistant manager. Sandra, this is Joe, the... assistant.'

Sandra winced. 'We've met. Brenda has also had that pleasure.'

'Brenda is third in command,' said Alexander. 'So now you've met all three bosses. Sandra, Joe is a friend of my brother Crispin. He'll be helping out on the tills and doing the compost runs. Please show him to the toilet. And Joe, when you've changed, see me in my office.'

Moments later, when I'd changed, I presented myself to Alexander in his office. A few of the staff had now arrived and were chattering amongst themselves like kids in a playground. No doubt Brenda had spilt the beans on my brazen show of nudity; she struck me as the gossiping type.

'Let's forget what just happened,' Alexander said, swiftly closing his office door. 'I don't know what you were playing at and I don't want to know. Just give me a few minutes and I'll show you around the place and introduce you to the staff.'

The "no pants" scandal forgotten, Alexander showed me everything a new employee of my stature needed to see. I was to be the 'chief sweeper', the 'chief bag lifter' and the 'chief person who puts the delivered plants out on display, ay'. Even Alexander - once the quintessential Englishman - had picked up the statutory Kiwi 'ay' at the end of every sentence.

The role of 'chief sweeper' was exactly that: I was in charge of sweeping the car park. 'Chief bag lifter' again was self-explanatory, but sounded like a homosexual Red Indian.

Grasping how to put the plants on display required at least a moment of my concentration. This was the procedure: the plants were delivered from wholesalers and dropped off around the back through a wire fence.

This was done twice a week. I had to move the plants from the back entrance to their individual sections, and arrange them neatly so the customers could take their pick of the stock. Alexander went though the procedure with me *four* times. Plants came in, plants went on display. Plants came in, plants went on display. It was thrilling stuff.

I met my first proper colleague (i.e. not 'I earn more money than you' management) in the car park before the expected rush hour. James was a peculiar kind of bloke: late twenties, five feet tall, wiry copper-coloured hair, goofy teeth, steel-rimmed glasses, long baggy shorts and over-sized brown labourer's boots. He looked like a Warner Brother's cartoon character.

'Listen up, Joe,' said Alexander, taking me to one side. 'James isn't like the other staff. He's kind of... different. Sometimes he doesn't understand things very well.'

'How so?'

'James once went with the delivery guys to an office in town. Some place near the waterfront. Anyway, there was a sign that said smoking wasn't allowed inside the building - you had to smoke outside. So James went to the nearest shop, bought a packet of cigarettes, and lit up outside the office.'

I shrugged. 'Sounds reasonable enough.'

'Yeah,' Alexander nodded, 'except James doesn't

smoke.'

'Ah.'

'Exactly. He tends to take things too... literally. Go easy on him.'

James stood with broom in hand, squinting at me through his glasses. He didn't say a word. I took this to be my chance to get in Alexander's good books; maybe I could become friends with James by initiating the conversation.

I raised a flat hand. 'How, James, I'm Chief Bag Lifter.'

He looked confused.

'Just kidding. I'm Joe. How long have you worked here?'

'My dog is called Baxter.'

'That's nice.'

'Baxter weighs more than me.'

I regarded his diminutive stature. 'I'm sure he does.'

'You know why? Coz he eats *two* tins of dog food for breakfast.'

I could see where this conversation was going. 'I'm going to be working with you for a few months,' I said, eager to change the topic. 'I'm hoping to go down south next year. Where do you think I should go? I've heard Nelson is nice.'

'Baxter's favourite flavour is beef!'

I liked James immediately, of course. He was all

foam and no beer; a true nutcase. He was going to be my friend and my wingman. I couldn't put my finger on what it was that made him 'different', but I liked his eccentricities and decided to play along with him.

But just as I was warming to James, things went disturbingly downhill. Whilst making a good fist of sweeping the car park Brenda was scowling at the main door.

'Brenda looks out for me,' James said, and then he pounded his chest with a fist. 'But *I* don't need looking after as much as she thinks.'

'So Brenda's your friend then?'

'Yes sir-ree.'

'But you can look after yourself, right?'

'That's *right*,' he said proudly, puffing out his bony chest.

I decided to step-up the conversation from dog food to women. 'So what types do you like, James? Blondes? Redheads? No, wait, I bet you go for brunettes, right? Me, too.'

Bad move. The next few seconds were a blur. Brenda clenched her fists and marched towards to us - in a fashion that suggested she was verging on extreme psychosis and that she was going to stomp me.

The look on her face still sends shivers down my spine. She was seething. I might as well have asked James what time he normally went grave-robbing.

'If I *ever* catch you taking to James about things like that again,' she hissed, 'I'll make sure they are your *last* words.' Brenda then dragged James back to the door like a spider reeling in a fly to its web.

Fortunately Alexander must have overheard some of this because he trotted over to the car park in a bid to consolidate me. He ran a hand through his sandy hair.

'I forgot to warn you, Joe. Try not to talk to James about women. It kind of sets him off.'

I felt sorry for James. So he had a few screws loose and he turns into a loony at the mere mention of girls. Don't we all? I'm sure Brenda felt it was absolutely necessary to protect him because his mentality is below par, but I just didn't think *talking* about women would prove so catastrophic. So, after that episode, I made a mental note to avoid any female-related conversations with James. Truly, the look Brenda had given me was horrific.

Fortunately all seemed to have calmed down, as soon after James danced out to help me finish the sweeping. Actually, this was strictly untrue. He somehow managed to sweep up everything I'd just swept up, only he kind of missed and sent piles of dry soil swishing into the air, so in fact we ended up going around in circles making *more* work for ourselves in a cloud of thick brown dust. When James had had enough, he beamed a likeable smile, expecting me to praise his enthusiasm. All I could do was lean on my broom, wipe the dust from my hair and say with as much virtue as I could muster, 'Thanks, James, I really couldn't have done it without you.' He then skipped off to harass the first attractive female customer of the day.

When I'd finished the sweeping, my next job was to open the pallets of compost and bark chippings. Most of the pallets were ditched at the far end of the car park by fork-lift truck, and were bound by thick polythene. Each pallet held about 50 bags. When busy I'd be shifting seven or eight pallets *a day*. To make matters worse, the scissors Brenda had equipped me with were blunt, so when I attacked the plastic covering it was like cutting through fillet steak with chopsticks. I reckon that Brenda had given me those scissors purely to test my patience; it's the very thing a hard-nosed Kiwi would have done to wind up a Pommie on his first day at work.

A quick word on the staff. After all, they were to be my colleagues for the foreseeable future.

I couldn't make up my mind about Sandra. As the deputy manager of Kings she had to be terse at times - and therefore wasn't the kind of woman I'd feel completely at ease with down a dark alley - but if it came down to a punch-up between her and Brenda, Sandra wouldn't stand a chance. Sandra demanded respect - no question - but she didn't possess the sheer terror that Brenda was able to wreak. If they both featured in *Top Trumps*, Sandra's Fear Factor rating would be 87. Brenda's would be 100.

I took to Patrick immediately because he was roughly my age - and hungover. Upon introduction his first words were, 'Hi mate. I've got a thumping head, ay.' Pat was working whilst studying at Auckland University and although his knowledge of plants was far superior to mine, he didn't like showing off his flair for remembering scientific names of fruit trees or identifying ten species of herbs just by their smell. Pat was carefree and modest, although I learnt very quickly he liked to drink and smoke with the best of them. I knew instantly we'd be great friends.

Grant was a burly local from Morningside who did for masculinity what Eddie 'The Eagle' Edwards did for aeronautics. The irony of a queen working at Kings didn't go unnoticed. His attire consisted of flimsy straw hats and pink socks, which were more suited to a Bangkok holiday with Julian Clary than working at a garden centre. Grant was a gentle giant and *overly* nice; there genuinely wasn't an ounce of hatred in his body. If you slapped him across the face with a wet flannel and called his mum a whore he'd apologise and buy you some cake.

Katherine and Brian were kind, healthy middle-agers who specialised in New Zealand natives (i.e. plants I couldn't identify, spell or pronounce). They both wore their yellow Kings sweaters with pride and you just *knew* they got a thrill wearing walking boots all day. Katherine and Brian adored 'tramping' in the 'bush', but whilst Katherine skated around the garden centre with so much energy it made you sick, Brian had all the get-up-and-go of a sedated sloth. Although I never doubted his catalogue of botanical knowledge, Brian came across as a bit 'slow'. He plodded along without a care in the world and he talked in a low drone ever so leisurely which made any real conversation really, really... (yawn) tedious.

The fork-lift truck drivers, Malcolm and Richard, loved their sport, beer and earrings. Both were suntanned and their hair bleached blonde. Nice lads, of course, and they had a strength that belied their skinny frames. You'd never think that Malcolm could lift a medium-sized potted orange tree from ground to lorry, but he achieved it with ease - even without James's assistance.

Sonya, Alice and Julie were a trio of amiable ladies who worked with the indoor plants and on the tills. Julie was the eldest of the three and possessed a cheeky wink that eased some pressure Brenda steered in my direction. We'd be mates, no problems there. Sonya was the youngest, whose sense of humour rivalled Grant's pink socks in the absurdity stakes. She was blonde and bubbly, a real livewire. Alice was down to earth -

earth being her obsession. She knew *everything* about potting mixes, fertilizers and composts. Her *Mastermind* introduction would be, '**Name**: Alice. **Occupation**: The Most Boring Person In The World. **Specialist Subject**: The properties and physiological qualities of Kings Plant Barn multi-purpose compost, and its subsequent use in maintaining New Zealand's flora in south-facing garden beds and frost-resistant pots.' Incidentally, Alice's boyfriend worked at the Remuera branch of Kings, so I bet their dinner times were *crammed* with stimulating conversation.

For the first few days at Kings Plant Barn most of the staff made puerile comments about the pastiness of my legs (bless 'em). It was very hard to get a suntan in Yorkshire, I told them - they should try it. The banter was harmless, but I just wished they'd poke fun at something more evident, like Grant's socks or Malcolm's overly peroxide hair.

Of more concern were the tills, and specifically, how to work the bastards. All three of them were huge - like oversized keyboards - but the buttons so tiny. Most customers preferred to pay with their debit or credit cards, but often these were chipped or 'maxed out', or had simply expired. The most frustrating aspect was inputting every purchase only to discover that the cards didn't work - and so the customer couldn't pay for anything - then having to ask another member of staff to return the goods to their precise location. Julie advised that some 'special' customers had been given loyalty cards, which permitted exclusive reductions on orders over $NZ 50. I quickly discovered it was a moot point what could be classed as an 'exclusive reduction'. When I'd run the plants and dry goods through the till, and then taken off the reduction from the loyalty card, quite often the customer gawped at me as if to say, 'Is that *all* the discount you're gonna give me, you tight-fisted cretin?'

More confusing were all the special offers. Kings was the largest garden centre in the country, so there were weekly special offers galore. There were special offers on bedding plants, bags of potting mix (two or more bags), bark chippings, compost (five bags), perennial shrubs, fruit trees, natives, indoor plants, dry goods, fertilizers... just about everything in the whole damn place except the ice lollies. They were all quality products at exceptional prices (hey, Big Boss Man Alexander, where's my commission?!) but that merely encouraged what felt like a quarter of Greater Auckland to descend on the same day in a bizarre "compost frenzy". Moreover, a great deal of them couldn't even speak English (or chose not to). What hope had I if an elderly Japanese lady demanded three dollars off a bag of potassium nitrate because she'd mistaken it for cat litter?

Usually there was a winning combination of Sonya,

Alice, Julie and me on the tills. We had a laugh. More specifically they laughed at my legs and I laughed at their accents. But till duty comprised a hidden risk. I believe Ogden Nash once said, 'People who work sitting down get paid more than people who work standing up.' In the shop area we were not allowed to sit down - even working on the tills - which was brutal. Occasionally, when Alexander wasn't looking, we leant on the flower stands. That was one of our perks. Of course, Brenda often witnessed this illicit act and scowled through suspicious spectacles (yeah, like *she* never leant on things).

I was starting to relax around with Brenda. It took a few days, certainly, but the old girl even engaged in something resembling banter. I asked her in which part of Australia she was raised, and she responded by inquiring about my taste in Welsh sheep. It was quite endearing. And once she cracked a joke: when I'd helped out with a savage order of potting mix, I asked how many people worked at Kings.

'About half of them,' she replied dryly. Unoriginal from the stone-faced one, but at least she was trying. To say that middle-aged Kiwis don't have a sense of humour is untrue.

She wouldn't admit it, of course, but Brenda was beginning to crumble. Underneath that hard exterior and anti-wrinkle cream was a heart of pure Kiwi gold. I'd just have to turn on the charm a bit more. I was fairly sure - no, positive - that it would only be a matter of time before we'd be good friends.

Chapter scorecard: A shaky start at work for the boy Varley. This is a case of an own goal versus consistent performance by the Captain, who, by 1770, had circumnavigated New Zealand and had charted both the North and South Islands. Cook finally gets off the mark.

CHAPTER 5

I held the beer mat in front of Crispin. 'Eleven numbers.'

'What?'

'Eleven numbers. These are the eleven numbers that stand between me and Miss New Zealand.'

Crispin scoffed. 'Don't be so dramatic.'

'C'mon, she was very, uh... she was beautiful!'

'If it's an "Eve" she's one pretty girl,' Crispin conceded. 'But if it's a "Steve", whose real name *is* Jeff... good work Joey - you've pulled the fittest bloke in Auckland!'

'She's definitely a girl,' I retorted, and we left it at that.

The beer mat could be my ticket to instant romance. But one thing I'd learnt is that you have to be wary with girls. Dating rules are not set in stone, but they exist for a reason. If you phone a girl too soon after the first encounter you'll mess things up. You don't want to seem too eager, but at the same time you don't want to give the impression of casual aloofness. It's a close call: desperation versus indifference. Two days, known as the 'industry standard', is just about right. Three days is also acceptable, whereas four days is asking for trouble. And if you go in with all guns blazing and call back within the first 24 hours it's committing social suicide.

Inclining to the side of caution, I made the call three days after the weekend using Crispin's mobile. Luckily the girl with the kissable lips answered by her name instead of an anonymous 'hello'. Crispin was proven wrong: her name was Jess, not Jeff, which, though unsurprising, was a huge relief.

But then, almost immediately, I wondered if Jess had been drunk and forgotten giving her number out in the first place, and then I'd be forced to say something humiliating to jog her memory - something along the lines of, 'It's *me*, remember? The pasty-looking English boy you met on Saturday night... uh-uh... you don't remember, huh? Very well. Good day to you.'

Thankfully Jess recalled everything about the night at The Temple, even the bit where I'd foolishly asked her if she knew the difference between compost and potting mix. Then she told me she didn't think I was a horticultural-obsessed, green-fingered nutcase, and that she was actually keen that we met up soon.

We made inconsequential small talk, and then a dangerous thing happened: I started thinking. Taking onboard her keenness, a few ideas skipped through my mind: she was lonely, she was a real goer, she'd seen *Fatal Attraction* once too often and was hoping I have a pet called Flopsy.

We agreed to meet at 8 PM at The Khuja Lounge, another Queen Street bar. I was on a roll. My New Zealand adventure was getting better and better. You could have seen my smile all the way from Sydney.

When I was at school, my only knowledge of New Zealand was watching their rugby players do that funny little dance before the match, then beating the shit out of the opposition. The mighty All Blacks were habitually the best in the world. They weren't described as anything other than 'mighty'. Powerful? Tough? Really good? Pah! They were *mighty*. The All Blacks had flair, skill and the strength of warriors - and they stuck their tongues out a lot. They were saying to their opponents, 'We both know we're going to kick your asses *and* we'll rub your faces in it by being rude.'

The famous *haka* war dance was performed by the All Blacks with such conviction they may have practiced in front of mirrors much like a ten-year-old girl might impersonate Madonna. Because I was young and ignorant, there was a fantastically barbaric and antiquated aura surrounding these so-called All Blacks. I really *did* think some of them were warriors, what with the long hair, tattoos and constipated facial expressions. During the *haka* they made wild gestures towards the heavens as if they were summoning demons. It made for a bloodcurdling show. It was pure theatre. But what did these All Blacks do when they got back to their mud huts? Did they walk around with fruit baskets on their heads? Did some live in trees and communicate with monkeys? More importantly, had they proper health insurance? At the time, I confess, I knew nothing about Kiwi history.

So before arriving in New Zealand I examined its mythology. According to Maori legend, everyone and everything lived in total darkness (nothing wrong with that, of course, if a little inconvenient). Fed up with bumping into each other, the sky and earth separated so that light could infiltrate the world. Many years later, after the forest god *Tane Mahuta* created a woman from a pile of dirt, the Polynesian demigod *Maui* went fishing in his canoe, accompanied by his five brothers. Reaching for his magic fishhook, *Maui* attached it to a rope and lobbed it overboard. Soon he had a bite. He yanked hard on the rope until a huge fish thrashed to the surface. As the legend goes, this marine mammoth became North Island. The fish's mouth developed into Wellington Harbour, with the East and West Coasts the two fins, and Northland the tail. South Island became the canoe in which *Maui* caught the fish, and Stewart Island moulded into the anchor that steadied the canoe as all this palaver was going on. This fable is undoubtedly bonkers - naturally - but its charm is there for all to see.

It was a magnificent Saturday. Crispin had been

summoned at the NIWA laboratory in Newmarket, so I took a solitary stroll around the city. I reminisced about watching the All Blacks on TV and considered what their country was like all those thousands of miles away. It may be true that some of the more distant, rural suburbs are a little old-fashioned, but here in downtown Auckland it was gleaming skyscrapers, verdant parks and elegant yachts cruising the wonderful Waitemata Harbour. The scene was picturesque without pretence, and the waterfront similarly impressed. The Ferry Building between Queens Wharf and Princes Wharf resembled a huge cricket pavilion - sandstone crossed with agreeable simplicity.

Westhaven Marina boasted thousands of boats bobbing contently on the azure water, and the National Maritime Museum is a must for salty seadogs. Famous Auckland Harbour Bridge - the kilometre long 'coat hanger' - offered tremendous views over the city. Although the bridge is by no means as celebrated as Sydney's landmark, it is a true New Zealand institution in its own right.

My friends had ventured to other cities with mixed reviews, namely New Delhi ('Noisy, smelly, over-crowded. Like Piccadilly Circus with athlete's foot'), Johannesburg ('Carjacking capital of the world... lovely') and Melbourne ('Nice enough, but full of Australians'), but on first impression Auckland was flawless. It was well organised and easy to commute, the people diverse and polite and the late spring weather was proving sultry yet bearable. More importantly, you could get a beer without queuing for half an hour.

But first impressions are deceptive. Despite the city centre's relative meagre dimensions in terms of area, Greater Auckland is among the world's largest cities. On a map it covers a random, expansive region some 5,000 square kilometres, which is about twice that of London. Auckland's magnitude, though, is a scam: the area is calculated from way up north where some people may not have *heard of* Queen Street, to as far south as the Bombay Hills. It's like saying London stretches from Cambridge to Brighton.

Auckland didn't feel like a crowded city. Inhabitants of rural New Zealand might disagree, but that's because some villages way out in the sticks comprise solely of a handful of sheep, a rusty tractor and Grandpa locked in a farmyard shack. A Londoner, for example, would consider Auckland a completely hassle-free utopia, free of smog and inner-city rush hours. In Auckland there was a noticeable lack of high-rise council flats and overcrowded tube stations. Pollution is minimal, and terrace houses are practically unheard of. Lush gardens are commonplace - even on the most basic properties - and the council does its fair share to keep the numerous parks litter-free. If there is one thing Auckland is not short of, it is space. It's like a giant playground for the fresh-air fiend.

I ambled along Waterloo Quadrant until I reached the university. The students reminded me of my studies in Wales, and I paused to wonder if there was some poor sod confined to a lecture room struggling with an essay on barnacles ('These gregarious creatures are very good at *clinging* to things'). I took respite in Albert Park, a divine retreat on the fringe of the university grounds. Albert Park was once the site of a Maori village, but now it seemed to have an identity crisis, unable to decide whether it's a popular attraction for tired tourists or a prime spot for brain-dead students to score dates. Selecting a place to recuperate under a palm tree, I smoked a Lucky and caught up on the country's current affairs in the *New Zealand Herald*.

By 4 PM all that sitting and reading and smoking must have taken its toll because I developed a sudden fatigue. The sun had sloped beneath the palm trees and a brisk breeze whirled amongst loose vegetation. It was home time. Fearing I was in bad shape, I decided to hike all the way up Queen Street to catch a bus to Kingsland. I managed 100 yards and then caught a taxi.

If you really have to be early you might as well do it in a bar, because booze is the only thing that will keep you entertained whilst waiting - and that's precisely why I will campaign for bars on all UK train stations by the year 2022.

It was 7.45PM when I arrived at The Khuja Lounge. It was located on the top floor of an art deco building. The bar was cool and dark, with the tables taken up with backpackers, smooching couples and young city slickers. I took a seat as a smiling barmaid approached me.

'Hiya. What can I get ya?'

I checked my watch. 'A Heineken, please.'

'You waiting for a girl?' she asked, bending down to fetch a bottle from the fridge.

'That obvious, huh?'

'Call it female intuition!' she laughed.

My position at the bar guaranteed a perfect view of the door. I was confident I'd be the first to spot Jess when she appeared, though I hoped she'd arrive at the exact time I ordered another beer so it'd seem I was talking to the bar staff instead of staring at the door desperately waiting for her.

Jess arrived at 8PM on the dot. This was pleasing for two reasons: either she was keen on me, or she'd mastered the art of telling the time. 'Keen' is an overused word in New Zealand. If a Kiwi, for instance, discussed a first date with a friend he would probably say something like, 'Was she keen on you, Bro?' At a party in New Zealand you'll hear people asking, 'You keen for a snog?' Whereas a Brit would use the word along the lines of, 'I trust madam was keen on the coq au vin?'

I kissed Jess on the cheek and led her to a window seat overlooking Queen Street. Etiquette usually dictated that the bloke buys the first drink, but Jess had none of it.

'Joe, it's your lucky night. My parents wired me some money today. Same again, or you keen for a voddie?'

'Voddie with tonnie please!'

Jess rolled her eyes, but smiled. The first opportunity to ogle her presented itself when she walked to the bar. This sounds wondrously sleazy, but I just couldn't resist. I couldn't keep my eyes off her. She was wearing thigh-hugging black trousers that stopped just above the ankle, a pink vest struggling to hide a black bra, and cute white pumps. She'd straightened her hair a little, too.

The vodka did what it does best: got the conversation flowing. We talked freely about our friends and our ideal job. Mine was a snooker player - 'All the fame and money without the exercise!' Jess wanted to be a professional dancer, so, after numerous "voddies", we inevitably found ourselves on the half-filled dancefloor.

A funky blend of jazz and soul boomed from the speakers. Jess built up a tempo and I smelled lemony hair. Whilst incredible, I just stood still looking gormless, like a kid who'd lost his pocket money, taking in her tight vest and feminine smells.

Three more large vodkas to the good, I began my

repertoire of dancing, which would be described, even on a good day, as an honourable failure. Clearly my definition of dancing was entirely different to hers; Jess had a natural swing in her hips that wouldn't be out of place at a Brazilian samba party. I bopped away like a war veteran with gout.

Soon a middle-aged man in a tight FCUK T-shirt boogied his way to my Dancing Queen. The predatory buffoon believed he was part of the 'young crowd' though he probably subscribed to *Knitting Your Way to the Top* magazine. His T-shirt was tucked snugly into even tighter stonewash denim, betraying a palpable paunch. Almost comically, he wore black sunglasses on a receding hairline. More *Agadon't* than *Agadoo*. Though we were competing for the same prize, a minute later he was nowhere to be seen - FCUKed off somewhere else, so to speak. Tonight I was some sort of disco god.

But, what with the loud music, not a conversationalist:

Me: So whereabouts in Christchurch are you from?

Jess: What?

Me: Whereabouts in *Christchurch* are you from?

Jess: Oh, right... New Brighton.

Me: Is it nice?

Jess: What?

Me: I said, *is it nice*?

Jess: Thanks, lots of ice.

Me: Any lime?

Jess: (Looking at her watch) It's quarter past ten.

Me: I think it's too loud to - '

Jess: Quick question: what's your pet hate?

Me: Well, he doesn't like things being shoved up his arse.

Jess: *What?*

Me: Er, what time do *you* make it?

Jess: Thanks, I'll have a G&T.

Me: You've got really lovely pixie ears.

It was hopeless. Dancefloors are designed for two things: for girls to exhibit flair, style and coordination, and for boys to display none of the above. They simply are not favourable for communication. Fed up with dancing like a drunken uncle at a wedding, I led Jess by the arm to the bar, where two girls were engaging in:

Random Bar Conversation

'How can you tell if you're falling for a bloke? Is it when you don't mind him wearing Spiderman socks in bed? Or is it when you come over all giggly and you forget what you're talking about?'

Jess concentrated so hard on the girls' conversation that she'd forgotten about me. Her back was turned, her attention gripped. I was completely invisible. I ordered a triple whiskey and retreated to a window seat. Queen

Street appeared grey and depressing.

Suddenly I felt dreadful. The Khuja Lounge was becoming my nemesis. I was angry for thinking such a stunner like Jess would happily spend a full evening alone with me. I thought back to Saturday night at The Temple when she'd sat near me; I doubted her motive. Was it some twisted bet with her girlfriends? Give out your number to a bloke and win 50 bucks?

I sunk my whiskey.

I needed out. I marched to the toilets to plot an escape. But after splashing my face with cold water I decided that although the coward's way out was more than acceptable, it was fundamentally not for me. I couldn't just leave without at least telling Jess. So in the mirror I practiced a few drunken excuses so we both retained some dignity:

1) I'm tired.

2) I'm a bit drunk.

3) Sorry, love, I'll come clean. I was born a woman and my real name is Josephine McTipsy.

The other two girls were still talking. Jess waved me over.

'Joe, where have you been? I've been looking all over for you.' She pointed to her new friends in turn. 'I'd like you to meet Chloe and Liz.'

I smiled weakly. 'Nice to meet you.' What an awful line: bland, unoriginal and delivered with all the zeal of a wet teabag.

'We've had such a lovely talk,' Jess beamed. 'Chloe is a student and Liz is a... sorry, Liz... ' Jess giggled. 'I've forgotten what you do! I thought you said something about, um, oh my God, how embarrassing, I've *completely* forgotten!'

Liz murmured something to Jess. They both laughed.

'Joe, this might sound a bit weird, but I just wanted to say... ' Jess laughed again. 'I just wanted to say I wouldn't care if you wore Spiderman socks in bed!'

Chloe and Liz sniggered, but Jess tried to keep a straight face. Aware of my alcoholic sway, I had to leave before I plunged deeper into humiliation.

'I'm so sorry. I've just remembered I need to, er, I need to go home.'

I walked to the door and called back to let Jess know I'd phone later on in the week ('when I've settled in at work'). She looked perplexed, and I didn't blame her.

Shuffling up Queen Street, a combination of booze took over logic. Whiskey fused with vodka with beer. I made it to K Road, dodging puddles of piss, and fell in a parked taxi.

'Kingsland, my good man!'

'Yeah, Bro.'

What had the girls said? More importantly, what had they implied? Jess said she wouldn't care if I wore *Spiderman socks in bed*. It was a strange thing to say, but the more I thought about it, and the more I reflected on the giggling and the loss of words, the more I was sure what Jess had implied.

On Third Avenue, I was *convinced* what Jess had implied: she was falling for me.

Chapter scorecard: A close call. In 1768, Cook was chosen to lead an expedition to the South Seas, ending up in Tahiti via Rio de Janeiro. Yes, the Captain didn't have many chances to enchant a girl so early in his travels, but one must assume that when he did get the chance on a rare shore-leave, at least he wouldn't chicken out. Cook takes a deserved lead.

VARLEY 1   COOK 2

Chapter 6

They say life is like a box of chocolates. If that's the case Kings Plant Barn was a tin of Quality Street and my job the warm toffee penny no one wanted.

It wasn't that I disliked the staff; I didn't. It wasn't that I detested the early starts; those I could handle. I supposed I was hacked off with sweeping the car park and lifting bags of 'matter' for a paltry nine bucks an hour. This may sound ungrateful, but if Dr Fish had told me I'd be sweeping up dust and lugging sacks of shit for a living I'd have punched him in the face.

Now with regular hours, the next few weeks at Kings Plant Barn were long, sweaty and exhausting, but they weren't without good times. Pat was rapidly becoming my best friend at Kings, as well as my most dependable ally. Whilst James's devotion to helping with the endless bags of bark chippings, compost and potting mix was admirable, his delicate frame limited physical input to a few minutes of assistance at any one time. Though my stamina was improving each day, the sheer number of customers and the searing heat meant I couldn't cope on my own. Pat often poked his head out from a crate of herbaceous shrubs and then, sensing my distress, desert his post and come to my rescue within a matter of seconds. When we shifted a few pallets of compost I gave him an obliging thumbs-up, but Pat merely deflected the praise with a 'no worries, mate.' Such gallant gestures were to become Pat's trademark.

I was also building up quite a rapport with most of the staff, as well as some of the customers. For instance, I knew when Sandra and Brenda took their lunch break (when they damn well pleased). I ascertained what Karen the landscape gardener from Epsom usually wanted (freebies and lots of compliments about her 'high protein physique'), and I knew what not to say to James if I was to enter Brenda's good books ('Hey James, did you see the tits on that? Bet you can't fit those in a suitcase').

On one notable day, when I'd watered all the bedding plants, Brenda gave me the go-ahead to relax in the resident café. This was unheard of.

'Have you taken your pills today?'

'Very funny, Joe. You want me to change my mind?'

'No, I don't want you to change it, Brenda. Your mind is perfection itself. It runs like a dream and is practically faultless in every - '

'You know where the café is. You've got thirty minutes.'

King's Café was run by a bloke called St. John, who occasionally gave me free carrot cake. He really was a saint. My favourite drink at the café was L&P - a strange-tasting fizzy tipple that is a Kiwi institution. L&P stands for Lemon and Paeroa - Paeroa being a small town in North Island noted for its spring water, and Lemon being the yellow citrus fruit found on trees and regularly sold in supermarkets. There's even a seven-metre high L&P bottle in Paeroa to mark its fame, and the drink is advertised around the country as 'world famous in New Zealand'. It's a great slogan, if it meant sense.

Random Bar / Café Conversation
'May I take your order, madam?'
'I'll have bacon, eggs, two hash browns, fried mushrooms, three rounds of toast, tomatoes and some fried bread. And a Coke.'
'Regular or sugar free?'
'Sugar free. I'm on a diet.'

The workload at Kings Plant Barn increased steadily. Whenever I was freed from the shackles of the tills or if ever there was a lull in the demand for compost, I was 'promoted' to organise the cargo of dry goods. This was not as exciting as it sounds, and even more intolerable.

'Dry goods' was a term used to describe anything sold that didn't require maintenance: in short, anything that wasn't living. Bags of fertilizer, insect powders, garden netting, hoses, wheelbarrows, wooden fencing and garden gloves - they all fell under this definition and none escaped my ardent attention. The obvious pleasure when dealing with dry goods was that they were packaged, so chucking them casually onto shelves was commonplace (well, with me, at any rate.) Bags of fertilizer were five kilos in weight and perfect in size for aerobatic tomfoolery - sometimes I flicked them up under my legs, circus-like, to land on the lower shelves, although Sandra's beady eye was never too far away, and Brenda had a nasty habit of appearing out of nowhere like the T-1000 in *Terminator 2*. It was about as fun as one could have in a garden centre.

Maybe I'm giving dry goods a bad name. Sometimes it was better working with dry goods under the shade of the shop than to endure the sweaty toil of the compost and bark chippings in the car park. The only advantage of lugging the compost around was you could chat to the customers and lose a bit of weight whilst doing so, although soon I became knackered and craved the indoor coolness.

Dry goods did have one major drawback: powdered insect repellent. It was disgusting. Routinely the plastic bottles arrived at Kings in a state that hinted they'd been stored on their side in a warehouse, thus resulting in the leakage of foul-smelling powder. When picked up in a bunch - like bowling pins - my hands were instantly smothered in the toxic mess. Most of the insect powders were an irritant beyond belief, so I ended up running around the shop like a madman looking for the nearest tap to wash off the damn stuff.

And the stench! Christ, most of the powders possessed the aroma of a cow burp - truly grotesque. To make things worse, my request to senior management for gloves and mouth protector was met with unsavoury howls of disdain.

Cutting the garden netting was also without its plus points. Unravelling the springy mesh was simple if you needed a short length, but anything more than five metres was truly tedious. The netting coiled and bended and twisted and generally did what the hell it pleased. Then, if a queue of customers formed behind me, I'd poke them in the eye with it or, worse, damaged their clothing. The only rational thing to do was hide in the café and then re-surface when customers had either gone home or reported me for gross insubordination.

Sheep pellets arrived in colossal cloth bags, and it was my duty to make sure a barrel at the entrance was regularly topped up so customers could help themselves, like Pick 'N' Mix. Each bag weighed in at 30 kilos, so it was a huge struggle to transport them to the barrel. Ideally the pellets would be poured into the barrel carefully to reduce spillage. To say this was difficult would be to grossly understate. After jostling with the bag for what seemed like an Ice Age you'd aim at the centre of the barrel. Then, with a steady exertion, you'd tip the bag at 45 degrees to fill said barrel. Judging when to stop proved impossible, and more often than not pellets would spill over the rim and skid along the floor like rice on a skating rink, resulting in a furious cleaning operation. Customers lined up specifically to watch this charade; it was their morning's amusement. When you'd emptied half the bag on the floor, they'd emit a low 'tut-tut' before sauntering to the garden netting and asking for six-and-a-half metres. It was never a *whole* metre.

'And watch my cashmere jumper, eh.'

Away from work, mid-October was stress-free because of the routine of leisure. Life with the boys was a blast. At weekends I joined Crispin, my boss and G on hedonistic jaunts. These included fantastic beaches, trips to national parks and over-indulgences in booze, cigarettes and drugs. A couple of examples:

1) Alexander drove us to the world famous surfing resort of Raglan, a small town three hours south of Auckland on the west coast - about 50 kilometres west of Hamilton. Raglan features in Bruce Brown's seminal 1964 surfing film *The Endless Summer*. Foolishly we swam in Manu Bay - the most famous surfing beach

in New Zealand which has one of the longest left-hand breaks in the world. Impressive stuff, but what does it mean? The boys hadn't brought any surfing gear (duh) but we were content bobbing about on the waves whilst the locals tried to take our heads off with their surfboards. A tattooed skinhead surfer came within six inches of my nose, prompting a stream of foul-mouthed obscenities. I yelled back, 'No need to apologise, mate, don't worry about it!' It was truly a Kiwi experience I'll treasure forever.

We spent a night there in a hostel called Raglan Wagon Cabins. The rooms were restored railway carriages. G observed, 'What a novel idea - sleeping on sleepers.' It was safer than in the sea, and after a crate of Speights and a packet of Luckies, I slept like a baby (I dribbled a lot).

In the morning, just before we left, a couple of local surfers picked a fight with Alexander because he had 'poofy hair'. It reminded me of the film *Point Break* where Keanu Reeves infiltrated a gang of criminal surfers. We drove off before the surfers noticed Crispin's girly locks. G wound down the window and yelled 'Gnarly, dude!' The locals started to chase after us, but decided to give up and instead just shook their fists.

2) Alexander, Crispin and I set off to Tongariro National Park. We slept in the car, ready to tackle Mount Tongariro in the early hours. Our expectations were

as high as the 2,000 metre volcano. The crossing is reckoned to be one of New Zealand's most enlightening hikes. Fitness wise, I was doomed from the start.

The national park (which is, incidentally, the oldest in New Zealand) was the setting for Mordor in *The Lord of the Rings* films - the place where nasty things happen to boys with protein deficiencies searching for old pieces of jewellery.

It was a sinister pitch black when we started out, so we fumbled over rugged terrain like geriatric drunks (it was even harder to light cigarettes!). The two brothers were kitted out in the latest North Face jackets and Salomon walking boots; my budget only catered for Hi-Tec trainers and purple leggings that may have been owned by an Elizabethan jester.

When darkness gave way to golden light, Alexander took out his Brunton GEO compass to determine exactly where we should be heading. I pointed at Tongariro's summit and declared, without sarcasm, 'We need to go *that* way.'

By the time we reached the top, I'd confirmed the hike as one of the most tiring in the country. My lungs wheezed like deflated balloons; my legs were liquorice laces. Across the valley lay the famous Emerald Lakes - a series of craters filled with deep green, mineral-laden water derived from the region's thermal activity. The wind was so severe it nearly blew me clean off. Aided by these gusts, it took a mere half an hour to scramble down to the bottom, skidding precariously on loose debris as though it were a natural escalator. It was terrific to get out in the great outdoors, but it just reminded me of how tremendously unfit I was. Note to self: gym membership cost $NZ 50 a month.

When we returned to Kingsland, our upstairs neighbour, Griff, invited us to sample his batch of 'electric puha' - Kiwi slang for marijuana. Griff had been growing it in plant pots on the roof for several weeks and was keen for some independent feedback. Although I'm generally against smoking dope (it turns a moron into a *complete* moron and, besides, I prefer crack!), I didn't want to be rude, so I asked for the biggest joint going. Griff handed me a seven-inch spliff that nearly took my eye out ('Joe, you need to put it in your mouth'), and once lit it was like inhaling the exhaust pipe of a London bus. I was combining the dope with plenty of Flame lager, so it was entirely predictable when, within the hour, I'd lost sense of both time and space. The last words I slurred that evening were, as far as I can recollect, 'You call it electric puha? But it's not even plugged in.'

A couple of days after Raglan, Alexander came round to the flat to announce a work update. I doubted he'd de-briefed every other member of staff at their home, so I was instantly suspicious.

And I was right to be. The gist was that I was to be on my best behaviour; over the next fortnight Kings Plant Barn was having one of their famous sales. Customers would double, with extra stock ordered to accommodate the increase. Profits and turnover would soar. Even the celebrated owner of the company, Mr King himself, would be there, undoubtedly strutting about like he owned not only the company but the whole damn city. I was not to be late. I was to be polite and 'customer-focused'. Even my uniform was to be clean. This was serious.

The next two weeks were going to be hell.

Chapter scorecard: Adventure coupled with obstacles means a varied month for Varley. Captain Cook was top-drawer for adventure, but who said the great man never had problems? It's a fair draw.

Chapter 7

Wherever you are in the world there will be one certainty: TV weather forecasters are all fallible. The pretty weather girl (I'm beginning to like her) advised today would be 'warm and sultry.' She had been glaringly misinformed - today was hotter than Satan's underpants, and it wasn't yet opening time.

I'd drunk a litre of water before leaving the flat, and a further bottle on Western Springs Road. I hadn't realised anywhere could be this humid so early in the morning. Liquid was pouring out of me. Perversely, the more I drank the thirstier I became. The sun was relentless. The moment I reached St Luke's I stole one of Brian's old fishing hats and strapped a piece of towelling around my ears. It was very *Lawrence of Arabia* and it served its purpose to a tee, but it made me look a bit of a twat.

It was mayhem. Customers flooded through the doors by the truckload like we were *giving* things away. By 9.30AM the garden centre was at bursting point. Alexander - and there was no denying the fact - was stressed to the max. He paraded around his office, clutching a notepad and pen, taking notes and making business calls like a Wall Street banker on a deadline.

Alexander just wanted everything to run like a well-oiled machine, so I retained a little sympathy for him.

I joined James and Malcolm in the car park to do what I did best - mainly leaking compost from split bags and amusing the customers (easy enough - a quick glance at my legs and they were in stitches). How envious I was of the staff. Even Judy - an experienced nature enthusiast from Greymouth who didn't *like* the sun - had wonderfully olive-brown skin. And Alexander! He boasted the most splendid legs one could ever hope to see (although his upper body was ghostly pale so he looked like a pint of Guinness).

The sun was ruthless; Helios was cracking his whip. Today was the hottest day of my working life. Inside three hours I'd produced enough sweat to water all the bedding plants and half the fruit trees.

Even with ear towelling it was intolerable. Regular breaks were necessary but risky (Sandra once caught Malcolm having a cigarette break and flicked his ear, *hard*). But these forbidden breathers gave me the chance to spy on customers. Observing them without their consent was terrific. What better place to 'people watch' than garden centres? Soon I could distinguish, say, a casual buyer from a mainstream purchaser, and an amateur horticulturist from a loner with simply nothing better to do. By my reckoning, there were three types of customer:

1) The Smash-and-Grabbers. These were high-powered professional landscapers or "trendy" garden designers who knew what they wanted and when they wanted it, goddamn it! Pat had another name for them: wankers. They had no time to stop and chat, were frequently rude, and undoubtedly drank 'mochaccinos' in pretentious coffee shops over conversations filled with compost and bullshit. They'd say, 'Right, you albino Pommie twerp, I'll get two dozen *Buxus*, five white *Camellia*, three ponga trunks and a bag of blood and bone. You fetch me five bags of sheep pellets, ten metres of garden netting and a bag of deluxe potting mix. Chop, chop! What are you waiting for? Winter?'

2) The Inquisitive Brigade. Usually locals with no social life who asked any gardening question, no matter how banal, stupid or bizarre. They'd turn up just to satisfy their sadistic craving for asking dumb questions. Some typical Q & As:

Question 1: 'Over here, you pasty-faced oaf. How much does this *Prunus* cost?'

Answer: (Looking an inch closer to the large, deliberately fluorescent price tag nobody in the Inquisitive Brigade seemed to notice, and said without a hint of contempt): 'Well, the price tag says thirty-nine dollars, so I'll put my neck on the line and say it costs thirty-nine dollars.'

Question 2: 'Tell me, young man, do I prefer the blue

or pink *Lobelia*?'

Answer: (Not spoken aloud): 'How the big bollocks should *I* know? It's your preference, not mine.' This was an infuriating line of questioning. How could *you* say what *they* preferred? It's like asking a barman if you want a pint of lager or a rum and Coke. It was ridiculous. And if you gave them the wrong answer, The Inquisitive Brigade looked at you like you'd insulted their sister.

Question 3: 'Do you happen to know the scientific name for the ubiquitous mountainous perennial gentian growing between twelve and fifteen inches, famed for its creamy white purpled-veined flowers, commonly found in fields in both North and South Islands?'

Answer: 'Er... no.'

What most riled me about The Inquisitive Brigade was that they didn't think before ploughing ahead with their stream of inane questions. How many times had customers interrupted me with the question, 'Oi, are you open yet?' You looked at the clock (which said 10.30) and you stared in disbelief at the obscene queues and you wanted to say, 'No, we're all here because we're homeless and we're incredibly bored.' Instead you sighed audibly and replied, 'Yes, we're open. Now, how may I help?'

'Do I prefer the blue or pink *Lobelia*?'

3) The Browsers. These were a strange breed. Regularly found at plant sales, this type of 'customer'

was anything but. Browsers had no intention of buying anything - be it garden hoses, alpine shrubbery or paving tiles - but favoured instead to saunter around wearyingly with an empty trolley until a member of staff asked if they needed any assistance. The answer, invariably: 'No thanks, just browsing.' After two hours The Browsers abandoned their trolley (obstructing the Smash-and-Grabbers, who'd instruct me to move the damn thing), head for the shop and, if daring, buy the cheapest ice-lolly on the way out.

The plant sale was a horticultural bloodbath. We had 20 St Luke's staff members, all of them dangerously over-worked. Malcolm and Richard careered around the car park in the fork-lift dumping endless pallets of potting mix, container mix, bark chippings and compost near the front doors. Pat, ever the trooper, worked the bedding plants whilst battling both heat and hangover. Brian soldiered on, because he was a tough-skinned Kiwi used to hard graft, and that's what they did. Grant dealt with three simultaneous sets of customers - cutting wooden fencing and answering questions about New Zealand natives - although how he did this I had precisely no idea. He had the knack of taking multi-tasking to new levels, and the thing was, everyone wanted his advice, so he must've been doing something right.

I was running tirelessly between the car park and the

herb displays - trying not to trip over split bark chippings and discarded trolleys - with the till queues rapidly increasing. Where had all these people come from? Had the Kings Plant Barn sale been advertised on national TV? Or Australasia FM? That was it - they'd flown from Brisbane just to make my life miserable.

By lunchtime the Tannoy system was on overdrive.

'Joe to the car park, please. Five bags of compost. Repeat - five bags of compost.'

'Five bags of compost in the car park, please. Repeat - *five* bags of compost.'

'Five bags of bark chipping, please. Repeat - *five* bags of bark chipping. Oh, and five bags of compost.'

I ached for anything - anything at all - but lugging warm compost to customers' cars. The problem was that the compost was on special offer: five bags for $NZ 20. Everyone was going compost mad - everyone except me. I was hot, sweaty and tired. I needed a beer. I needed Jess.

'Five bags of compost in the car park, please. Repeat - *five* bags of compost.'

And it was Alice speaking on the tannoy! Her voice was irritating at close range; at this volume it was unbearable. She sounded like a Whoopee cushion gradually being let down, only more grating. The phrase 'Five bags of compost' later produced endless nightmares. I wanted to bellow '*Oh-my-God-stop-pronouncing-bags-as-biggs!*'

and crawl under a large plant pot, pretending compost did not exist.

But we all knew it did, and we all knew compost was king.

The next day at work was 27 degrees, easy. The intensity of the Kiwi sun couldn't be underestimated. Alexander was away 'on business' (skiving on the second day of the sale!) and Sandra had taken charge, but she was busy with fertilizer orders, so Brenda kept things ticking over.

Such was the overwhelming humidity Pat needed help hosing the bedding plants, which was practically a constant job. Saturated soil could be reduced to a dry, crumbly mess in a matter of hours. The dangers of over-watering are well documented, but the plants really did need endless dousing. Hose in hands, Pat and I developed a horticultural symbiotic relationship, drenching each other with pressure hoses when the need arose. It was quite cute.

And for the time being I kept Brenda at bay. She even bought me cheesecake from the café, which I suppose was the Kiwi equivalent of patting me on the back and saying, 'You know, I thought all you Pommies were sickly, work-shy gobshites, but you haven't cocked up yet - so good on yer.' Encouragement indeed.

This might sound crazy - and a little contradictory - but I was looking forward to the next few days. Not so much because I was taking pleasure from the lifting and the sweeping and the watering and the constant heckling. It was because I'd lost so much weight that my body now resembled what a 23-year-old boy's body should.

And my knowledge of the native Kiwi plants was forever expanding, which was a minor victory in itself. Not that I despised plants or paid no attention to the countryside or anything flora-related. Animals are superior because they actually *do* stuff. A dog will meet you at the door after you've been away for years - recognising you instantly - and will give the impression that it has genuinely missed you with a series of tail-wagging and face-licking. Though I'm not overwhelmed by cats (they're selfish and they piss in your shoes) at least they try to make friends with you - until they realize you don't carry tins of sardines in your back pockets - and when you become bored of their grooming habits you can kick them out so your neighbour can take care of them. Horses are muscular and intelligent and they have that menacing glint in their eye which says, 'Make no mistake, pal, I'm the Daddy. Come any closer and I'll stomp on your nuts.' You know where you are with horses. And barnacles... well...

Plants, essentially, are dull: they stay in one place, have no charisma and they can't fetch the morning paper. I don't know why, but I've never really developed a rapport with plants. Some people - incredibly - will part with huge sums of cash for a plant merely because it smells nice: as long as it releases an odour which doesn't make you recoil in disgust, well that's all right. You can glue three packets of air freshener to a hat stand for the same effect. Plants are popular gifts - be it for birthdays, weddings or as a Mother's Day present - although the logic behind this mystifies me. What use to anybody is something that looks pretty if it's going to curl up and die within 72 hours? And what is it with people *talking* to plants? They have no nervous system. Granted, an increase in carbon dioxide may stimulate plant growth, but you don't need to greet them or apologise to them or recite to them verses of Act II from *King Lear*. Breathing on them will do.

Nevertheless, my horticultural knowledge was growing by the day. I familiarised myself with the usual suspects and could identify a few plants without reading the labels: *Begonia*, *Lobelia*, marigolds, *Fuchsia*, *Chrysanthemum*, pansies, *Geranium*, *Buxus*, *Cordyline* and *Cotoneaster*. And the herbs (once so difficult to differentiate) were also beginning to make sense with all their individual, aromatic smells: sweet marjoram, leafy basil, scented iron-rich thyme, beautiful coriander, spicy fennel. Christ, the heat was really getting to me.

Chapter scorecard: Varley rises to the challenge of the plant sale, earning himself kudos in the process. By

1770, Cook had sailed along the east coast of Australia, but came a cropper when he got his calculations wrong and crashed into the Great Barrier Reef. Such incompetence is demoralising for the Captain, and so the young pretender draws level.

VARLEY 2   COOK 2

Chapter 8

Working life at Kings Plant Barn zoomed by in a pungent blur of compost, bark chippings and bedding plants. Had I really been in New Zealand for a few weeks? It was time to think about my plans for next year, and travelling to South Island seemed a necessity.

'If you don't haul your ass down there,' Brian warned me, 'you'll regret it for the rest of your life. You just make damn sure you get down there, boy, or I'll hunt you down with a kitchen knife, ay.' Being threatened with a 'kitchen knife, ay' seemed a bit harsh, but the thing was, Brian really *meant* it. Kiwis must hold South Island in the highest regard - even Aucklanders - and all the photos I'd seen in travel books indicated a sacred wilderness that was pretty much incomparable with anywhere else in the world.

Of course, my South Island plans for the New Year depended on finance, but if it was a choice between saving a few dollars or being hunted by Brian, I'd go for the former every time. Hopefully I'd be there for the winter, even though I hate skiing, have a noteworthy indifference to the cold and I can't snowboard. It should be fun.

Malcolm and Richard were madmen. The car park was teeming with cars and delivery trucks and customers struggling with bags of compost, yet the two lads were quite content competing in some form of fork-lift freestyle. Malcolm was at the wheel, giving the rusty vehicle plenty of gas. Richard stood in front, a dirty rag raised high above his head. Malcolm feathered the accelerator and the fork-lift hissed in anticipation. It was nearly show time.

'Ready, Mal?' said Richard.

'Just give me the nod, mate,' Malcolm said with a wicked grin.

Richard then brought down the makeshift flag to begin the contest. Malcolm put the fork-lift into first gear and he was off. Under a dense cloud of dust the fork-lift chugged across the car park. After only a few yards Malcolm slammed on the breaks, jolting the fork-lift at right angles to an abrupt halt. This mechanical U-turn was remarkable and as Malcolm struggled with the steering wheel for the return leg, Richard suddenly grabbed my arm.

'Better give him a wide berth, Joe. You don't wanna get impaled on those forks, ay!'

Malcolm careered back as the forks wobbled under two tonnes of roaring metal. As the petrol canister bubbled with ferocity under the sheer acceleration, Malcolm gleefully crossed the imaginary line. Richard looked at his watch.

'And we have ourselves a new Kings record for the Car Park Olympics!'

Malcolm jumped from the front seat and performed a victory dance.

'That felt good, eh. I knew it was a quick 'un.'

'Hey, you wanna have a go, Joe?' said Richard. 'Mal did it in twenty-three seconds. Rickon you could beat that?'

'Well, I haven't driven in about a year and I don't really know if - '

'Course he wants a go,' said Malcolm, thrusting the keys into my hand. 'Poms are so competitive - they'll have a go at anything.'

And so I found myself climbing cautiously into the fork-lift. Although I passed my driving test three years ago, the fork-lift was a different beast altogether. It was on par with winning junior gymkhana and then trying your luck in a Wild West rodeo. The fork-lift was a spluttering, oil-leaking, compost-lifting mean machine. I struggle to operate a Renault Clio.

'Better be quick,' warned Richard. 'Don't want the boss catching us again.'

'Again? Alexander has already caught you?'

'Just the once!'

I made myself comfortable as the fork-lift once again wheezed into life. My hands were slimy with sweat and hose water after a session in the bedding plants with Patrick. I wiped them on my shorts and glanced nervously to the entrance to see if Alexander was hiding in some sort of disciplinary ambush. The last thing I wanted was for him to see me racing the fork-lift when I should've been helping the customers.

'Ready, Joe?'

'I guess.'

'Okay, three, two, one... *go!*'

At first the accelerator jammed. There was either a certain technique to it, or else I wasn't putting my foot down hard enough. To my left a stream of cars glistened under the sun on St Luke's Road. To my right, an assortment of tropical shrubs and fruit trees behind the wire fencing. Straight ahead was smooth tarmac, surrounded by parked cars.

The fork-lift reared into action. I felt immediately the power that these things could generate. It was the Sherman tank of the horticultural world. The steering wheel felt heavy but I didn't need to use it until I braked for the second leg of the race.

And therein lay the problem: I didn't know *how* to brake.

The fork-lift was only going at ten miles per hour but speed was not the issue with this wrecking ball on wheels. When the halfway mark was in sight I tried the brakes. Nothing happened. I looked back frantically at the boys. Richard was studying his watch. Malcolm had his head in his hands.

'Help!' I squealed.

'Brake!' screamed Malcolm. 'Joe - *brake!*'

This was bad. I looked to my right, where the big yellow Kings logo stood proudly over the door. Though I couldn't see any customers it'd only be a matter of seconds before they started pushing their plant-laden trolleys to their cars. Only a blind man would fail to see a fork-lift truck rampaging across the car park, so at least for now the potential for human fatality was pretty slim - but how to stop this madness?

A black Mercedes was five yards away. There was only one thing for it - I'd have to deliberately crash into the first expendable object I could find and hope the fork-lift wouldn't spontaneously combust in a ball of petrol-induced flames. That would surely send Alexander over the edge, and me to the nearest hospital.

Just ahead, to my right, a large plant pot accommodated a tropical palm tree. The pot was a bulky wooden barrel - much like a beer barrel - and though it looked sturdy I still fancied my chances colliding into this than a car - particularly a brand new Mercedes. Crashing into a customer's sports car would've not only hindered any chances of promotion, but also increased the likelihood of instant deportation.

So I wrestled with the steering wheel, eventually

turned it clockwise, shut my eyes, and hoped for the best.

Boom!

I felt a sudden jolt. My body was thrown forwards, and my ribcage jarred in agony. The exposed rusty metal dashboard stopped any further progress. There was a smell of leaking oil and hot steam. I heard Malcolm yelling something, but the words were fuddled.

A few seconds passed. Then the words became clear: 'Get out! Joe - *get out!* She's gonna *blow!*'

Registering a dull throbbing behind my eyes I clambered down from the fork-lift. A moment of composure later, I took heed of Malcolm's warning and hobbled across a patch of greenery before diving headlong into a nearby rhododendron bush to protect myself from the impending blast.

Nothing happened.

I stayed crouched underneath the cool vegetation, hands covering my ears to protect myself from the deafening explosion. Still nothing.

Malcolm and Richard stared at me. They were both quite casual. Fork-lift trucks smashing into plant pots might've been a daily occurrence to them.

'You can come out now, Joe,' said Malcolm.

'... Is it safe?'

'She'll be right. If she was gonna blow she would have done it by now, ay.'

I brushed myself clean of the dried debris. For now

only my pride was damaged.

Malcolm padded across the car park. 'Give me the keys, Joe. I'll drive her back to the compost. Jeez, I hope Alexander didn't see that.'

Alexander didn't, but Sandra did. Sandra saw every manic second. She emerged from the shopping area and advanced on me. She had the same look in her eye as Brenda a few weeks ago: menace and fury.

'Did I just see what I thought I saw?'

No Sandra, it was a mirage. You've been hallucinating. Have a lie down.

'I was just - '

'Who said you could drive the fork-lift? Only Richard and Malcolm have the authority. This is totally unacceptable. See me in Alexander's office. Now!'

I turned to the boys for support but their expressions were blank. I'd have to take one for the team.

I followed my now livid deputy manager into the office, grateful at least that Alexander seemed to be busy elsewhere. Sandra pointed to the nearest chair. 'Sit.' I duly complied.

'Well? What have you got to say for yourself?'

'I thought it'd be a good idea to have a go, just in case I was needed to drive it if Malcolm and Richard are off sick.' Not the most convincing lie, but certainly not the worst.

'That's no excuse. What you just did could have

seriously injured somebody, or worse. Alexander is in Takapuna so I'm going to have to tell him when he returns.'

'Please Sandra, don't do that. Please.' I was grovelling, but this was pretty serious.

'Why shouldn't I, Joe? Unless you think that careering around the car park on a fork-lift represents reasonable behaviour?'

'Of course not. I'm really terribly sorry.' I was shocked at how English I came across. I'd never before said I was 'really terribly sorry'. It sounded like I was apologising to the Queen for kicking one of her corgis.

Sandra and I shared the office in silence. I hoped she was mulling my apology over, deciding whether telling Alexander would've been such a wise move. Sometimes I had the feeling that Sandra really did like me and that I was doing my best to please her, like a batty old aunt happy to be in the company of her favourite nephew. But now I was scared I'd thrown all that away for the sake of fork-lift lunacy.

'Well,' said Sandra finally, 'I really should tell Alexander. You went too far, there's no doubt about that. But you're a good worker, Joe, so I'll give you a second chance.'

'Thank you, Auntie Sandra. It'll never happen again.'

'I know it won't. You *don't* want to know what will happen if you pull that stunt again. Now go and help

Julie on the tills. It's chaos out there. Then you can do some weeding. Go!'

Although Mal and Richard's antics had not been malicious, I had succumbed to their powers of persuasion, and that calamitous escapade confirmed a few things I needed to be aware of. At the time my little fork-lift adventure seemed nothing more than horseplay; crashing didn't seem a reality. If things got out of hand the plan was simply to stop and let the boys get on with their fun by themselves. But some gentle cajoling on the boys' part was my downfall. I couldn't blame naivety - what caused my predicament was youthful exuberance and my desire to appease my two colleagues.

Sandra's leniency proved obliging, even compassionate. She'd previously dished out punishment to staff - Patrick told me she threatened to tweak his nose for taking an extended lunch break - so I was thankful she wouldn't tell Alexander. But now I needed to repay her tolerance by keeping my head down and grafting to the best of my ability. God knows what Sandra will do if she caught me on the fork-lift again. Most probably kick me in the balls and report me to the British Embassy.

After the tills I weeded in-between the flagstones outside the toilets (ah, the glamour!) and by closing time I needed to let off more steam than the fork-lift. I'd arranged an impromptu drinking session with Jess, something which I'd wanted to do for a long time. We ended up in Embargo, one of the more popular bars near Queen Street.

The evening was warm and still and the air full of promise ('I promise to behave myself!'). Jess hadn't made plans for the next day, so she too could let her hair down. Tomorrow morning would bring fresh crates of bark chippings that would be snapped up in no time and lugging bags of plant substrate for eight hours in unbearable heat was bad enough without the added torment of a hangover. I had to be sensible; I'd stick to just the ten beers.

In Embargo we mingled with drunken travellers sharing stories of bravado and tomfoolery. We ghosted from group to group, bouncing from story to story, until settling on a gang of three South Islanders from Invercargill. All were young and unshaven and wore jeans and chequered shirts. Instantly I thought: farmers.

After sinking a few 'Steinies' - a Steinie being the local brew Steinlager - Jess and I began to flirt shamelessly. Steinlager is well-known in New Zealand for being a famous beer outside New Zealand, but what it is that it's famous for outside New Zealand seems to be this evening's moot point. Jess claimed that it'd won a few 'gold awards', but apparently only Aucklanders drank the stuff. This made no sense. But Jess really was having a good time and eventually we clicked bottles and made a toast to Steinlager - famous for making you talk utter nonsense. When Jess smiled at me I felt a gooey warmth deep in my stomach. Tonight was shaping up to be something special.

By 10 PM we were both pretty drunk, so in my 'casual' state I took out a week's wages with my new bankcard and handed some notes to Jess.

'Buy whatever you want!'

'Gosh, Joe, you can't afford it. You don't have to do this.'

'I can afford it and I do have to do this. You're my queen and queens warrant the best things in life.'

'Like crowns?'

'Yes! Crowns! You deserve a crown!'

Jess faked a punch to my shoulder. 'You're crazy.'

'You're right, Jess. I am crazy. I'm soooo crazzzzy, crazy for lovin' youuuuu!'

When Jess stopped laughing she stepped closer. I ran a hand through her hair. She looked into my eyes.

'You may kiss the queen now.'

'Don't mind if I do.'

In one fraction of a millisecond, as our lips met, everything was assigned to obscurity. I smelt raspberry and sweet breath and I didn't want to come up for air. My hands moved up to her neck where they pulled her harder to my mouth. Even David Copperfield couldn't pull off this kind of magic.

Seeking another drink, Jess and I wandered drunkenly onto Ponsonby Road. The Safari Lounge was an aptly named bar, with pictures of antelopes on the walls and gorillas asking for ID.

Random Bar Conversation
'You got proof of age?'

'No.'

'Why not?'

'Coz I left it at school.'

We settled down with two large gin and tonics. A fat, sweaty American oaf waddled over. He'd heard my English accent and wanted to know my concerns about BP. My only concerns, I told him, were that he doesn't kill me with his odour and that he doesn't get stuck in the door on the way out. Then he started talking about nuking whales. Jess was a keen animal lover, so this Yankee imbecile was in water more dangerous than one of the marine behemoths in Norwegian seas. Jess remained unflustered, calmly telling him he should feel some empathy towards flabby mammals.

'It's ironic, isn't it' she mused, 'that blubber is used to make soap, but the ones who closely resemble whales don't use it?'

Boss Hog finally backed down and disappeared to pester the bouncers on the door. I had to hand it to

Jess. Brains, beauty and a killer kiss - it was a winning combination.

Next up was Grand Central, a New York styled bar farther down Ponsonby Road. It was neither grand nor central but small and funky and highly recommended. The staff were fun and obliging, refilling our glasses without delay or reservation. Grand Central was the type of place where, if your mission was to get as drunk as possible, a barmaid would sidle on over, place a beer mat in front of you and say, 'Now there's a fine idea. Here's a large vodka on the house to help you on your way.' Having Jess all to myself in an intimate bar made me the happiest boy in the Southern Hemisphere.

Then disaster struck. We danced for a while (my gout had returned), then tucked into pungent - and possibly fatal - cocktails in a bar farther still down Ponsonby Road. The only thing I remembered was surfboards for tables and weird tropical flowers and fisherman's netting on the ceiling, and I was lying on cold concrete with my legs in the air howling like a wolf.

The transformation from English gentleman to idiotic drunkard progressed in a flash. What was so cruel were the effects of alcohol were irreversible; once you reach the stage where you're howling like a wolf, it's impossible to regain the decorum needed to convince your date that you are, by all accounts, a perfectly decent human being. To the person who invents an "instant sobriety" pill will bring global admiration and a whopping bank balance. I needed one now.

The combination of Steinlager, gin and miscellaneous cocktails was devastating. Vision was blurred and general coordination had thrown in the towel. Even standing up - the most elementary of functions - was taxing. When I managed this feat on the seventh attempt (like a tortoise struggling to its feet after being laid on its shell) I opened my mouth to say something - anything at all - but was capable only of producing a thick droop of saliva that dribbled down my chin and settled crudely on my left shoe. I then needed to relieve myself, so I wrestled with my zip, but instead only managed to loosen my belt, so my trousers dropped to the pavement in a shameful display of drunken nudity.

Patches of the evening were precisely that. I recalled climbing a tree to snare a wood pigeon, but the bird smelt my booze-breath and flied to safety, leaving me stranded for half an hour in a maze of tangled branches. I remembered also using an empty beer can as a microphone to serenade Jess with a rendition of *Zoom* by Fat Larry's Band. By this stage I was singing to whoever would listen, be it nearby neighbours, tuxedo-wearing gorillas or stray cats. A karaoke classic it was not, but at least the effort was there.

The rest of the evening descended into oblivion. I forgot which country I was in. Suddenly Jess was nowhere to be seen. I looked around, half in panic, half blind drunk, but she was gone. And my ear was bleeding, which was unaccountable. And that was the last of my memory.

For the time being, my angel had flown.

Chapter scorecard: After a promising night on the tiles, Varley loses his girl, and - who knows? - any chance he had with the lovely Jess. The Captain wins this one.

Chapter 9

Weekends in Auckland were bliss. Even on a Saturday shopping wasn't a chore, and the city offered an astonishing range of activities. Crispin often drove me around, stopping off for a bite to eat, do some window-shopping, maybe relaxing on a beach for a few hours. It was this last leisure pastime that I enjoyed the most, but on the day after my drunken shambles, the sun proved to be my downfall.

I'd taken the day off work. I felt terrible. Alexander was unaware that I'd got sincerely annihilated last night so I hadn't given him the gory details - I just told him I had a stomach bug. My boss wasn't naturally suspicious, but when I'd made the phone call he must have suspected foul play. Even *I* could hear my voice sounded like I'd been on the pop all night.

Crispin recommended Mission Bay, a popular beach a few kilometres east of the city. It was mid-afternoon, and the music from last night was still audible. I hoped the fresh sea air would perk me up; I needed something to bring me back to life.

Crispin parked the Toyota overlooking the sea. We bought battered snapper and chips from The Fish Pot, a delectable café on Tamaki Drive. The food was just what I needed, but my mind was on Jess. Where had she gone? Was it something I'd said? Or worse, something I'd done? Had I insulted both her but her entire family and kin before passing out with the booze? Never had alcoholic memory loss been more distressing. I didn't even remember getting back from to Kingsland. From Ponsonby it's within walking distance, but for an unfit drunk the journey was pretty much unachievable.

'Don't worry about Jess,' Crispin said, chomping on a vinegar-sodden chip. 'She'll be fine. I'm sure there was a nice big Dutchman to look after her when she got back to the backpackers.'

I didn't take the bait. My temples throbbed, activated by the belting sun. It was *so* hot. There were fine views of Rangitoto Island - a peculiar 600-year-old volcanic cone ten kilometres out into the Hauraki Gulf. It rises gently to its central summit as though someone has pinched it in the middle. The island boasts crisp black basalt deposits, a population of orchids, and the largest pohutukawa forest in the world.

'We'll have to kayak over there sometime,' Crispin yelled from his car. 'It'll be awesome.'

I stared blankly towards the horizon. It appeared miles away. 'Yeah, awesome.'

During summer Mission Bay is crammed with tourists, cyclists and rollerbladers. The tourists want a little peace and quiet, the cyclists cycle, and the rollerbladers show off their oh-so brown legs under fluorescent spandex. Tamaki Drive, the main road leading back to Auckland, is a cyclist's wet dream. The smooth road snakes between blue waters and steep, rising crags. There are superb panoramic views of the Auckland skyline, too, with the Sky Tower never looking so striking. I'd be having a great time if I didn't think I was dying.

The sun was barely tolerable. Crispin reminded me of New Zealand's short burning time and asked if I was wearing sunblock. I told him to mind his own business. My friend shrugged, mumbling something about 'mad dogs and Englishmen'. It's *my* skin, I told him, and I'll do what I damn well want with it. But, by Christ, it was *soooo* hot.

Shortly my eyes grew heavy. I passed out on the beach wearing only my shorts. The scorching heat and seductively lapping waves were a calming lullaby. Soon blackness turned to sleep. I didn't dream about anything.

Something was wrong. Something was very wrong. When I woke my head felt lighter, but my legs were immobilised, like they'd been tied to blocks of lead piping. I rubbed my eyes, adjusting to the light. I saw two black objects stretched out in front of me. I needed to focus to confirm their identity. Unfortunately, the two black objects were attached to my body.

My first reaction was one of alarm. Had Crispin buried

my legs in the sand and replaced them with charred slats of wood? And why was breathing difficult? Dizziness and dry throat completed the horrific situation. I'd been sunburnt. Badly.

Now, if you think you've had sunburn before, the chances are you haven't - you'd know about it. If you've turned a tender pink, suffered from sweats or if you've had minor skin blisters, consider yourself very lucky. I laugh in your face if you've ever been severely dehydrated or had heatstroke. No exaggeration - I'd been roasted alive.

Crispin padded down to the beach. His face told the story. Initially he was too shocked to speak. Then he simply said, 'Fuck me, Joey, you've gone all black.'

I remained rigid in the sand, paranoid that my legs would snap like charcoal sticks. 'All black, like the rugby team?'

'Jesus, this is no time for jokes. You're fried!'

I was, too. The sun had acted like a giant grill and sautéed my entire body.

My friend sprung into action, hoisting me up on the sand under my armpits. I kept my legs completely taut lest the skin cracked the surface. I felt like a barbecued chicken, and a stupid one at that.

'I told you to cover up,' Crispin reiterated, shaking his head in disbelief, 'but noooooo, you wouldn't listen. And you've been asleep for less than... ' He looked at his watch. 'Less than *two hours!* It's not even four o'clock yet.'

The awful truth about this mishap wasn't the awkwardness of walking to the car like an elderly incontinent; I'd been embarrassing myself for the past 23 years and was warming to it. No, the worst part was ignoring sensible advice from those in the know.

The ride back was agony. My blackened feet poked out from the Toyota's window, like a scene from a gangster film. Along Tamaki Drive the breeze zipped up along my legs, not cooling them, but making them feel... overcooked.

Back at the flat, I waddled onto the balcony in a fashion John Wayne would have been proud of. A warm, sickly heat hit us both as Crispin plumped up two cushions to accommodate me on the sofa. Immediately after, he recommended I took a shower. I returned his suggestion with a sharp look of pain.

'No use arguing, baby. I genuinely think it will help.'

'How? How can a shower possibly help? Look at me, Crispin. I look like a chipolata on twiglets.'

Then G-Man walked through the door, whistling cheerfully. 'Alright lads? Today's been amazing. Guess what I did when... *fuck me Joey!* What happened to you, man?'

'Sunburn,' Crispin said gravely.

'*Please* tell me you used sunblock.'

I swallowed hard. 'I know-I know-I know-I know. You don't need to tell me, G.'

'You need to get in the shower, quick,' said G-Man. 'It'll get the sand out of your skin.'

'That's what I said,' Crispin added, already lifting me from the sofa. 'C'mon, G. Give me a hand.'

In no condition to put up a fight, my friends bundled me into the shower. Cold water trickled down my blackened torso. My chest resembled the surface of the moon: huge blisters erupted from taut, shiny skin. Water invaded defenceless nooks; blisters grew into transparent black balloons. I had shiny black sacs ten inches in circumference growing all over my body.

My friends jabbed the balloons with inquisitive fingers, hoping they'd pop like water bombs. It was weirdly fascinating watching these sacs expand with water, like I had a special power only stupid English boys would ever know. But after a while, when the boys had had their fun, I felt ashamed and embarrassed, like The Elephant Man, so I ordered them both out of the cubicle. A packet of painkillers later I passed out for the second time that day.

I was a shell of a man. Crispin phoned his brother to inform him of my predicament. The outcome: I couldn't work for the next few days. Alexander wasn't lying. I was totally sofa-ridden, forced to watch appalling TV. It was torture.

'Good news, Joey. Alexander said it's fine and to get well soon.'

'Really?'

'Yup. The bad news: he wants you to write 'I am a fool who doesn't respect the sun' two hundred times before you go back to work. He said it'll remind you to wear sunblock.'

'Is he joking?'

'Alexander doesn't joke, my friend.'

'How true.'

My friends only wanted me to be careful, but writing lines was like being back at school. That said, it hammered home the fact I was still learning about New Zealand. G-Man fetched me a Biro and a pad of paper. Grimacing on the sofa, I began my punishment without protest.

I am a fool who doesn't respect the sun
I am a fool who doesn't respect the sun
I am a fool who doesn't respect the sun
I am a fool who doesn't...

Chapter scorecard: Cook sailed west to Java to repair his ship, but his crew were not accustomed to such exotic environs, and some of them caught fever and keeled over. The Captain, however, was making breakthroughs in science and managed to save a few lives. The boy

Varley, in contrast, gets obscenely sunburnt. Varley must get his head straight, and in the meantime, Cook adds to his lead.

VARLEY 2   COOK 4

Chapter 10

'Oh, Joe! What happened to you? You look *terrible*.'

'Thanks Jess.'

Three days later, I was still a slave to the sofa. I'd phoned Jess but my voice cracked up so she assumed I was having a seizure or something. She caught a taxi immediately.

Jess brought cold beer and a copy of *Maxim*. Then she filled me in on what had happened on Ponsonby Road the other night. It wasn't easy listening. I'd got into a scuffle with one of the barmen, and started surfing on a table while singing the *Hawaii Five-O* theme tune. Then I'd caught my ear on an overhead fan, which explained the pain. When it started bleeding, Jess thought it best to go home alone. Events after that remained unknown.

Jess was spot-on - I did look terrible. Crispin had positioned a mirror on the coffee table so I could gauge my recovery, which only confirmed I'd been a shit-for-brains imbecile. I'd not slept much and I was sweating heavily. My legs were paler but now variegated in hue, alternating between black and pink, like sticks of liquorice rock.

'Is there anything I can do?' asked Jess, protectively.

'Anything at all? Do you want some water? Or aspirin? Let me get you some water. Tap or bottled? Bottled, right? From the fridge? It'll be colder.'

'Thanks Sweetie, but do you think we've got *bottled* water?'

'Fair point.'

I asked Jess to close the blinds and fetch me a damp towel. She cradled my head on her lap and began dabbing my forehead in gentle, deliberate strokes. I grew sleepy.

'I used to be a nurse, you know,' said Jess.

I stifled a yawn. 'Really?'

'Well, a junior one. In Christchurch. Does that count?'

'Of course it does.'

'Yes, I suppose it does. I really enjoyed it. Lousy pay of course, but the job was sweet as. Oh, you should have seen me, Joe! I was really good at it.'

'I can imagine.'

'I even enjoyed wearing the uniform. To tell you the truth, it was kind of kinky. It sort of turned me on. I used to put the uniform on and pretend that I could make all the patients do whatever I wanted - that I had complete control over them and that I could - '

I'd have to hear that story another time, I thought, as I dozed off under the therapeutic dabbing of my very own Kiwi nurse.

My first day back at Kings Plant Barn was embarrassing.

I didn't have suitable trousers to wear (I'd be far too hot in my jeans), so my striped legs were the day's big talking point. Banter included such gems as: 'Give us a hand over here, zebra boy', 'They should have closed down that tanning parlour ages ago, ay,' and, 'Lovely. We've got an awning in just the same colours.'

I couldn't work properly, which was frustrating, and I badly needed sleep. Walking was just about bearable, but bending down or stretching was tricky because my skin hurt too much. I had to use a set of steps just to reach a packet of fertilizer from the top shelf when, under normal circumstances, it would have been a piece of cake. My condition was farcical.

And when I asked Brenda to go home early, she told me I needed Sandra's permission, but Sandra had to ask Alexander, who just laughed in my face. Worse still, Alexander photocopied my 'I am a fool who doesn't respect the sun' lines and posted them all over the staff room. Amusing, yes, and I could take a joke, but had I really come half way round the world to be laughed at?

Work that week was slow, uncomfortable and humiliating. Even James - who usually didn't have a clue what was going on - ridiculed me about my 200 lines in the staff kitchen. By Friday I just wanted out of Auckland for the next couple of days.

Fortunately Crispin arranged to meet his friend Matt

in Tauranga for a Halloween party. G said I didn't need a costume.

We set off at 6 PM. G-Man cracked open a few beers for the journey (Lion Red, the redneck's choice) and began guzzling with alarming enthusiasm.

'We'll be there by nine o'clock, easy,' said Crispin with steely determination. I needed this; I needed to be out of Auckland and away from work. I needed to stick up two fingers at Kings Plant Barn and vowed to have revenge on the suntanned staff.

In two hours my wish was granted. We were out of Auckland and in redneck country. Even the sheep had mullets. It was eerie, so quiet. Were those sparkling eyes in dense roadside thickets *watching* us? I was reminded of an answer to a question in a local pub quiz: "Which word means a favour granted to members of the same family?" Answer: "Incest".

Sucking on my beer I thought about *The Texas Chainsaw Massacre*. I remembered jerky camera angles and snaggle-toothed hicks intent on kidnap. Despite the title, the film isn't especially gruesome - it mesmerizes its audience with a disturbing aura right until the terrifying finale. Paranoia set in now, and I panicked about breaking down in this agricultural wilderness. Though our chances of encountering cross-dressing psychopaths were slim, I was super alert for buzzing chainsaw sounds in decrepit farmhouses. The country can be a dangerous place for city slickers.

Tauranga (pronounced 'Toe-runga') lies on the East Coast about three hours from Auckland. It's a pretty large town by New Zealand's standards - the population nudges 130,000. There were roads here with *two* lanes.

The surrounding region is known as The Bay of Plenty - named by the great Captain - although what there was plenty of was uncertain. When Tauranga is mentioned in a travel book, they'd be a photograph of a farmer wearing a straw hat with the caption, 'My sister is my aunt', and very little else. Tauranga is noted for its kiwi fruit and big game fishing, but not a lot more besides. Unlike L&P, it's famous for not being famous for anything. There's a petrol refinery, and it may very well have the highest concentration of rednecks per square kilometre anywhere in North Island, but that's about it.

On the strength of Crispin's excellent East Coast knowledge ('Tauranga means 'sheltered anchorage'') we let him choose our night's accommodation - a cosy hostel with 'Duck' in the title - something like The Furry Duck, or The Duck's Bill or Duck! Low Ceilings. The hostel was cheap and spot-on in most departments, and had clean linen and taps that produced water, but we shared a room with a handlebar-moustached German who littered the room with beige underwear. He insisted on calling me 'Mike, yah.' I named him Fritz.

By ten o'clock - in a whirl of drunken furore - we had showered, necked some more beers and hailed a taxi for Matt's Halloween party. Fritz was keen to tag along but, as he was wearing knee-length socks and sandals, we politely shook him off. It was Halloween, but socks and sandals were a little *too* scary.

At Matt's house a zombie with warts and a blood-splattered face thrust beer cans into our grateful hands. After brief introductions to a skeleton, Dracula and a guy wrapped in a bed sheet, we gathered in the sitting room, cross-legged, and played a drinking game common in New Zealand called Circle of Death. The formalities were hazy - and not vital - but the idea was that the loser ended up being legless, and that was just after one game. We played five games.

We quaffed crates of Speights. The beer slipped down a treat, and then down my clothes. A couple of hours later - after my stomach could no longer hold any more liquid - things went sensationally downhill. I may have lost three games, which went a long way to explain the evening's outcome.

I didn't remember anything. Not a bean.

So the next morning, shuffling sheepishly down an unfamiliar road, Crispin filled me in as best he could on our first and only night in Tauranga.

'We left Matt's house,' he explained with grave detail, 'and then we headed into town. You got barred from a pub, and then smoked some dope by the waterfront. You tried to pull some guy's mullet off but he wasn't wearing a wig. Then you broke into that strip club... what was it called? *Nick-Er-Less*? You got thrown out and started running over parked cars.'

'Wow. Is that it?'

'Then you got arrested.'

'Eh? All in one night?'

'You're lucky, Joey. The cops went easy on you. They could have turned nasty, you being a disrespectful Pom and all that.'

Ah, yes - the local police station. What a cheap, refreshing night's accommodation you were. It was coming back to me now. I'd been 'coaxed' into the station by two robust officers, where the word *detox* had been stamped in red ink across an admittance form I had signed. More specifically, an admittance form I had scribbled, wheezed and possibly dribbled on. How I got to the police station remained a mystery, although police car was a strong possibility. As for my lodgings, again there was some ambiguity. I couldn't say which cell I'd slept in, with whom, or even if there had been a bed. Presumably my cell had a floor, unless gravity is an alien concept in Tauranga.

The New Zealand Police are notorious for their uncompromising attitude towards drunk drivers and dangerous criminals, but they aren't total strangers to empathy. A well-known story describes a drunken Kiwi man referring to New Zealand's law enforcement as "pigs" - insisting that the dictionary acknowledged the word to describe police officers - but he wasn't thrown in jail or kicked in the shins. Instead he was sent to a farm and ordered to write an essay highlighting the differences between police officers and pigs. In another example, a man was instructed to send flowers to his mother as an apology for urinating in the street.

So I'd like to thank New Zealand's police force. I could have been robbed, beaten with truncheons or sent back to the UK, but instead they'd looked after my wallet and given me Weetabix for breakfast. What champs! In fact, because all the bars in Tauranga had refused to serve me, I'd actually *saved* money.

I later learn that G-Man lost his bankcard, Crispin fell over a table, and Matt puked on a girl called Lisa. Kids, don't try Circle of Death at home.

Chapter scorecard: A cracking night for Varley, but he falls foul of the long arm of the law. On his ship, Cook was the law. A mixed bag of emotions, so a score draw.

VARLEY 2   COOK 4

Chapter 11

We quickly checked-out of our hostel to avoid Fritz, who wanted to show us his sock collection.

'Beige, yah. Nice colour, yes?'

We met up with Matt and ventured to the famous beach at Mt Maunganui. I hoped its big swell would ease my hangover. Graham revealed he had a big swell when he woke up. I ignored him.

On Ocean Beach Road we unloaded equipment from the Toyota's roof rack. The boys brought *Rip Curl* wetsuits, recently waxed surfboards, St Tropez sunblock and bottles of pre-chilled mineral water. I had a snorkel and mask, and a warm bottle of Pepsi.

Gorgeous yellow beams cut across the bay, illuminating the expansive but largely deserted beach. The waves looked menacing, rearing up from the horizon with venom. The swell was six or seven feet high, which was daunting for a professional paddler with the shakes.

Crispin zipped up his wetsuit, eager to lead by example. He bound ungainly towards the sea, surfboard under arm. G-Man sprinted after him, yelling 'Whoa!' and 'Come on!' I brought up the rear with a clumsy waddle, struggling to keep my shorts up. Damn that cheap, Taiwanese cord! Matt wore black sunglasses and complained of dehydration, like a Hollywood star out of rehab. He was going nowhere near the ocean.

Thunderous waves cracked my head. A large, salty washing machine was miraculous for my hangover; highly recommended. I was treated like a rag doll, and twice I was tossed in somersaults, my head bouncing along the seabed like a cartoon character falling down stairs. And there were *rocks* down there.

But we were suitably revitalised, and could now function properly. We felt like action. So when Matt suggested we go for a cruise in his boat, we jumped at the chance.

'It's moored on the other side of town,' he said. 'Joe, want a go at the wheel?'

'I nearly crashed a fork-lift a few weeks ago, mate,' I said.

'He did as well!' piped up Crispin.

'Well,' said Matt, 'I'm sure you'll be fine.'

'Yes, but what about us?' G-Man said.

The boat was moored at Tauranga Harbour. She was a 'beaut'. Handsomely painted in navy blue and white, the Sea Boss 620 had all the necessary qualities I looked for in a boat, namely... no holes.

Matt made a sweeping gesture. 'She's over twenty feet long, has a mono hull with four-stroke ninety HP Mercury engine, and boasts a single axle unbraked trailer configuration.'

'Does it work?' I asked, but G-Man and Crispin were already onboard and waving me in. Matt started her up. The four-stroke 90 HP engine growled with menace. Never before had the Sea Boss 620 hosted so many deluded sailors.

But that didn't deter Matt. Once we were in open water, he stepped back from the wheel and, with what I could only assume was misguided confidence, offered me the wheel.

'There you go, Joe. She's all yours.'

To say I felt like the great Captain would be to understate. Cook would have been impressed - even proud. I was King of the Ocean, and I was going in a straight line. As my confidence grew, so did the boat's speed; the Sea Boss 620 was up to twenty knots.

'Who's the Boss of the Sea now?' I hollered, weaving between bright orange buoys. G-Man vomited in the frothy surf, and Crispin threatened to jump overboard unless I slowed down. It was a fair request, since I didn't know what I was doing.

We said a hearty farewell to Matt the next day. Crispin checked the tyre pressure, filled up on petrol and cut the Toyota south. We were heading to Rotorua.

If you talk at length about Rotorua to any Kiwi, they'll establish at some point that it's the most popular tourist spot on North Island; Fenton Street has one of the longest stretch of motels in the country. But what Rotorua is most famous for are its geysers, thermal springs, Maori history and its rather unfortunate smell. Apparently it's a thriving town of around 70,000, but the only people visible were riding in the Toyota. Where *was* everyone?

A lot has been written about Rotorua. One thing I know was that it's a peculiar old town with a couple of nicknames: 'Roto-Vegas' because of the 'overwhelming' tourism, and 'Sulphur City' because of the presence (and smell) of hydrogen sulphide. As every budding chemist knows, hydrogen sulphide is a colourless gas produced as a by-product of rotting sulphur-containing matter. It's also extremely toxic. And we were standing outside a café deciding whether to go for the spicy bean burger or the chilli con carne.

I quite liked Rotorua. I wouldn't want to live there, but it was okay for standing outside cafés slowly getting corroded. Maybe I felt sorry for Rotorua; El Dorado was the 'City of Gold', Argentina is the 'Silver State', and poor Rotorua is named after a dull yellow element that smells of flatulence. You had to feel some sympathy towards it.

We chose burgers, which tasted better than Wendy's because the acidic atmosphere gave them some edge. We then parted with $NZ 30 (say what?) to go on the

Skyline Rotorua go-karts (or 'luges', as they're known). A rickety cable car hauled us to 500 metres above sea level to the summit of Mt Ngongotaha (pronounced as it reads) where the views over Lake Rotorua were magnificent. Company policy dictated we had to start on the easiest course - just to warm up - but after that test-run our egos prevailed and we turned into Formula 1 drivers. The boys rammed into each another, testosterone surging. I enjoyed the ride because it was one activity that didn't require experience to succeed; gravity was all one needed. I came away with a hole in my T-shirt and a patch of my sunburnt skin stuck to the tarmac. Great fun, though.

There were plenty more attractions on offer in Rotorua. The town was ideal to sample a *hangi* - a traditional Maori oven in the ground where fresh meat is steam-cooked to perfection. You could take part in just about any sport, as well as view some of the country's best Maori art and culture, and the Rainbow Springs Wildlife Park hosts kiwis, keas and the coffin-dodging tuatara. We just had time to eat a burger and hurtle down a hill on a tea tray.

Graham elected to drive back to Auckland. I saluted smelly Rotorua, vowing to stay longer on my next visit. The back seat was my bed for three hours; the drinking and the paddling and the go-karting had taken immediate effect. Tomorrow at Kings was going to be tough. It was going to be another scorcher, maybe thirty degrees.

I couldn't recall returning home to Kingsland. My memory was waking up on the sofa at 6AM, wrapped in a duvet, with a glass of milk and a blueberry cookie on the coffee table. The boys must have carried me from the car, down onto the balcony and into the flat. The cookie was stale, but it was a nice touch.

Chapter scorecard: Varley has a whale of a time on the East Coast, but his strict schedule dictates he can't see as much of it as he would have liked. Cook, meanwhile, was putting his troubles in Indonesia behind him and, in 1773, he became the first sailor to cross the Antarctic Circle: another point for the Captain. This is getting pretty desperate for the young pretender.

Chapter 12

So that was my weekend trip to The Bay of Plenty and Rotorua. The next week passed by largely without incident. Crispin and G took holiday leave, and went to Taupo to catch 'monster' trout that lurk in the eponymous lake. The fish are legendary, and Lake Taupo is one of the world's few lakes where fishermen return home after a gruelling day's angling and boast, 'Really, it was *this* big', without stretching the truth even moderately.

I had the flat to myself. Normally this would've meant getting Jess tiddly and inviting her to hide the sausage ('C'mon, you've only had thirteen beers - another won't hurt!') but sadly it wasn't to be: she had taken a three-day break to Whangarei in Northland with her friends Liz and Chloe. And Patrick was at a music festival somewhere to the south of Fuck-Knows-Ville.

It was strange being alone. I'd flown 11,000 miles to a country I'd previously never imagined flying to, and now I was sitting on a second-hand sofa in an empty flat in suburban Auckland watching reruns of *Shortland Street*. The acting was awful.

November brought more searing heat to Greater

Auckland. Mirages appeared through fingers of heat rising from the tarmac and wavering in dense air.

Unfortunately the demand for compost and bark chippings didn't dwindle; the warmth was nature's own marketing tool, coaxing extra customers to the Plant Barn - and all they wanted was compost. It was hard work - or 'hard yakka' as the Kiwis say. I developed sores, blisters, creaking knees and, once, a sprained elbow. Some customers appreciated my efforts, and gladly gave encouragement (Go on, boy, you can carry three bags at once'), and one even gave advice ('Go into management... ha ha ha!'), but often they failed to notice I was overworked, underpaid, tired, sweaty and irritable.

'Hurry up, ay' one man said. 'I need to pick up my woman in ten minutes. And my wife will go *mad* if she finds out.'

The worst culprits were customers in overalls and work boots who refused to help. If a smartly dressed businessman or -woman declined to get their hands dirty it was understandable, but these blokes were *already* grubby. Sometimes I'd lift two bags precariously and wobble to their ute in the hope they'd rush over and take the extra weight off my hands. Invariably, they'd light up a cigarette and laugh in my face.

Kings brought in temporary staff to keep things ticking over. Several were recent graduates who didn't know a lemon tree from a lemon meringue pie. Alexander and

Sandra hired them to help with the car park runs, thus relieving Malcolm and Richard's duties on the fork-lift, and my aching muscles. But with the new staff brought new customers. They just kept piling in, and most were The Inquisitive Brigade:

'Excuse me, can you tell me which annuals thrive in damp potting mix?'

'I have slugs in my garden. How do I get rid of them... humanely?'

'Garden stakes or plastic poles - which do I prefer?'

'How much is this mini cyclamen?' (Answer: 'From what I can gather by reading the information on the price tag wafting in front of your asinine face, *Sir*, I can confirm the mini cyclamen costs one cent shy of ten dollars.')

Needless to say my lunch breaks were glorious. For nearly an hour I avoided all contact with both humans and plants. I was at peace. Bark chippings, bedding plants, compost and idiotic customers didn't exist. Everything was calm. Everything was serene. For nearly sixty minutes I didn't have to -

'Call for Joe, five biggs of compost in the car park... repeat, *five biggs of compost! Get a move on, you cretin!*'

Outside working hours I tried to catch up on my e-mails (though I'm generally technophobic, e-mails are useful, and in New Zealand the Internet cafés are clean, efficient and cheap). Most messages were from friends wanting to know if I'd been sacked yet, and from companies kindly offering an extension of my manhood for a 'bargain $79'.

Two e-mails caught my eye, both from university friends. Kate's e-mail was simply entitled 'AUCKLAND!!' She'd been living 'The Australian Dream' for the past four weeks, which sounded superb until I realised she'd spent thirty days in a stuffy 'Fun Bus' avoiding hormone-driven advances of spotty teenagers desperate for their first shag. Now Kate was at a Queen Street backpackers, waiting for my response.

Chris's e-mail was entitled 'BOOZING'. He is one of my university drinking partners, with an insatiable appetite for high jinks. His rather muddled e-mail stated he'd be soon flying out and he'd ring G when he wanted picking up from the airport. Chris is an impulsive fellow, but spontaneity can bring calamity. I recalled in our second year at university we'd arranged a trip to the tiny resort of Borth, near Aberystwyth, to see the zoo. I waited for the whole afternoon to discover Chris was in a bar - in Birmingham. I hoped his spontaneity in New Zealand would bring no calamity. Well, maybe just a little.

With Kate's arrival, things didn't so much move fast as spiral out of control.

Crispin and G had returned from Taupo and Jess and

I met them at Grand Central. G had bought the seventh round of gin and tonics when Crispin received a sudden call from Kate, who was drinking on the waterfront. Downing our gins, we jumped into a taxi and met our friend in the Loaded Hog - a large chain pub on Quay Street about as Kiwi as the Big Mac.

It was bizarre seeing someone for first time in months half way around the world, and more bizarre that I was seeing two Kates at this stage. She looked the same as I remembered - a bit more tanned, maybe - and we hugged like long-lost relatives before buying more drinks for everybody. Kate brought along her travelling companions Jenny and Jane and we all got on splendidly (although there was the usual boy / girl divide).

Hours of solid drinking ensued. Some danced on tables; some lost the power of speech; some kissed a barman (which Crispin regretted). At 4.30 AM (work in four hours!) we retired back to Kingsland and crashed out in front of *Cheers* on our wooden TV. In this episode the dim-witted Woody was extra funny. Not only is he so dopey, he always provoked exactly the right response from the extra deadpan barstool favourite, Norm.

Woody: Can I pour you a draft, Mr Peterson?
Norm: A little early, isn't it Woody?
Woody: For a beer?
Norm: No - for stupid questions!

Early afternoon. Monolithic hangover. I didn't phone in sick. There was a brief period where I thought I'd be in trouble, but it soon passed as the second wave of my hangover kicked in, acute pain replaced by lethargic apathy.

G emerged from his room. His 'bed hair' was caveman-like and his skin was nearly green.

'Joe,' he croaked. 'Got a mouth like Ghandi's flip-flop.'

'Me too.'

'Just remembered - we need to get to the airport.'

'Are you *insane?*'

'We need to pick up Chris. He phoned last night. His plane gets in at three-thirty.'

G said I'd spoken to Chris late last night, though at the time I was checking if my boxer shorts were my own. They were. It said 'J. Varley, Class 5B'. I really needed to throw them away.

Astonishingly G and I were on the road twenty minutes later. G is a decent driver, but he was clearly still over the limit.

'How do you work this thing?'

'Toyotas work in a similar fashion to most cars, G-Man. The ignition needs a key.'

We couldn't find Chris at the airport. Maybe he'd been detained for pineapple smuggling. Suddenly G's phone buzzed. It was Chris. He'd messed up his times and was wandering around aimlessly in the city fringes: a British idiot lost in Auckland. So began the calamity. G mumbled a couple of things, burped loudly, and said we'd meet him in Kingsland.

During the return journey, the garden centre was my main concern; maybe I was sobering up. I should've phoned Alexander to verify my absence, to confirm his suspicions that sometimes I could be a drunken degenerate, but something had stopped me. What was it? My hangover? Guilt? Maybe I just didn't care.

I hadn't much time to think about the reasons; in just 20 minutes we were in Sandringham, then approaching Kingsland. G's phone buzzed again. Chris was already loitering on our sloping garden in Third Avenue, basking in the sun.

'If Griff from upstairs offers you some dope,' G advised, 'don't smoke it, it's strong! Okay, Chrissie, we'll be over there as soon as.'

Chris had already met Griff. They were both sitting in the garden, their grins sloppy. A six-inch joint hung loosely from Chris's mouth. His cropped brown UK hair had been replaced by a shiny 'cue ball' summer plumage.

'G-Man,' Chris drawled, 'you weren't lying. This gear *is* strong, ay.' He'd already picked up on the Kiwi diction.

'Well, there's only one thing for it,' I said, stooping down to plant a kiss on Chris's cheek. 'Griff, my good man, beers all round!'

The rest of the day involved more beer and a little dope. We showed Chris around the flat and in particular the TV, the blinds, the wooden floor and my room where he'd be staying - all the interesting parts.

'Nice TV,' observed Chris, particularly smitten. Then on closer inspection: 'A little old school, though... does it work?'

Reluctant to go on an elaborate spree again, we stayed in with two bottles of duty-free rum. It tasted like soap, but both bottles vanished with gusto. Seeing Chris again was terrific.

'It is a silly fish that is caught twice with the same bait.'

Tuesday at work was tough. Some staff thought it amusing I hadn't shown up yesterday. Alexander didn't. Sandra didn't. Brenda *certainly* didn't. I took grovelling to a new level, but my apologies were futile: Alexander called me a 'drunken moron', Sandra labelled me a 'fool', and Brenda chipped in with 'lazy, English bum'. The comments were generally reasonable, but did Brenda have to mention my nationality? I was assigned to lug terracotta pots from one side of the garden centre to the other. But for what purpose? Punishment, most probably. And it was.

Just for the hell of it, the next day we took Chris out

to Ponsonby Road (again, on a school night!). There was a large crowd: the boys, Jess and friends Liz and Chloe, Kate and her friends Jane and Jenny, Griff, and Patrick and Malcolm, who were both superstars: I wouldn't be the only staff member at Kings suffering tomorrow.

'Joe, I've got tomorrow off,' said Malcolm.

'Sorry mate, me too,' said Pat.

Shit.

The evening flashed by in a haze...

... The next day I surfaced at 4 PM (*4 PM!*). My mouth tasted like a pig fart in an ashtray. I swayed under the shower. I checked the clock: 4.12PM. I was nearly eight hours late for work. Work?...Work? I'd forgotten I had a job. What would Alexander think? I would know in an hour.

Breakfast was my usual Lucky Strike and Fresh Mint mouthwash, which this time was surprisingly flavoursome. I was making coffee in my dressing gown (the coffee was in a mug - not actually *in* my dressing gown) when, like a hideous mirage, Alexander appeared at the door. He didn't knock, he just barged in. He was livid. So livid, in fact, that he was unable to speak. I'd never known anyone so incensed as to be genuinely speechless. His face was bright red and he stood there with steam whistling cartoon-like from his ears. No, that was the coffee.

Maybe Alexander was bowled over by my

Thundercats dressing gown. That was unlikely, but I gave it a try.

'I am Mumm-Ra the Ever-Living!'

Then I burst out laughing. I couldn't help it. It was utterly uncontrollable, and Alexander's contrasting yellow hair and crimson face merely exacerbated my outburst. Perhaps I was still drunk. Whatever the reason, I found Alexander decidedly amusing.

At last my boss spoke. He'd recovered the power of speech! 'Make tomorrow your last day,' he growled. 'You're fired.' Then he left. Just like that - a man of few words.

I stood in my dressing gown dripping cold water onto the wooden floor, then collapsed onto the sofa in a fit of derision. It was so intense I nearly choked. When my coughing subsided I slowly grasped the harsh reality of the situation before saying out aloud, 'He's sacked me. That fucker just *sacked* me.'

The only person who could realistically help me was Crispin. I called him at his NIWA office, and relayed what I'd done (or specifically what I hadn't done). My friend had sympathy, but he, too, was unhappy. Alexander is his older brother after all; I'd let both of them down.

'You have to do something, baby,' stressed Crispin.

'Like what?' I heard my own exasperation.

'*I* don't know. What did Alexander say exactly?'

'Er... he said 'make tomorrow your last day.' I think.'

'That's not good. He doesn't usually say things like that.' Crispin thought for a while. 'Okay, baby,' he said. 'I think you should write him a letter. You know, to apologise. You never know, it might work.'

I didn't have anything better to do - and I like the dying art of letter writing - so I rustled one up in a few minutes. G-Man drove me to Alexander's flat in Mt Eden when he'd returned from work. I folded the letter with the precision one usually associated with the shakes, and stuffed it through Alexander's cat flap. It read:

Alexander,
I know I've let you down. I suppose I've let Crispin down as well. I am ashamed and hungover in equal measure. I got carried away with seeing Chris after such a long time. I'm sure you would have done the same. Actually, you're too old and sensible for that.
I'd just like to say that it won't happen again because - well, because you sacked me. Anyway, I must go now. Please accept my humble apology and I look forward to seeing you on a non-working basis.
Kind Regards,
Joe V
P.S. If there is a stain on this letter, blame your cat

I didn't want the boys to read it because they'd tell me to rewrite it. Plus, Alexander would be even more angry.

I liked Alexander - he *could* be a laugh... sometimes - but his position at the Plant Barn dictated he had to be conventional. I only wanted to humour the guy. He should lighten up: he was an Englishman in New Zealand, after all. Some people would've given their left kidney to be in his shoes.

That night I didn't sleep well. I was thinking about tomorrow - my last day at Kings Plant Barn. I wished Alexander had sacked me there and then, not forced me to work an extra day with my stripy legs. What kind of a sadist was he?

Friday - my last working day at Kings - was uneventful. I worked mainly with Patrick sorting out the bedding plants, because my friend was perhaps the only person who pitied my predicament. James was as inquisitive as I'd allow, mainly because he didn't know why I was leaving and he wouldn't have understood even if I'd told him. That said, he knew something was wrong. He followed me like a lovesick puppy wanting to know why Alexander and I weren't talking, and why Brenda crinkled her face whenever I came within earshot of her. The lad had persistence, I'll give him that.

By 5.30PM, I slunk along St Luke's Road alone. Apparently my work here was done. If I were a dog, my tail would be between my legs. Or they'd put me down.

I relaxed at the weekend - walked down to the harbour, browsed in bookshops, visited Auckland Library. Looking back, maybe I did go too far. Maybe I should have waited until the weekend before drinking with Chris and Kate. Yachts bobbed on the sparkling waters and I dreamt of taking Jess out on the high seas. I closed my eyes and pictured us travelling the world with no concerns other than when our next cocktails were coming from. My concern now was no dream, but very real. The reality was I was drunken moron and a fool; the reality was that I was 11,000 miles from home with hardly any money and I was unemployed. The reality was frightening. I needed Jess.

I walked back home, thinking my fitness had improved. There was laughter on the balcony; my boys were in high spirits. How could they be having fun in my miserable state?

'Joey!' shrieked Crispin.

'Here he is!' said Chris.

'How's it going lads?'

Crispin handed me a beer-stained piece of paper, then a can of VB.

'Read it and weep... with joy!'

The document was a formal written warning from Alexander, printed on official letter-headed paper. My letter must have worked - I'd been given one last chance. The warning stated that if I was late for work again without 'suitable explanation' the penalty would be 'instant dismissal'.

Suddenly I was back in work, and back in the money. Alexander wasn't so callous after all.

We celebrated my re-employment with *a few* beers on Sunday, although I felt somewhat weird: happy, guilty, foolish, puzzled and love-struck. I blamed everything on the fact I was in an unfamiliar country and that it was a new and wonderful experience that would only strengthen my character. And for the fact that I was an idiot (but - come on Brenda! - not a lazy bum!)

Chapter scorecard: Varley joins up with old friends but his wild behaviour almost costs him dear. And yet the Captain had his share of scrapes and didn't get where he was by avoiding risks. It's another draw, but the Captain's lead is daunting.

VARLEY 2   COOK 5

Chapter 13

A BRIEF WORK SUMMARY

Plus points:

1) I was still working.

2) Brenda was still speaking to me.

3) Julie brought me home-cooked food as she thought I wasn't 'eating properly.' Her lasagne was delicious, if a little overcooked. Overcooked pasta is a basic error, but it was ungrateful to mention it.

4) We had a 'work's dinner' last week, bought for us by the bosses at Kings. It was a Thai restaurant in Kingsland, but only Pat and I drank. Maybe Alexander had one beer.

5) I was being coaxed from the tills and car park to the more pleasant outdoors working on the fruit trees.

6) My sunburn was turning into suntan.

Minus points:

1) Rumours flew about that Alexander only took me back because I was his brother's friend. Not totally inaccurate, but a little harsh.

2) James kept asking me about girls, but I couldn't answer him because it'd 'set him off'. I hated lying to him.

3) In true festive spirit, there wouldn't be staff Christmas bonuses.

4) See Plus Point number 2.

The next Saturday the boys went skydiving. I'm a keen sportsman and enjoy most activities, but I declined the opportunity on the grounds that:

1) I'm petrified of heights.

2) My finances wouldn't allow me to cover the exorbitant $NZ 300 fee.

3) I felt sick.

4) If there's a more ridiculous pastime than paying a week's wages to strap yourself to someone in boiler suit and Biggles goggles and throw yourself from a tiny aircraft a few thousand feet in the air whilst controlling the action of your rectum, I've yet to hear it.

So-called 'adrenaline junkies' often praise the benefits of such 'thrills'. Are they insane? Give me a beer and a copy of *Playboy* any day. New Zealand is surely the world's premier location for adventure sport, but would a vegetarian in Paris tuck into a beef bourguignon simply because France is the gastronomic capital of the world? And the follies of jumping from a plane is endorsed with the quote, 'If at first you don't succeed, then maybe skydiving isn't for you.'

Chris added extra spice to the skydiving ordeal by serving kebabs for breakfast. It was a vile concoction of whatever he found in the fridge: mince, red peppers, cayenne pepper, carrots, white bread and parsley. The meal had zero aesthetic qualities, but we managed to keep the food down - aided by copious cups of hot coffee, which proved a masterstroke because it actually heated up the meat.

Suitably refreshed, we rolled into the Toyota and made our way to the skydiving site, an hour south of Auckland. The route was torturous on our kebab-rich stomachs. Even Crispin - usually the epitome of eagerness - was now doubting the whole *let's-throw-ourselves-from-a-plane-just-for-the-hell-of-it* idea. 'I'm going to puke. Lads, I think I'm going to puke...'

Crammed in the musty Toyota for 60 minutes was one of the most unpleasant experiences of my life - and I've been to Scunthorpe. At the airfield we inhaled gallons of fresh air.

'Chrissie, please don't make kebabs ever again.'

'Gotcha.'

The boys stumbled into the skydiving office to register their details. They looked ill. Graham was turning purple. Poor Chrissie displayed the signs of jaundice. And Crispin... there were no words.

Navy blue jumpsuits and goggles are never going to be fashionable, and the boys proved the point exactly. As far as I could tell, their training was in three stages:

1) How to jump out of a plane (Say what? They're

attached to instructors).

2) How to panic in a calm and orderly fashion if the parachute fails (Here Crispin excelled).

3) How to adopt the position if plummeting towards tarmac at 250 mph without attached instructor and parachute (Protect the head (?!))

'It's a bloody long way up,' observed Chris.

'Yup, mate, the sky usually is.'

G-Man was now actually quite composed; Chris still marvelled at the sky's altitude; Crispin, the poor boy, was supremely hesitant. He gave me a sideways glance, undoubtedly hoping I'd intervene at the last minute and pull him back, pleading, 'Don't do it! *Please*, in the name of God, *don't do it!*' I didn't, of course.

And away they went. Soon they were 12,000 feet up - beautiful black specks in the sky. I was assigned to take pictures of the sadistic ordeal, flapping my arms and pressing random buttons.

It was precisely then that I remembered reading about a veteran parachutist named Ivan McGuire. In the spring of 1988, Mr McGuire decided to film his students skydiving in North Carolina. Just for research, like you do. However, much to his chagrin, he made one fundamental error: he jumped out of the plane without a parachute on his back. As he hurtled towards some woods, which were two kilometres from the airfield, the video camera attached to his helmet recorded his final words, which were, 'Uh-oh.' When the dust settled, Captain Ralph Brown, the local sheriff, scratched his head and said, rather plainly, 'A man who has jumped eight hundred times ought to remember his parachute.'

This was worrying. If the experienced Ivan could make such an elementary mistake, would my boys become three unidentified splodges of kebab?

Amazingly the boys landed safely. How they fell from 4,000 metres - and combated high winds, mainly from the kebabs - and landed in the same area from where they'd taken off was nothing short of a marvel.

'That was amazing!... *awesome*, man... '

'What a rush! What a pure adrenaline rush, man! I wanna do it again!'

'Un-fucking-*believable*!'

'Excuse me, Crispin, but you have some sick on your shoulder.'

Sunday was the big boxing fight between David Tua and Lennox Lewis. We took the ferry to Devonport to watch the fight in The Masonic Tavern. Pat wagered us a crate of beer that Tua (the pot-bellied, Auckland-based Samoan brawler) would beat Lewis (the lean, fleet-of-foot, British fighter). Were all Kiwis this confident in their compatriots, or were they just plain stupid? The beer was ours before the first bell.

Devonport is a tranquil suburb across the waters

from the harbour. Access is over Harbour Bridge, past Takapuna, but the ferry remains a popular method for locals and tourists alike. We set out to the bar to capture the best seats. I stopped an ageing local for directions.

'It's behind you,' he said.

'So it is. Thanks. Who's going to win today?

'Pommies, eh? The All Blacks will kick your asses.'

I told him his wires were crossed. 'Sir, the All Blacks aren't even - '

'You're telling me the All Blacks *won't* win?' He stared at me that said: 'Say that again you snivelling turd.' I said I hoped the All Blacks would win, too, and then scampered to the bar.

It was bustling, mostly with die-hard Tua fans. The fight started as expected: the two boxers circled each other before Lewis threw caution to the wind and threw a punch. Our man then bombarded the big-haired Tua with right-handed jabs. Lewis's considerable height advantage and superior agility proved more than a handful for the rotund Tua. Lewis was sponsored by Nike; Tua may have signed a deal with KFC.

A few minutes passed. Tua wheezed and lurched, hobbling like a drunkard. The chubby native then wobbled from side to side. Everyone booed. Tua, arguably, had thrown a single punch, and that connected dramatically with fresh air.

The fight ended, and we knew the beer was ours.

Everyone booed again. G leapt in delight, then regretted this when he remembered we were outnumbered by a mob of angry, drunken Kiwis.

We snuck out and walked, with a hint of strut, along the promenade, engrossed by the wonderful Auckland skyline. Waitemata Harbour looked gorgeous.

'I told you Poms the All Blacks would win!" yelled the elderly Kiwi gentleman, who'd spotted us and blatantly had nothing better to do.

'But did they?' I said. 'Did they?'

Despite my recent behaviour, I was keyed up for the working week ahead. It'd give me the chance to prove that I was a good worker, and that Alexander did a wise thing by reinstating me. I'd arrive early, just to make a point. It wouldn't do any harm. Brenda, surely, would welcome me with open arms.

Chapter scorecard: Varley wins beer from his colleagues, something he feels confident that the steely mariner never managed, being stuck in the colder, more hostile Antarctica. Winning a cleverly placed bet earns Varley a point - and not too soon for the up-and-coming freshman intercontinental traveller.

VARLEY 3   COOK 5

Chapter 14

Brenda watched me skulk through the doors. We hadn't spoken properly since my cock-up. She held a cup of coffee in one hand and a price gun in the other, her podgy finger gripping the trigger. I didn't know whether she was pleased to see me, or whether she wished the price gun was a Smith & Wesson - and loaded.

'So, Alexander has given you another chance, ay?'

I sighed. 'Look, Brenda, let's not talk about it, okay?'

She paused, taken aback by my aggressive response. 'Fine... Listen, are you feeling all right, Joe?'

Brenda was asking *me* if I was okay. Brenda - the stone-faced, Pommie-bashing Kiwi - was concerned for me. Perhaps she didn't think I was English scum after all.

'I'm fine, thanks, Brenda.'

'Okay, then. Now, there are five pallets of bark chippings near the café that need uncovering. James will help you.'

Brenda's behaviour was frustrating. Though she didn't go overboard to welcome me back (nor did I expect it), she really *was* pleased to see me. And the look she gave might've been Kiwi-speak for: 'You're all right, really.' If she liked having me around, I wished she'd just say so. Some Kiwis could be so stubborn.

December brought more heat, and more surprises: Chris scored a job.

'I just walked into it,' he shrugged. 'I put on a suit, grinned like a maniac, and they gave me a job.'

'That's great, Chrissie, really fantastic. Who're you working for?'

'A marketing company. Baker Street.'

'How much do you get?'

'There's the rub, Joey. It's 100% commission.'

I was sceptical. 'Hmmm. What will you be *doing*, exactly?'

'Selling stuff door-to-door: video membership, gym cards - that kind of crap. I get eighteen dollars for each sale.'

It sounded too easy, but I was jealous. My job was secure and my pay check regular, but Chris would earn so much more because he had the gift-of-the-gab. Apparently all you needed was the ability to talk a large amount of bollocks. If I got tired of Kings (or sacked again) I could do a lot worse.

Christmas Day was approaching. Crispin hired some camping gear and took us to the Northland settlement of Whananaki, southeast of the celebrated Bay of

Islands. The area around Whananaki was as unspoilt and picturesque as it must have been hundreds of years ago. Splendid coves dotted the coastline, the waters clear and inviting. Nowhere had I encountered a more idyllic setting, and it was as close to paradise as I'd ever likely get. But did some poor sap have to name the main beach Sandy Bay? Well, *duh*. Littorally.

We hired kayaks from a friendly old man in a navy sailor's cap, and explored the islands. It was Captain Cook-esque, and frequently I capsized my dinky vessel, which I fondly christened 'The Scamp'. She was bright orange and battered, but I liked her all the same. The old girl had character - and she didn't answer back.

By the time of landing on our third beach we were exhausted (even for young men with lusty physiques). But the beach was perfect for what we came here to achieve: to etch in the sand in giant letters HAPPY CHRISTMAS, and then to take photos of us all in the background to use as Christmas cards. We were crazy.

The rest of the day was excellent. On Sandy Beach we swam, snorkelled and rolled about like kids - it was all *Lord of the Flies*. I mentioned this to Crispin, who called me Piggy. I called him Ralph.

'Wasn't he the cool one?'

I collected kindling whilst the boys caught fish with abandoned netting. They snared seven of the beasts and cooked them in tinfoil on a beach fire. We felt like primitive savages: down-and-out castaways marooned from the outside world, surviving on natural instincts and intrinsic prowess. But then, just as we were about to fall asleep on the warm sand under a blanket of twinkling stars, a local yelled out, 'Say, have you boys left your car lights on?' and Crispin trudged back across the beach to revive the car battery.

The next day, on the crest of adventure, we snorkelled the coast at Goat Island Marine Reserve. Snorkelling was becoming my favourite beach activity. Because I had neither the ability nor inclination to surf, I felt inadequate without alternative accessory. Both Alexander and G are accomplished surfers, and what Crispin and Chris lacked in aptitude they made up for with enthusiasm. I was the outcast when it came to surfing, but my snorkel kept me happy, and served as my weekend comfort blanket.

The boys squeezed into wetsuits and Crispin gave us the lowdown on the area. As chief expert in marine and freshwater biology, Crispin was justly proud of his knowledge of both local wildlife and Goat Island itself, which became NZ's first marine reserve in 1975. The water's visibility, he claimed, was about ten metres most of the time. He really was insightful, and reported that it was like 'an underwater zoo'. I told him he meant 'an aquarium'. He told me to piss off.

Well, what an experience! Goat Island was a

submerged nirvana, a biologist's dream. The tiny resort was a menagerie for exotic fish of all colours. Large brutes roamed amongst sharp crags; brightly-marked tiddlers darted about like luminous bullets. The University of Auckland elected Goat Island for the site of their research facility, and they'd chosen well. We spent two hours exploring small underwater caves in transparent waters. I duelled with a crayfish, its pincers advancing belligerently. It snapped and attacked and was really quite vicious, although I managed to get a left-hand jab to its head and we called it a draw.

Once dried off we played Frisbee with a truly remarkable lack of accuracy. Chris hit a dog.

This spontaneous surge in activity gave us a second wind. Crispin wanted to show us Pakiri Beach, so when Chris apologised to the dog owner ('Sorry mate, I thought he'd catch it'), we drove 10 kilometres north along serpentine roads towards the hidden gem.

I admire anyone who can locate a secluded spot without the need for maps. Crispin had been to Pakiri twice before, but road signs seemed non-existent and the beach wasn't visible from the main road, so I admired The Master of the Toyota when we arrived without misdemeanour or wrong turnings.

Pakiri was undeniably stunning. White-sand dunes interspersed with gnarly shrubs. The waves were hypnotic. There couldn't be a more accurate term than the aforementioned 'hidden gem'. We collapsed on the sand, thankful that Crispin had provided us - his young Northland protégés - with a venue so gorgeous I'd happily have *paid* to come here. Suddenly Chris bolted upright and pointed out to sea.

'Christ, boys, look! It's a shark! Fucking hell, it's a *shark*!'

Thirty feet from the shore, a grey dorsal fin skimmed through the water. It dipped below the surface and then, without warning, shot back up. I'd never before seen a shark in the wild (and never had the desire to see one), but this was truly a once-in-a-lifetime sighting.

'Well spotted, Chrissie,' nodded Crispin, a flat hand across his forehead to get a better view, 'but sorry to correct you. That's a dolphin. It's more *Flipper* than *Jaws*.'

A shark sighting perhaps would have provided us with more of a pub yarn ('We were fighting for our lives, ten metres from its gaping mouth, full of fearsome sharp teeth... ') but, in my mind at least, seeing a dolphin was an equally memorable episode. It was one of my best days ever, although I wished Jess was here.

Christmas Eve is my birthday. As a special treat I left work early to allow for more drinking time. Brenda and Sandra clubbed together and bought me two presents: a gold bottle opener shaped like a kiwi, and a stone 'thing'. It could have been a paperweight, or just a stone. But either way I was content; the two strict Kiwi ladies could've bought me squat, and they'd come up trumps. They were definitely warming to me.

I didn't tell Jess it was my birthday. I wanted to, but felt the day should be set aside for the boys. It was hard to explain. Maybe I realised how much I owed Crispin: he'd found our flat, drove me around the city and beyond, secured my job at Kings... hell, he'd been the one that got me to New Zealand in the first place. After numerous beers I didn't think about the situation. I'd be with Jess soon, but for now I was with my boys. Alexander even allowed himself a drink (which I paid for and *still* didn't finish).

We spent Christmas morning suffering at Piha, a celebrated raging black-sand surf beach on the West Coast. Like Cathedral Cove, Piha is another 'picturesque postcard' destination, and the view from Lion Rock - a rock shaped like a lion - is top-notch. Many surfers have come a cropper in Piha's treacherous waters, so dry land was the place for me. This was no beach for a green horn - even for one armed with a snorkel. From Lion Rock the horizon seemed never-ending. Somewhere out there, I thought, was England.

Piha is usually crammed with longhaired surfers looking for the 'perfect break', but on this special day we *owned* the beach. Several houses in the surrounding fertile hills are amongst the most desirable in Greater Auckland. Artists and hippies mix with businessmen and -women - a contrast of urban-gained wealth and countryside apathy.

Alexander cooked Christmas lunch at his Mt Eden flat: roast chicken (dry), raw onion stuffing (still raw), roast potatoes (magnificent), gravy (so-so) and a variety of local vegetables - I ate my first sweet potato, or *kumara* to the Maori. After the sumptuous feast we watched *The Perfect Storm*, which is a film about some people in a storm; hardly *Santa Claus: The Movie*, but tolerable. I soon fell asleep, but then Alexander kicked me awake to wash the dishes.

Christmas Day so far from home was surreal. There were no Christmas lights, decorated spruce trees or re-runs of *Goldfinger* on the telly. I didn't receive warm bottles of festive ale, socks, or a hideous jumper three sizes too large. It was tremendous. And Alexander also seemed in good spirits because he gave me a few days off work (possibly as thanks for my admirable washing up skills). My batteries needed restoring and I deserved the rest. All I needed now was to kick back and wait for the New Year to arrive.

Chapter scorecard: Varley is living the 'working holiday' dream, but must watch his money. Cook's fame meant he had gold coins coming out of his ears. A draw seems fair enough.

Chapter 15

In January, though, out of the blue, an era came to an end - I left Kings Plant Barn. It was on happy terms, although Alexander's reasoning was that the busiest part of the gardening season was over (yeah, right - in the middle of summer!), and there was no need to keep me on the payroll. At his desk he reminded me that the job 'wouldn't last forever.' True enough, but I felt there was a sinister ulterior motive, like I was a liability - the weak, pasty clog in the corporate garden centre machine. Maybe I was that barnacle just clinging to things after all.

'What else could you do?' asked Alexander, a pencil probing his ear. He was blatantly uninterested, and not listening.

'Oh, *I* don't know. Architect, movie star... conceptual artist specialising in photorealism.'

'Huh-huh.'

'So I *could* design the next government building?'

'Huh-huh.'

'And you think I'd excel in Tom Cruise's next film?'

'... Oh, yeah, sure.'

'Thanks for your input - truly inspiring.'

Finally, after he stopped his ear-jabbing, Alexander said, 'Well, what degree did you take?'

'You already know - I took zoology.'

Alexander clapped his hands in delight. 'There you go, then.'

'There I go, *what*?'

'Get a job at the zoo. I hear it's one of the best in the southern hemisphere.'

'The zoo?'

'Why not? I'd be happy to provide them with an adequate reference.'

'An *adequate* reference? Thanks, Alexander, but I'll try to find something a little more... demanding.'

Alexander shrugged as if to say, 'Well, good luck. You're going to need it, my compost-carrying schmuck. Close the door on your way out.'

So that was that. Four months of hard graft helping Kings Plant Barn maintain their status as the premier horticultural corporation in New Zealand had been tossed aside like a soiled tissue. I handed in my name badge and uniform, although I kept one pair of shorts. They cost $NZ 60.

I was already thinking about South Island, but I didn't know whether to ask Jess to come; she's *from* South Island. It probably wouldn't appeal to her. It'd be like her flying to the UK and asking me if I wanted to go to the Yorkshire Dales. What if she laughed in my face? What if she collapsed on her back in a fit of hilarity, repeating over and over again, 'You want me to... ha ha ha... you want me to go with *you* to South Island for the... sorry, let me compose myself... for the *whole winter*?' I couldn't handle that.

I'd travel down south in a few weeks. That was my plan. I'd made my mind up. My only hope was that I'd get a job, because I couldn't survive solely on my Kings wages. I hadn't saved a cent.

In the afternoon I waded through the Auckland phone book and *Yellow Pages* searching for suitable recruitment agencies: 'suitable' meaning anyone willing to interview a redundant compost carrier with no prospects and no CV.

Several agencies were dotted around Queen Street. I convinced one agency - Man-Hire or Boy-Zone - that I was a highly motivated, astute Englishman with excellent credentials, and scored an interview.

That was easy. Now I had to persuade the main agency man, Dennis Lewis, that I was a hard-working, Kiwi-loving golden boy who'd once again toil sweat and blood for minimum wage. As an introduction to my plight, I told him the reason I had a year's work permit but sadly out-of- work was because 'the busiest part of the garden centre season was over.'

'Correct me if I'm wrong,' said Mr Lewis, 'but isn't summer *the* busiest season?'

'You'd have thought so, wouldn't you!'

'I'm no gardener, Mr Varley, but why are you no longer being employed by... where was it?'

'Kings Plant Barn.'

'Ah yes, Kings Plant Barn.'

'Because my contract ran out.'

'In summer?'

I nodded gravely. 'Uh-huh, in summer.'

'Okay, let's change tactics. Have you any bar experience?'

'Well, I've been in a few!'

'I see. And what are your qualifications?'

'Bachelors degree in zoology, Sir, and I have a badge for the two hundred-metre butterfly.'

Mr Lewis crinkled his eyebrows. 'Let's just concentrate on your degree, ay? Zoology is an interesting subject, anyone ever tell you that? There aren't many zoology graduates out there. Let me ask you something. I don't suppose you've ever thought about working at the - '

Don't say it, Mr Lewis. Please *don't say it. If you say it, I may have to bang my head repeatedly on your desk and vault headlong through the open window right onto Queen Street where I'll get scraped up and sold as food for the warthogs at the -*

' - zoo?'

Nooooo! Jesus Christ, *no!* I held my head in despair. Was I destined to work around filth and mud and animals and plants for the rest of my life? I could picture Dr Fish handing me my degree with a peculiar grin on his face, knowing a zoology degree meant a lifetime of shit-shovelling.

I composed myself and played along with Mr Lewis's suggestion. 'Well, I can't say I've thought about the zoo, no. What would it involve?'

Mr Lewis rummaged through a filing cabinet, pulled out a folder and studied a few papers.

'Ah, here it is. Zoo assistant. Let's see now, duties include... helping the keepers with feeding... assisting with cleaning the animal quarters... moving matter... '

'Matter?'

'That's animal matter, Mr Varley.'

Huh-huh. Animal shit. Despite the progression from working with plant matter to working with animal matter being a perfectly natural one, I couldn't face any more lifting of 'matter'. I adopted the 'thanks but no thanks' response before Mr Lewis asked what other qualifications I'd acquired. 'Apart from your swimming credentials,' he added.

I racked my brains, then played my trump card. 'Well, I did take a home course in private investigation.'

His eyes widened. 'Private investigation? Phoor!

Now we're talking!'

'We weren't talking already?'

'No, what I mean is, I may be able to help you, Mr Varley. You see, I have a friend who works as a private detective.'

'Crikey!'

'Well, in his spare time. In fact, he helped me out once. Thorough job he did, too.'

Work permits should be used for precisely this: investigative work in the hot, concrete jungle. I sweated in anticipation.

'May I have your friend's address, Mr Lewis?'

Mr Lewis turned in his swivel chair, stared out of the window. He was thinking. 'Yes, it was a very thorough job. He provided me with all sorts of details: times, dates, photos.' Mr Lewis at once turned bright pink. He slammed a chubby fist onto the table. 'The scheming *bitch* didn't have a leg to stand on!'

'Uh, excuse me Mr Lewis, about this address... '

'Yeah, I caught her in the act, the two-faced bitch. Tried to deny everything, of course. She said it was somebody that *looked like* her. Can you believe that? Pah! I showed her the pictures in all their vulgarity and all she could do was laugh! And we'd been married for eighteen months. *Eighteen months* for God's sake! She'd been playing me for a fool all along. Little *bitch*!'

Mr Lewis whimpered like an injured dog, then his

pain progressed to a torrent of tears. He was blubbering like a drunk at last orders. I felt uncomfortable; first he suggested lifting animal shit for a living, then he revealed his wife had been cheating on him. I couldn't come up with anything constructive, so I just said, 'So can I have your mate's address, or what?'

Mr Lewis's acquaintance, Terence Woods, lived in Point Chevalier, ironically near Auckland Zoo. I took a late afternoon bus to his house. It was small and compact, much like any other residential building in the city: symmetrical roof, narrow wooden panelling, and adequate decking overlooking a neat, square garden.

Terence was short and rotund with patchy brown hair and questionable oral hygiene, but seemed pleasant enough. I explained that Mr Lewis should have phoned to tell him I was coming.

'Of course, no problem,' he said jovially, inviting me inside. 'I generally work by myself, but Dennis is a mate. Damn shame about his wife.'

'I heard she was a bitch.'

We had a cup of tea together, then I launched into a barrage of questions: do you deal mainly with cheating wives (or husbands, for that matter?). Have you ever been threatened by irate husbands (or wives, for that matter?). Do you always take pictures? Have you been hired by celebrities? Have you ever been tempted to drive a red

Ferrari, wear an Hawaiian shirt and call yourself Woods PI?

Terence liked my youthful enthusiasm. 'All will be revealed in good time, Joe.'

'So are you currently on a job?'

'Oh yes. A husband in Mt Albert wants me to sting his wife. He suspects her of having an affair in Avondale. In fact, I could use your help.'

'Seriously?'

Terence nodded. 'But it's a one-off job, Joe, you understand. We'll probably never see each other again.'

I caught a whiff of his breath, not entirely ungrateful. 'That's all right, Terence. I understand.'

'Okay, here's how it works. We'll cruise over to the house in Avondale with a package to be signed by the wife. You'll be wearing a blue shirt and a cap, like a delivery boy. I'll give you a form for her to sign and date, alongside the address. When she answers the door, I'll take her picture from the car.'

'What if the man answers the door?'

'He won't.'

'How do you know?'

'He works until nine in the evening.' Terence tapped the side of his head. 'Inside information, see.'

'Will this be enough evidence?'

'I reckon. How else would you explain a woman accused of adultery being at another man's house in the evening? Trust me. This'll be *all* the proof we need. She's going down, partner.'

I didn't think this would be the concrete evidence a court would use, or even a husband would need, but I supposed if I saw photos of *my* wife answering the door to another man's house, *I'd* want a few questions answered. Or at least reduce her monthly allowance.

Technicalities aside, this was exciting. I thought about phoning the boys to them I was on a 'stakeout to bust some bitch's ass', but I backed out on the grounds of professional confidentiality. Plus they wouldn't believe me.

Terence would pay me $NZ 250 to be the bogus delivery boy. I would've taken half that amount. Terence had a baseball cap that he'd made just for these very occasions - dark green with the fake logo 'ABC Deliveries'. It was a bit corny, but he said it had worked on 'numerous affairs'.

The house was on Orchard Street, off Rosebank Road. Several bushy shrubs provided ideal cover for Terence's car with just enough of a view to capture the all important photo. I spotted a lovely white blackthorn shrub (*Prunus spinosa*); maybe Brenda had taught me something after all.

I put on my cap. Terence revealed a small cardboard package wrapped with parcel tape. Inside, apparently, was a cheap cuddly toy.

'It's a rat,' Terence said, grinning. 'It's my little joke. You know, like they're rats for cheating on their partners.'

This Terence was okay. I kind of liked him.

'Right, Joe, first ring the doorbell.'

'Good idea.'

'Ask the lady *politely* to sign the package, and to print her name, sign, to write down the date and time. If she asks any questions, tell her she may have won a competition. People fill out so many damn competition forms these days they forget which ones they've entered.'

'No problem, Terry.'

'Good lad,' he said, and got his trusty Nikon ready for action.

I rang the doorbell, which went as smoothly as anticipated. Almost immediately, a leggy 40-something blonde answered. She was wearing a dressing gown and smelt of cheap perfume: a dead giveaway, for sure.

I was initially nervous and actually pointed (*pointed!)* to my cap, informing the woman I was from ABC Deliveries, as if she needed further proof. I told her the occupants of the house had won a prize and that the package required a signature. She told me she didn't live there but was merely 'house sitting for a friend'. Oh, didn't I know *that*; sitting *on* a friend, more like it. But I was remarkably persuasive and the randy old girl wrote the incriminating evidence on the fake form. I thanked her kindly, tipped my cap, and handed over the package. I walked briskly back to the car, handing Terrence the form.

'Great work, Joe! She was even in a *dressing gown*!' Terence yelped with delight. 'We're gonna nail this woman, no question! My client will be very happy.'

And I was very happy, too. 250 dollars were coming my way and, more importantly, I earned it. So it wasn't hard graft or anything too strenuous or demanding. I didn't care. It was a job - albeit a strange one - and I was proud to work with a true professional.

I learnt that morals are nonexistent in detective work; I didn't have any qualms about 'nailing' that woman. It was her fault; no one forced her to have an affair. We were just doing a job. Shit happens in the concrete jungle. I could see myself doing it again, so I asked Terence if there was much need for private detectives in Auckland.

'Uh, not really. I only do this in my spare time. Normally I'm a librarian.'

A librarian? That destroyed my image of cigar-chomping gumshoes fighting off women with a stick. Surely Magnum PI never said, 'Sorry, love, not tonight, I have to sorted out the science fiction by Thursday.'

Still, when we returned to Point Chevalier, Terence counted out five 50 dollar notes. I thanked him earnestly.

'Don't thank me, Joe. Thank the rich husband with a naughty wife.'

'Get in touch with Mr Lewis if you need any more help.'

He winked. 'I'll let you know, kidda... I'll let you know.'

And then he disappeared. Terence certainly talked like a private dick. Maybe he'd read too many crime novels.

Chapter scorecard: Varley is back in the money thanks to a randy local philanderer, which is certainly an experience the honourable Captain was unlikely to have experienced. An ecstatic Varley takes a point.

Chapter 16

Things suddenly started to pick up; my private detective earnings proved to be the catalyst for more work.

'I've sorted it, man!' yelled Chris, falling over himself with excitement. 'We're gonna be working together! Won't it be great? We'll conquer the whole fucking *city*!'

So the news of a job with Baker Street Marketing signalled the start of my first - and short - sales career. The words 'sales' and 'career' had me in panic sweats but Chris assured me it was easy money. How wrong he was.

The owner of the company, Paul Baker, was a multi-millionaire with a Hollywood smile. He wore dark blue suits and silk ties fashioned Windsor-style, his two-tone shoes created from thick-hided animals. I liked him instantly, although when he called me 'sport' I disliked him quicker than I'd instantly liked him.

The company had a routine ('regime' was more accurate). Paul dropped off his workers in his flash Porsche in remote suburbs, did a little door-to-door selling himself - gym membership, book clubs, car rentals, anything people didn't have and didn't need - and then picked them up late at night to take them back to Auckland city centre. What a gent. What a kind, rich gent. He'd then put the cash earned by his staff into a currency-counting machine and book his next holiday to the Cayman Islands.

'You might get a few tough customers,' warned Chris, 'but if you don't get lucky with the first, Joey, you can bet you'll be successful with the second.'

Chris was becoming a cause for concern. When he first came to New Zealand he wore *Lacoste* T-shirts, baggy shorts and sunglasses. Now he was sporting a white business shirt, red tie, shiny black shoes and sunglasses... on his head. He was even talking like a salesman, waxing lyrical about 'gross profits' and 'productive marketing pitches'. Soon, no doubt, he'd be asking if I wanted to 'do lunch'.

That evening Chris introduced me to fellow sales-pitchers in a bar near Auckland cemetery. The cemetery - resting place for the dead. Claudia was a young fast-talking 'go-getter' who favoured pin-striped 'power suits'. She was pleasant, though she talked constantly about her boyfriend, as though he was the Master of the Universe... or at least Mr New Zealand. Shane was just as young and 'fast climbing the sales rungs'. His aspirations for this year were to 'reach the thirty K target, ay.' Smooth-talking Marcus was from Melbourne who was under no illusion - as was I - that he could sell make-up to the Mona Lisa. All three reeked of bullshit.

I didn't fit in. I had no idea what they were rabbiting on about. The conversation was pitches, profits and margins, but I just registered hard cash. After all, this was what I needed to travel down south, and to impress Jess with what little time I had.

Nevertheless, the next Monday I attended an 'observation exercise' with Chris. It went well - Chris sold nine 'Flying Fit' gym membership cards, which meant $NZ 160 in his back pocket. This was three times my daily rate at Kings. The marketing game was starting to add up: we smiled, charmed house-owners with quaint English accents... and then took their money. Was it this easy all the time? Surely in a couple of days I could afford to take Jess out for a slap-up meal; she might even sleep with me.

Tuesday, 27 degrees, the first day in my new sales career. I was wearing a suit and tie for the first time in over a year. I stared hard in the mirror. I slapped myself in the face three times to get motivated. 'I *am* a salesman. I *will* sell... stuff. I am a TIGER! Grrrrrrrrrr!'

My boss - the aforementioned well-dressed multi-millionaire by the name of Paul Baker - drove us to North Shore in his sporty Porsche with aerofoil and electric windows. Squeezed into his penis extension were Chris, Shane, Marcus and a motor-mouthed Aussie called Summer, whose interests were fake tan, talking, lipstick and talking about fake tan and lipstick. Claudia wasn't working today; apparently her boyfriend had a cold.

I nudged Paul and said, 'Summer can talk for Oz. Too much fake, not enough tan, too.'

'She's my girlfriend, mate,' he said, his eyes fixed on the road. The tie around my neck felt tighter...

Paul dropped us off on a nondescript street in North Shore. 'See you at five,' he said. 'Go get 'em,' and used every horsepower of his Porsche to accelerate from 0 to 60 kph in about two seconds.

We were selling *Video Ezy* membership cards. We had our clipboards, pens and membership forms at the ready. Right away Summer asserted her position of Boss Banger by giving me 'the heads up'.

'What you have to do,' she twittered, 'is present your pitch to the customer as if you're their friend. A happy pitcher is a successful pitcher. You don't want to come across too hard-out or you'll just alienate them. And-we-wouldn't-want-that, would we? I like to think sales and marketing is all about friendship.'

When she stopped talking to me like I'd just struggled out of nappies, I asked her how long she'd been working in Sales and Marketing.

'Oh, it's not how *long* you've been doing it,' she said. 'It's how successful you strive to be.'

'Well, okay, but how long?'

'Try not to think about Sales and Marketing in terms of *time*. Think about S&M along the lines of V.L.E.'

'V.L.E?'

'Valuable Life Experience, silly.'

'Okay... but how long *have* you been working?'

'I try to define the term 'work' as merely the state of well-being in a positive environment whilst - '

'Not long, then.'

Summer glared at me. 'It really doesn't *matter* how long you've been doing S&M,' she finally said, and stomped off in a huff. S&M? Christ - I wish someone *would* gag her.

North Shore was no place to be dressed like an accountant. Real estate in the area was rocketing, as was business. Clearly this was where rich people lived. North Shore is as affluent as Auckland gets, like Solihull with a beach. Though North Shore was a nice change from the city centre, to be here in a shirt and tie in a heat wave was really quite distressing. It was sweltering. Heat mirages flickered in the air; there wasn't a cloud for miles around. My white shirt was now grey.

We dispersed randomly. Chris eyed up a row of extravagant houses, straightened his tie, and pointed to a pristine white pebbledash villa. Pink hibiscus (*Hibiscus*) and cabbage trees (*Cordyline australis*) thrived in soil bordered lavishly with bark chippings. The expansive lawn had been precisely mowed into three distinct shades of green. Sparkling white chip garnished a curvaceous drive. This was a serious house built with serious cash.

'Looks like a good start for a beginner,' Chris stated confidently. 'There's no 'Beware of Dog' sign. Right, Big Boy, let's go to work.'

Aware of my apprehension, Chris massaged my shoulders like a boxing trainer relaxing his protégé before a big fight.

'Don't worry, Joey. Have no fear. Believe in yourself. You can overcome anything when you put your mind to it. It's all about self-confidence. This is why you've got your visa. If you think they're not interested, hang on in there. Don't be put off by first appearances. Remember, they want these video membership cards. They *need* them. They know it, you know it. Just don't let them - '

'Chrissie?'

'Yes, Joe?'

'Shut the fuck up, okay?'

'Okay.'

I walked up the drive. Approaching the door I looked back for a sign of encouragement. Chris pumped his fist. I gulped, took a deep breath, and straightened my tie. Just for measure I rubbed my shoes on the back of my leg for that extra 'salesman shine'. I was ready.

The door opened without a knock, like the occupant had been waiting for me all morning. She was an old Maori woman with a prune-like face. She stood defiantly in the doorway, an apron tied around her podgy waist. In her ursine hand was a large rolling pin. I was reminded of the faceless housewife in the *Tom & Jerry* cartoons.

'Yis?'

'Good day to you, ma'am.'

'Yis, can I help you?'

I chin nodded at her rolling pin. 'Have I interrupted your baking?'

'What do you want?'

'It certainly smells nice whatever it is.'

'What do you *want?*'

'Er... right, okay. Let's get down to business, ha ha ha! I'm representing the North Shore gymnasium... I mean the North Shore Video-Ezy branch, and I was wondering - '

'Yis?'

'I was wondering if you'd be interested in buying some gym membership?'

'Excuse me?'

'Video membership. I meant video membership.'

'Are you sure?' she asked.

'What?'

'Are you sure you're selling video membership?'

'Yes.'

'You don't sound too sure to me, ay.'

'Well, I am.'

'And how much is it going to cost?'

'Right, let me see. They've given me so many forms I forget which ones to use, ha ha ha! Ah yes, here we are. Okay, so if you wanted to buy... let's see... you'd probably want to start off with a month's... hang on... a *week's* trial and then move onto our special offer of... umm... sorry, I've forgotten what... er, to be honest, this is my first - '

'I'm not interested,' she said, and closed the door.

'Okay then, have a nice day.'

My first house was conquered. I'd made a fool of myself, certainly, but at least I could go on to bigger and better things.

Actually, neither Chris nor I sold anything at all that day. For eight hours we traipsed around North Shore receiving similar responses. One teenager even told me to 'rack off.' Utterly dejected, we concluded that trudging around the suburbs of Greater Auckland wearing cheap polyester shirts in the searing summer heat without earning a penny was a seriously shit job. I guess S&M just didn't do anything for us.

It was a depressing day. I lost a pound through sweat but gained nothing in my wallet. Paul Baker would have to put his Cayman Island holiday on hold. We'd worked in the blistering heat of North Shore selling video cards and tolerated verbal lashings from the general public - all for nothing. I assumed those who didn't exercise would want video membership, and vice versa, but sadly this was the real world and it didn't happen. All commission-based jobs are a waste of time. More than anything, I wanted to kill Paul Baker with his Hollywood smile and his sporty little Porsche with aerofoil and electric windows.

I packed in the job and went drinking.

To cap off an entirely miserable week, Chris also quit Baker Street Marketing on Friday and joined me in getting horribly liquored up at Hugo's Frog Bar in Newmarket. We were the Auckland Rat Pack, quaffing gin and tonics and Long Island Iced Teas in sweaty (and very unsuccessful) salesman clothing.

Random Bar Conversation

'Nice suntan. Been anywhere nice?'
'The Executive Tanning Parlour.'

'Bollocks to sales and marketing,' slurred Chris, clinking my glass. 'Here's to manual labour.'

'To manual labour.'

'Here's to hard graft,' my friend mumbled, slamming his glass against mine.

'To hard graft.' I hiccupped. 'Here's to getting an overdraft.'

'Yeah man. To an overdraft.'

By now intoxicated, we hailed a taxi home. 'It'll be

thirty bucks, fellas,' insisted our driver.

'Thirty bucks!' snorted Chris. 'To Kingsland? You know that Paul Baker is my *boss?!*'

'*Was* your boss,' I corrected him.

The driver persisted. 'Thirty bucks, fellas.'

'I demand to see your manager!' yelled Chris. '*Now!*'

Dumped brusquely on the pavement we began the arduous walk of shame to Kingsland. It took nearly three hours. Chris found an unlocked fish van parked on Kingsland Avenue and climbed inside, ready for an unconventional - and very pungent - night's sleep. I noted with glee that his head was slumped directly on a red snapper. He seemed comfortable enough, but the fish looked horrified.

Meanwhile I located an abandoned shopping trolley outside our flat and decided, rather unwisely, to clamber inside and hurtle down the wooden stairs to our balcony. In doing this, I dived headfirst over the trolley and got wedged inside the metal cage for the next hour. It hurt like hell. It then started raining so ferociously the fish van might be swept away and I'd never see Chris again.

Then my saviour: our lounge light came on. G-Man appeared wearily, scratched his bollocks, then his head. He quickly assessed the situation, and identified me as a drunken idiot. He took my hand and pulled. I emerged from the trolley with a wet, sloppy *pop*.

'Joe,' he sighed. 'Sometimes you go too far.'

'I know G, thanks mate. Fancy some video membership?'

Chapter scorecard: The boy Varley wastes time working for nothing, and then nearly breaks his neck. Fresh from his Antarctic experience, Cook was again bitten by the travel bug and, in early 1774, he set off to Easter Island and New Caledonia. The Captain scores again.

VARLEY 4   COOK 6

Chapter 17

'She was a lovely girl. Our courtship was fast and furious - I was fast and she was furious.' *Max Kauffmann*

I spent the next few days avoiding supermarket trolleys and trying to sort out my life. This wasn't easy. I had to face a few home truths, namely:

1) I was 11,000 miles from home and out-of-work.

2) Rent didn't pay itself.

3) My bank balance had dropped to an all time low of $NZ 90 and 36 cents. This was not good.

4) Asking for a (strictly illegal) overdraft was looking increasingly likely...

5) ... As was working at a K Road sex shop.

6) I had hardly anything to offer Jess.

The bank balance, work issues and my lack of esteem? That was nothing. The last point really hurt the most.

'You're thinking about working *where*?' gasped Jess, sipping on an iced tea in Eon, a trendy Kingsland café just up the road from the flat.

'The *Den*.'

Jess winced. 'Joe! Isn't that a porn shop?'

'And not even a good one at that. So I've heard.'

'Jeez, are things really that bad?'

'Well, Jess, let's see. I have ninety dollars to my name. And I'm out-of-work. You know that Baker Street job I was telling you about?'

'Door-to-door selling?'

'Yeah, video membership cards. It was all bollocks. I couldn't *give* them away. No one wanted anything. I quit, and so did Chris.'

'Oh Joe, I'm so sorry. Come here.'

Jess gave me a reassuring hug. I felt better instantly, but I spotted our waitress shaking her head, thinking, 'What's that outstandingly good-looking girl doing with that broke English tosspot?'

To make things worse, Jess offered to pay the bill. 'I do have more money than you,' she stated stoically.

A fair - yet brutal - point well made.

February made for a gruelling job-hunting session in town. It was the hottest month in Auckland: the equivalent of an English August, except it didn't rain. Patrick told me of an assistant's position at Jansen's Pet and Aquarium Centre on Mt Eden Road, and he helped me write a CV ('The manager doesn't need to know that you consider yourself good-looking, eh.'). At Pat's house I rang the Centre and arranged an immediate interview. Desperation makes for a potent catalyst in career development.

I wore a new / old tie I found in a dustbin on New North Road. It was at least 50% polyester and a very nice pale green. My hair was styled with some of Crispin's wax, and I wore a pair of Chrissie's salesman shoes. I had in my pocket a recent bill with my address, and my passport and work visa. I had high expectations.

The manager - a wiry, moustached man with dubious armpit patches and whose name I didn't recall - invited me into the store. The shop area was clouded by a disagreeable odour of stale water, green algae and fish flakes. To the left, an assortment of aquariums bubbled away under the lazy scrutiny of multi-coloured tropical fish.

The manager interrogated me on everything piscine, from fish tank maintenance and water pumps to filters and substrates, from java ferns, speckled guppies and brine shrimps to God knows what else. The *one* time in my life where degree-level knowledge of barnacles might have been favourable was swept aside in a shambolic display of how not to conduct a job interview.

I bombed - badly. The manager wasn't even impressed that the illustrious Dr Fish, author of *A student's guide to the seashore* and the leading boffin in West Wales on the *subject of* fish, had taught me marine biology. He thought I was joking. I thought he was joking when he asked me to leave. He wasn't.

Changing tactics, I tried my luck at Glengarry's Liquor Store on Ponsonby Road ('We're waiting to hear back from a deaf refugee, but we'll keep you in mind, ay!'), the Edinburgh Castle pub on Symonds Street ('Don't call us, we'll call you'), and another soulless employment agency on Queen Street with all the vigour of one of Jansen's speckled guppies. However, I left with a handful of vacancies, and read them outside Myers Park.

All the agency vacancies insisted on 'drive and enthusiasm' with a 'can-do attitude' and an 'eye for detail', and for candidates to possess 'excellent communication skills', which must be the most hackneyed phrase in job specifications ('Tell me about your excellent communication skills.' 'Well, uh, I really am a very exceptional communic... sorry, can you repeat the question?'). Honestly, a job description that requires 'excellent communication skills' means practically nothing at all.

In fact, the term 'excellent communication skills' had me fuming, and this led me to reflect on a handful of things that truly exasperated me. In no specific order of irritation the culprits were as follows:

1) Commuters talking on mobile phones on public transport ('Hi dear... I'm on the train... you remember that spreadsheet I was working on last night? I didn't

save it properly... hmmm, as you can imagine it was a nightmare, and the office today was just *ghastly*... chicken supreme sounds wonderful... I'll see you in five minutes... love you, too'). I've lost count of the number of times I've wanted to grab them by both ears and scream in their face, '*If you're going to see them in* five *minutes then why the hell are you telling them so everyone in carriage C can hear you?*' Turn it off and shut up.

2) Tiny luggage bags with inconceivably long handles. These are infuriating. When you get stuck behind one on a train platform it'll hold you up for *hours* - and then trip you up for good measure.

3) Alcohol-free lager. There is no place for this in society. It is solely for people who want to *look like* they're drinking proper lager because they can't drink and drive. Have a soft drink. Also, alcohol-free lager costs as much as the real stuff and tastes like mildew.

4) An old classic: The overuse of the word 'literally'. Example: 'That new Tarantino film literally blew me away.' The only person who may accurately say they were literally blown away is an anorexic in a tornado.

5) The reluctant general public joining gyms in January in a bid to rid themselves of their 'Christmas excess', only to give up by February because they're too lazy to continue. Every year they do it, then from February to December they'll stuff their faces with

Wheat Crunchies and goose fat, wondering why they've gained 43 kilos in the process.

6) Bars and pubs "enticing" customers with slogans like, "SIT, DRINK, RELAX". Seldom have I have been so confused in a pub that I have to be *notified* how to conduct myself. Never have I walked into a bar and asked myself, 'Now, if it wasn't for that slogan I'd never think to have a seat, purchase a drink and start to unwind.'

7) Noel Edmonds.

But recruitment agency job descriptions put them all to shame. Trawling through them was as depressing an activity imaginable without attending a funeral. There was *not one* job that didn't require 'excellent communication skills'. The agency might as well have written, 'Candidates must have a basic grasp of English. Use of own vocal chords desirable but not essential.' It's always '*excellent* communication skills', too. It's never 'exceptional' or 'top-notch' or 'outstanding'. And candidates must always be proficient at 'multi-tasking'. How many people, when asked if they can 'multi-task', reply, 'Now that you mention it, *no*, I can do only *one thing at a time*'? It's tedious to the point of nauseating. To say Goofy could write these job descriptions would be a disservice to Disney.

With my bank balance at a now laughable $NZ 46, I had reached my job-hunting nadir. Having no other viable alternative, I decided to bite the bullet: I had to grovel to the bank. It was the most unlikely of sources, but if the young, friendly, super-efficient professionals at ANZ couldn't help me, then I was screwed. I hoped my excellent communication skills would hit the mark.

I approached the Queen Street branch of ANZ with unadulterated fear. Their glass doors exposed a forehead lined with sweat. I was just as nervous (perhaps more so) in front of the *Tom & Jerry* housewife in North Shore. I straightened my tie (don't we all?) and stepped inside.

The queue was as downcast as I imagined; each person had their own financial quandaries, and each looked as wretched as the next. When I waited for perhaps four days it was my turn to beg. I shook off my cramp and edged towards a desk. The clerk - an impeccably groomed young lady - eyed me cagily. I didn't blame her; I was wearing a tramps' tie. She beckoned me forward, took a quick examination, and slowly reached below her desk. Was she reaching for the panic button?

'Good afternoon, how may I help you?'

'Hello. My name is Mr Varley.'

'Hello Mr Varley. How may I help you?'

'I bank with you.'

'I hope you do.' She smiled thinly. 'Do you require assistance with anything?'

'Er... yes. With my finances. You see, I don't have

any... *finances*. I need an overdraft.'

'I see. Are you a resident?'

'Yes... well, I live here... sort of.'

'You're not a New Zealand citizen?'

'Er, no.'

'May I see your papers and passport?'

'Of course.' I pulled out my paperwork. 'All present and correct!'

The lady studied them and scanned between my passport photo and my face.

'That photo doesn't do me justice!' I said. God, I was nervous. I put on a Baker Street Marketing smile. 'I need an overdraft please.'

'But you're not a New Zealand citizen,' she said. She tapped her biro on her desk to stress the fact. I didn't like that: she was getting impatient.

'Yes, I realise that.'

'Then I'm sorry, but we can't offer you an overdraft. There are some very reasonable loan companies out there.'

'But you don't understand,' I pleaded. 'If you don't lend me some money I'll have to live like a dog on the streets. I'll become a beggar... I'll have to rummage through people's bins. Do you want me to rummage through *your* bins?'

'I beg your pardon?'

'I'll do it. I'll find out where you live and I'll come

round and rummage through your bins!'

The poor clerk was alarmed. 'Did you say you'll come round to my *house?*'

'Sorry, forget that. I didn't mean it. I'm just trying to say that I'm desperate.' That last word hit me hard. I was a failure. I was a *begging* failure.

The clerk pursed her lips. 'You're that desperate?'

'Truly. If you can find it in your heart to give me an overdraft I'll be forever grateful. Let's see... eight hundred dollars isn't a lot, is it?' I actually had my hands clasped together in a prayer.

'The amount is irrelevant, Mr Varley.'

'What's eight hundred dollars? I mean for a good-looking, intelligent professional like yourself? It's peanuts, right?'

'This is highly irregular.'

'Maybe, but it would be highly *generous* if you would - '

'But it's not our policy to - '

'Oh you won't regret this Mrs - '

'It's *Miss* Bentley.'

'You won't regret this, Miss Bentley.'

'... I do hope not.'

I rubbed my temples in relief. 'Hey, maybe we could go for a celebratory drink.'

'Don't push it.'

'Fair enough.'

'And Mr Varley?'

'Yes, Miss Bentley?'

'You can get up from your knees, now. You look pathetic. Besides, we have some paperwork to sort out.'

'I knew it!' exclaimed Jess, sipping a Heineken I bought her with my temporary wealth. 'New Zealand women are a pushover for down-on-their-luck English boys.'

'When you say down-on-their-luck, you mean pathetic, right? That's what the bank clerk, Miss Bentley, called me.'

'Well... '

'I admit it was a bit humiliating.'

'But you got what you wanted, right?'

I rubbed together my thumb and forefinger triumphantly. 'Yup. Eight hundred dollars should keep me going for a bit.'

'Like I said, a pushover.'

'Does that mean you're a pushover, too, Jess?'

'For down-on-their-luck English boys? Well, I suppose I am.'

'Good, because I want to take you out for dinner.'

Jess stepped back for effect, her eyes widening with surprise. 'Whoa - that's a bit flash.'

'It doesn't matter. You're worth it.'

'How cute. And I thought you Pommie blokes didn't

know how to treat a lady.'

The stars were twinkling in Parnell - an expensive and oh-so trendy suburb a short walk east of the city centre. It's the kind of place anyone connected with the America's Cup chooses to pig out on caviar and crabsticks. We'd downed a few tequilas previously in a bar on Wellesley Street, so by the time we reached the posh restaurant we were 'merry'.

And posh it was, although the atmosphere was relaxed - helped by the potent Argentinian Malbec I'd ordered. We clicked our glasses and Jess whispered, 'Thank you.'

'For what?'

'For this... for this evening. It's perfect.'

'It'll get better,' I said.

'Oh, will it now?' Jess gulped her wine and smiled.

The waiter took our order. Jess asked for grilled lemon sole and I opted for the steak, mainly to enhance my status as a red-blooded male, but truthfully it was because half the dishes on the menu were unpronounceable.

Whilst chewing the fat (the steak wasn't as lean as I'd hoped for), I learnt that Jess was: 1) enjoying her fish, 2) getting drunk, and 3) becoming frisky. All three revelations were terrific, but the outcome ultimately depended on me, and my timing. So once Jess finished her meal to 'powder her nose', I had a few minutes to come up with the best line I could think of. Crucially, was

Jess *expecting* me to ask her back to the flat? I couldn't blow it. I refilled her wine glass to consider matters.

I only appreciated how wonderful she looked when she returned to our table. Her sleek black dinner dress sparkled under the subtle lighting, her buttocks like two billiard balls wrapped in a handkerchief. She was strikingly gorgeous - a glossy magazine model. Her dress wasn't typical of a traveller, so I assumed it was hired especially for the evening. I had to admire her; she must've been the classiest traveller in North Island.

'This wine is delicious,' she said, drinking half of her glass. 'Can I have some more?'

'Certainly.' I filled her glass to the brim (poor etiquette but absolutely required). 'Would you like dessert?'

'Yes, I would, Joe... but it's not on the menu.'

'Ummm... are you saying that... Jess, are you... '

'Yes, Joe.'

I was shocked by her bluntness, and decided to be equally brazen. 'Wanna come back to mine?'

Jess took a gulp of Malbec. Her lips were inches away from my ear. 'Well, Joseph, in that case I'd be delighted.'

I drained my glass and called the waiter over, peeling off a wad of crisp ten-dollar notes. I tipped him generously and took Jess's hand. On the way out, I winked at the doorman. He winked back. I was back in the money, and we both knew it.

Back at the flat, 1.15 AM, a bit worse for wear.

'You got a Frenchie?' panted Jess in between furious bouts of tonsil-tennis.

'A what?'

'A Frenchie.'

'What's a Frenchie?'

'You know - a condom.'

'A Frenchie is a condom?'

Jess bit my tongue. 'Uh-huh.'

'We call Frenchie's love-bites.'

'Yeah?'

'Yeah.'

'Didn't know that. So, you got a Frenchie then?'

I rooted around in my pockets. 'Uh, hang on.'

Our lips untangled, she kicked off her heels, losing four inches in height. She unzipped her dress. I dribbled like a six-year-old who'd just seen Santa. Then, holding my gaze, Jess removed her bra in one fluid movement. She had the most fantastic breasts I'd ever seen (including on TV). They were berry brown and wholly magnificent - large enough to balance a beer can on, each small enough to fit into a cereal bowl.

We moved to my room. I lay down on my back, then proceeded to engage in something resembling hanky-panky. Jess trailed her tongue over my chest and down my torso until it settled lazily on my belly button. It wasn't unpleasant - far from it - but when her tongue poked my stomach I was aware that the lack of recent work coupled with formidable alcohol consumption had left my body in a far from desirable condition. Body a temple? More like a bouncy castle.

Jess thrust her tongue in my mouth, eager to clash teeth again. When we're done, she smiled wickedly and gasped, 'Joe, I want you *now*.'

Certain my flesh trombone was ready to play its tune, I put on the 'Frenchie' and we grappled like Greek wrestlers. We then had 'noisy sex' - I kneed her in the groin.

'Awwwww... ooowwww!' yelped Jess.

'Sorry.'

My second attempt was more fruitful. Jess lied on her back, eyes closed, hair fanned like a mermaid's tail, probably dreaming about Brad Pitt. Meanwhile, I was doing my best with what I'd got: dwindling confidence but faultless bedside manners.

So, as the moon shimmered in the clearest of night skies, and with the murmur of crickets from the open window, I nibbled on her ear and smothered her neck with soft kisses. Jess gently guided me inside her and after two or three passionate thrusts I bit her neck and engaged my fingers with hers so it felt more romantic, and as I thought how nice she smelt and all the immoral things I could do to her I... shot my load in about 10 seconds.

I collapsed like a marathon runner crawling to the

finish line. A sheet of sweat zigzagged across my chest. Worse still, Jess lay there looking at her watch as if to say, 'Is that all you've got, Big Boy?'

Ever competitive, I dug out another 'Frenchie' and gave it another go. I put the first attempt down to impatience.

The same thing happened, but this time I lasted a good 45 seconds. I couldn't believe it. This was not happening to me. Just before a career-best *third* go Jess brushed away her hair, balanced on one elbow, greedily licked her lips, and went down on my cock.

Her method was faultless, but then an incredible thing happened. Weird, actually: Jess began talking to my penis.

'Talking' not as in polite conversation, along the lines of, 'Nice evening, isn't it?' or 'Been to the new shopping mall yet?' or 'Where's the best place to buy curtains?' It was more like she was *encouraging* it: 'Come on, fella, you can do it' and 'Don't be shy, it'll be all right'... and then something *really* bizarre: 'There, there, it's okay. Do it for England.'

I put her voice out of my mind, and put my palm on her head, just to guide her, but she pushed it to one side; she was in absolute control. I couldn't stand it anymore. I gritted my teeth, seized up, and then came right in her mouth.

'Eeeeugh!' she hollered, rather curtly. She wiped her

mouth with the corner of my pillow. 'What did you do *that* for?' She was mildly irritated. I'd be, too, but I'd never allow myself to be put in that situation in the first place.

'I thought it was the right thing to do.'

'Well it wasn't.'

'Sorry. So, wanna do something else?'

'Like what?'

'You can choose.'

'How about making me a cup of tea?'

'What?'

'You heard, lover boy.'

Smashing - one cup of PG Tips coming up. Hey, Jess, I'll try not to make it too quickly.

I ducked out from beneath the duvet. Jess was on her side, knees tucked up to her chin. She was in the foetal position... or was it the trauma position? Yep, there it was - I'd traumatised her. Maybe a cup of tea wasn't such a bad idea.

Thrilled by not fucking up the tea-making process, I returned to the bedroom to find Jess facing the wall. I put her tea on the floor and stroked her hair. Jess purred in response. She soon fell asleep.

I snuggled with her and contemplated my future in New Zealand. Would Jess come with me to South Island, or did she think I was an inept Pommie with nothing to offer but well-made tea? I was at a lost. I fell asleep, too, in no time.

It was late morning when I woke. Jess was in the shower.

Crispin and G were having breakfast - Crispin was burning toast and G was on the veranda puffing on a Marlboro.

'Aye aye,' Crispin said. 'Good night, baby?'

'Sort of.'

'Restaurant not up to scratch?'

'It was fine.'

'We heard you come in. Good work getting Jess to stay the night.'

'Yeah... I thought you boys were going out last night.'

'We were, but Chrissie bought a bottle of rum so we just drank that here instead. We all crashed out at about midnight.'

G rapped a knuckle on the open veranda window. 'Hey, Casanova, how about making me a cup of tea?'

'Sure, G-Man.'

'Better make it two,' said Crispin.

'No problem.'

'And baby?'

'Yeah?'

'Do it for England. C'mon, I know you can do it.'

Damn those thin Kiwi walls.

Chapter scorecard: The boy Varley scores points for scoring, but cocks things up with his cock. Perhaps the Captain also had his lesser such moments. A dubious score draw.

Chapter 18

For three days Jess barely spoke to me. It'd been a peculiar night. Sure, we'd shared a romantic evening at one of Auckland's premier restaurants and the conversation had been deliciously flirtatious, but the post-dinner shenanigans had been somewhat of a letdown. I wanted it to be perfect - and it so nearly was - but I felt things would never be the same again.

I didn't think Jess wanted to come with me to South Island. Even though she may have to go back soon to Christchurch, she'd want to do that by herself - not tag along with a 24-year-old ex compost-lifter and Auckland's Most Unsuccessful Salesman.

But I had to move on. Living in Auckland was glorious - surpassing my wildest dreams - but I couldn't face coming this far just to spend twelve months in the same city. That would be too depressing, even with Jess by my side. And anyway, Captain Cook would disapprove if he knew I'd bottled such a golden opportunity. The score was tight enough without emotions influencing the competition.

So I had three plans in mind:

1) Hitchhike to Wellington, catch the ferry to Picton and take a train to Christchurch, where I'd spend a couple of days looking around the largest city on South Island. Then hitch to Queenstown, where I'd be a dogsbody and live off cheese sandwiches and cold beer.

2) Hop on a night train to Wellington, catch the ferry to Picton, a train from Picton to Christchurch, and then a minibus from Christchurch to Queenstown, where I'd be a dogsbody and live off cheese sandwiches and cold beer.

3) Sod the trains and fly to Queenstown, where I'd be a dogsbody and live off cheese sandwiches and cold beer.

Hitchhiking is generally safe in New Zealand, but you can't be too careful; the very notion you might get picked up by a crazed lunatic makes hitchhiking in any foreign country risky. I'd save money, sure, but it remains unpredictable and somewhat dangerous. Flying is quicker and offers views of the legendary Kiwi scenery, but is more expensive. For once on this trip, common sense prevailed; I chose the second option.

A quick note on New Zealand trains. Though adequate, the Kiwis don't use them often. There are nearly 4,000 kilometres of train track in the country, set amongst some of the most jaw-dropping landscape in the world, but the truth is that most Kiwis simply prefer driving, hitching, cycling or taking a bus.

Trains are cheap, which is helpful. A ticket from Auckland to Christchurch is a relatively paltry $NZ 125, which includes the infamous three-hour ferry trip over the Cook Strait - that's about 40 quid covering the same distance from Aberdeen to Penzance. Using the extra money I'd acquired from my illicit overdraft I immediately booked a train ticket - then realised I hadn't asked Jess if she wanted to come. It'd be a nonstarter anyway.

Additionally I faxed my CV to several Queenstown hotels. You had to get in early, as competition in the hospitality industry is perennially fierce. The hotels on my hit list were: The Copthorne, Queenstown Parkroyal, Alpine Village Motor Inn and Novotel Queenstown. I was confident at least one would take me on board. I'd be willing to work front-of-house, scrub floors, wash dishes... and Alexander - this *really* was the icing on the cake - had mentioned in my reference that I was a 'nice, amiable lad'. I bet he hated writing that.

During the fortnight before leaving I did a few things on a limited budget. Though constant work dried up, I managed to scrape a few dollars together mowing lawns, doing housework and general garden maintenance ('Look at my reference - the manager of Kings Plant Barn said I'm a nice, amiable lad!'). The work was reasonable, the pay lousy, but the customers were in awe of my horticultural knowledge ('Were you aware your *Hebe speciosa* has a bad case of the cottony rots?').

The boys helped me out whenever required. Crispin and G-Man sometimes put in extra money for rent, and Chris took me out for drinks and Wendy's meals. He also splashed out on tickets for New Zealand v Sri Lanka at nearby Eden Park. It was a splendid day, chugging Bundaberg rum in the sun with likeminded cricket fans, and hounded by Kiwi girls who wanted my autograph because they'd mistook me for a famous British film actor ('Kenneth Williams?' asked Crispin later). For the time being, living on the breadline had never been so enjoyable.

During the week before I left for South Island, I struck gold with Mrs Brewer. She was a decrepit hag with cracked piano key teeth, but her heart was in the right place (or at least I hoped it is - it's hard to tell with the elderly).

I knocked on her door hoping to sell my horticultural services. Mrs Brewer ushered me inside for a 'nice chat'. For the first hour I was offered three cups of tea and a home-made cherry scones; was she just lonely and wanted company all afternoon? I sat there politely, complimenting her baking, until restlessness turned to agitation.

'I could polish your silverware.'

'Oh no,' she said, 'I like to do that myself.'

'How about the vacuuming?'

'Sorry young man, no need.'

'Washing-up?'

'All done.'

'Ironing?'

'My sister comes round to do that.'

'How about I take you outside and give you a slap for wasting my time?'

I didn't say that, but came close.

'Well,' she croaked, 'there's a pile of concrete paving next to the fence.' She pointed to slabs of concrete paving next to the fence; there was nothing wrong with her eyesight. 'I want you to move them to the black bin near the back gate.'

I saw the bin near the back gate - again, Mrs Brewer's excellent vision came to the fore.

'Okay. No problem at all.'

'You may want to take off your T-shirt,' she said. 'It'll be hot work out here.'

'I'm fine thanks, Mrs Brewer. It won't take me long.'

'I really would advise it.'

'I'm fine, really.'

Her eyes narrowed. 'If you want to get paid, sonny, I suggest you take off your shirt. I'll be watching you from the sitting room.'

The lecherous crone disappeared briefly, only to present herself in full view in a rocking chair behind some sliding doors. For a second I was nonplussed. I desperately needed the cash, but was this bordering on prostitution? People her age should be content with central heating and mint humbugs. Not Mrs Brewer. Now she was getting comfy with a tartan rug and another cup of tea and... Christ, were they binoculars? She wanted close-ups!

I walked towards the paving slabs and began a few light stretches - touching the toes, windmill arm circles, that type of thing - until I was ready for action.

Thwack! There was a loud crack on the glass doors. Mrs Brewer was rocking herself into a frenzy, and was now armed with a walking stick. Grinning manically she pointed to her cardigan, indicating she wanted me to succumb to her lusty demands and work bare-chested. I needed the money *so* badly.

I submitted, and Mrs Brewer actually *applauded*. Each paving slab weighed no more than a bag of compost, so the job would be easy; the sooner I finished the sooner I could get my mitts on the old bag's money. But the thought of Mrs Brewer getting her rocks off in her rocking chair was a little off-putting.

For once I surprised myself. Not 20 minutes had passed and all the concrete slabs were near the black bin, and they were all neatly arranged, to boot.

Mrs Brewer beckoned me inside her lusty lair with a hooked finger.

'Very good show, young man. Here - don't spend this all at once.' She pulled a wad of cash from her beige handbag, handing over nine green notes, pausing to caress my hand. I'd earned $NZ 180 for 20 minutes work!

'Thank you, ma'am. Just out of interest, why did you want the stones moving?'

'I didn't,' she cackled .

'Good day to you, then.'

24 hours until departure.

G-Man reckoned he'd meet me soon in South Island, with Crispin and Chris both vowing to join us in July. Theoretically this was viable, but I had doubts. For starters, Crispin and Graham had secure, well-paid jobs at the research lab, and if they sauntered off to Queenstown for a few weeks then they could kiss those well-paid jobs goodbye. I knew what it was like to be penniless, so I expected them to stay put.

Chris was more promising. June was a long time away, so he could work odd jobs and visit in the winter. I didn't think the weather in South Island would suit Crispin. Whilst Chrissie dabbled in skiing and snowboarding, Crispin was useless at both and had grown to love the muggier northern climate, so having to wear earmuffs and woolly mittens wouldn't appeal to him, or his fashion sense.

I had a sinking feeling I'd have to do the South Island Experience alone.

Chapter scorecard: Varley makes up his mind and follows his dream down south. Cook may well have been homesick by now. The Captain is fortunate to escape with a draw.

PART 2

South Island

Chapter 19

Waving farewell to the boys at Auckland train station was difficult; that sinking feeling proved to be accurate. Leaving Auckland was heartbreaking. It'd been my home for seven months, and I'd grown a soft spot for the City of Sails. Had what started off as a yearning to establish myself in a foreign place in this brave new world really flourished into reality? Had I survived relatively unscathed in a place I'd only read about? Probably. True, there'd been a few hiccups along the way: the work had been tough and grossly underpaid, I'd nearly run out of money, and I'd been fried alive - but that didn't matter. I had to focus on the future. Dreaming about the snow-tipped mountains, raging rivers and sweeping plains that belong to South Island was enough to persuade me that I had to make the crossing single-handedly. I was supposed to be cut from the same cloth as a certain Captain James Cook. I had to *travel*; I knew it, and Cook knew it.

But then, moments before departure, Jess turned up out of nowhere.

I considered pretending I hadn't seen her. I could board the train and duck behind a seat, hidden until the train pulled away. That would've extinguished awkward silences or niggling pangs of infatuation I might've had. But that would've been too easy. New Zealand was making a man of me. I had to see her.

Jess spoke first. 'I don't really know what I'm doing here.'

'You're here to say goodbye and that you hope to see me when I get back and... you *are* here to say that, right?'

'Something like that.'

And then a longer pause - The Inevitable Silence. I didn't want this. I wanted for the conversation to be natural, but evidently for both of us it wasn't to be. Instead I shook out two Luckies, lit both, and handed one to Jess.

'Listen,' she said, taking a deep drag. 'You don't have to go. You could stay here and - '

'Please don't do this.'

'I'm sorry. It's just...' Her head sank. She stared at the platform.

'I know, Jess. I know.'

But I didn't really know. I didn't know why Jess was here at all. If my memory served true, the last time I saw her after I'd slept with her was at Kings, just before I said farewell to the staff. I'd bought her a triple-layered chocolate cake and a cappuccino with a few chocolate sprinkles, just the way she liked it. She was wearing a black vest and knee-length shorts, her ankle socks peeking out from a new pair of white pumps. She'd sat behind a lime tree in a heavily-set glazed pot, and when she spoke a citrus waft caught in the breeze.

That much I did remember. But now?

The train was about to leave.

'When are you coming back?' she asked.

'Don't know for sure.' I inhaled smoke. 'End of August?'

'The end of the ski season?'

'I suppose so, yeah.'

'I didn't know you could ski.'

'I can't. Never tried, in fact.'

'Thought so.'

'Oh you did, did you?'

'Listen,' said Jess. 'It's a fact the English can't ski.'

I held up my hands in defence. 'I don't even like skiing. Once you start it's downhill all the way.'

We shared a smile, then stubbed out our cigarettes. Looking at her almost killed me.

'Listen, Jess. I really have to go.'

I wanted her to hug me. I thought she knew this, too, but she held back for a second, as though she was testing how I'd react.

I stepped forward, and we met halfway.

She wrapped her arms around me. Her face squashed against my chest. It was clumsy, but it felt right.

A whistle in the distance...

Jess stepped away from the platform. A tear trickled down her cheek. It landed onto my cigarette butt; the flame of love had been extinguished.

Jess waved a feeble goodbye. She blew me a kiss.

Jess turned to leave.

I picked up my cigarette butt and put it in my pocket.

And then I was alone.

The *Northerner* was the rickety overnight train that ran from Auckland to Wellington. I shared a compartment with a young Latvian, built like an oak, sporting a blond pony tail and wearing a floral duvet as a jacket. Erik was visiting his sister, Elena, in the capital, where she earned her crust as a museum administrator. He smiled at me and then raised an index finger, as though he'd just remembered a long overdue answer to a quiz question. Erik pulled out a small plastic food bag from his rucksack, fiddled with the opening, decided that was too difficult, ripped it open with impatient teeth, then unleashed the contents all over his lap. Instantly the compartment filled with a sardine / sauerkraut stench so bad I cursed when my window refused to open.

Erik remained unruffled and began scooping his dinner from his crotch, relishing every mouthful as though he was dining at The Ritz; he even used an expensive-looking napkin to dab his lips. It occurred to me I hadn't eaten all day, and the notion of sleep was looking my best bet, but Erik was keen to prove that was going to be a nonstarter.

'Latvia, yes, you been?'

'No.'

'Riga, yes?'

'I haven't been to Latvia at all.'

'I'm from Latvia.'

'Indeed you are.'

'And you not visited there?'

'No, I haven't had the time since you last asked.'

Eventually Erik acknowledged I hadn't set foot in his home country and returned his now empty food / sick bag to his rucksack. The smell lingered terribly.

'Maybe you visit me in Latvia? Riga, yes?'

'That would be lovely, Erik. I'll provide you with my contact details and we'll convene next year. Would you like my PIN number too?'

Erik grinned a tad too manically, like he'd just noticed we were alone in the compartment (and for all I knew the whole train) and that he could, if the desire took him, take me hostage and relieve me of all my belongings and possibly a limb or two.

'Elena, she work in Wellington. You go?'

'This train goes to Wellington.'

'So you go?'

'Umm... yes. Listen Erik, I need to sleep, if you don't mind. Long journey.'

I settled down, tied my bag around my ankle (a cautious habit), until my eyelids grew heavy. My deep snooze brought a dream of vast landscapes and jagged mountains dusted with snow. I roamed my kingdom on horseback, a sword by my side, searching for something, or more likely someone. Birds with huge wingspans soared in pink skies. Far away was a village of wooden shacks, smoke billowing from primitive chimneys. It could have been a clip from a fantasy film, but more probable a precursor of my destiny in a new land. The images were captivating and thrilling, and as I slept I felt comfortable about my future. The dream was a promo for my winter activities. I'd be a successful South Island worker, a nomadic warrior surveying my territory. I'd be Mad Max, an untouchable. I sensed great adventures in the great outdoors, battling with job seekers amidst the rivalry in the most famous small town in the world. I sensed, too, the toils ahead, the blood and the sweat, and the unmistakably smell of sauerkraut and... was that sardines?

'So you come to Riga, yes?'

Erik was next to me, a muscled arm around my shoulder. His breath of fermented cabbage and pickled fish was as effective as any alarm clock (note to entrepreneurs: bottle that aroma and sell it as a wake-up call). I was immediately alert, aware of my safety.

Erik then let out the loudest fart. He wasn't

embarrassed; in fact enormously proud.

'Riga, yes?'

'Yes, I'll go to fucking Riga,' I barked, and escaped to the farthest compartment on the train.

Strange folk, the Latvians.

Erik didn't follow me. I sat nervously and hoped I'd soon be in Wellington - the nation's capital and self-proclaimed 'Windy City'. I hoped the nickname was strictly meteorological.

Wellington lies at the very bottom of North Island. It gained city status in the mid 19th century and is the world's most southern capital city, though this must be put into perspective - with a greater urban population just approaching the 420,000 mark, in many countries Wellington would be classed as a large town. The population of Greater Leeds, for example, is nearly double that of Wellington, and most Londoners don't know where Leeds is. (Generally, Londoners become flummoxed anywhere north of Stevenage.)

Wellington is NZ's coffee drinking capital, with reputably more cafés *per capita* than New York. This may be so (who's to know?) but I've always been suspicious of the phrase '*per capita*'. Any fact proceeded with '*per capita*' should be treated with the utmost conjecture. Consider the following:

1. The seaside town Ilfracombe boasts more one-

legged Sagittarians *per capita* than anywhere in the South West.

2. There are more competitive worm charmers in the Cheshire town Willaston *per capita* than anywhere in the UK.

3. Ramsbottom has more black pudding throwers *per capita* than any other UK town.

4. *Per capita*, there are more eleven-toed albino TV evangelists in Mississippi than any other US state.

5. The British Royal Family, *per capita*, gains the most income for the least amount of work than any other UK family.

6. The NZ city Whanganui claims the most Goldie Hawn fans *per capita* anywhere in the world. This is fictitious (indeed, as are all of the above); if *Private Benjamin* is your favourite film, don't rush to the city to meet like-minded enthusiasts. You will be disappointed.

So, the phrase *per capita* is open to speculation. What is an accepted opinion, however, is that Wellington is a nice city. It's compact (even the unfit find it manageable), vibrant (by New Zealand's standards), cosmopolitan (rough figures are 67% European / New Zealand, 13% Maori, 10% Asian, 8% Pacific Island, 2 % 'Other' - largely Latin American, African and Middle East), and by most accounts a very pleasurable city in which to reside (In 2018 Deutsche Bank named it the city with the best quality of life, beating 50 global cities to the top prize.). The income to property price ratio is better than most, and Wellingtonians have never heard of pollution. There is hardly any traffic, and the city can verify over 100 parks and playgrounds.

Wellington is the country's capital of culture. The national museum Te Papa, which dominates the waterfront, is hard to beat. Costing $NZ 317 million, the museum took four years to construct (using 80,000 cubic metres of concrete), and weighs 64,000 tonnes (though why you'd want to know this is questionable). For a few years it housed the *Lord of the Rings* touring exhibition, as well as 27,000 nerds dressed in cloth bags referring to dwarf tossing and Aragorn, son of Arathorn.

Quaint stores and outdoor coffee shops crammed the downtown area. I wandered idly, yearning for a beer, but as it was 9AM I settled for a cup of coffee (what else?) and found myself on Civic Square, a cool 'art deco' complex, a bit like a Venetian mezzanine. It was here that Wellington's 'air of sophistication' came into its own, with metal palm trees dotting the surroundings. Maybe these were created on a meaningless whim, but one thing was certain: like most of New Zealand, Civic Square lacked the pretence associated with other cities.

Crossing the bridge over Jervois Quay, colourful wooden houses above Frank Kitts Park formed a picturesque suburbia so typical of laid-back New Zealand. The slapdash, haphazard architecture gave the city both a pleasing and disorganized aura. I took in the sights, filled my lungs with unpolluted air, replaced that with a Lucky Strike, and felt electric knowing I was as south on North Island as one could be.

I was lonely, though, and decided to walk to Aotea Quay to wait for my ferry. Wellington had given me good vibes: it hadn't been sunny, I hadn't met many locals, and the place *was* a bit windy, but I liked it immensely. So much so I took in the scattered wooden shacks on the craggy hills for the last time and chain-smoked until boarding my transport for pastures new. There was no sign of Erik.

'I knew I shouldn't have eaten that cheeseburger in Palmerston North, Sybil.'

'Which one, Carl? The fourth or fifth?'

Carl, the podgy American in Bermuda shirt and combat shorts, was feeling seasick. Doubled over the railing of the Interislander ferry, Carl was in bad shape. His wife Sybil, decked out in black sunglasses and chic poncho, was not the sympathetic type.

'I think I'm going to be sick,' moaned Carl.

'Do you have to be sick here?' retorted Sybil sharply. 'Can't you wait until we *at least* get to Picton?'

'For God's *sake*, Sybil!'

It was certainly entertaining, but I reserved some empathy for old Carl. When I was a kid we took regular family holidays to the Scilly Isles. From Penzance we boarded the *Scillonian*, a white ship that transported passengers to the beautiful islands via the stormy North Atlantic. Just the thought of the journey made me queasy. For a young kid it was daunting, and I wonder if Captain Cook suffered similar woes. I still remember the acute nausea that accompanied the weaving and bobbing of the ship. I was sick into the salty froth below precisely four times on my first outing. It wasn't fun. What made it worse was the taste of the anti-seasickness tablets, which was at best revolting. They were bright pink and came in silver foil packets. Immediately after I swallowed the first pill I brought it back up over the top railing, splattering a curious seagull. The next two pills suffered the same fate. I never recovered until we reached dry land, which never stayed dry for long because of my unfortunate custom to vomit on my shoes before we had left the harbour. So, even on a bad day, I always reserve some condolence to the severely sick at sea.

I touched Carl's shoulder. 'You'll be okay, big man.'

Sybil raised her sunglasses. 'Aw, thanks for your concern, hon. He'll be fine and dandy in a few minutes. He just needs some air.'

The Wellington skyline evolved into a grey flicker, the ferry chugging across the wicked Cook Strait waters. Volatile waters threw Carl's vast bulk dangerously closer over the railings. He moaned and clutched his stomach, unaware his cheeks were turning both chubbier and a shade of green somewhere between Emerald Glade and Fresh Sage.

'Maybe I should get some tablets or something,' I offered. 'There might be a shop below deck.'

'Carl, honey? Do you want this nice young man to fetch you some tablets?'

'Sybil, will you stop talking to me like I'm some goddamn infant!'

Sybil reeled away, mortified by her husband's riposte. I backed away, too, desperate not to get involved in a maritime marital feud. Then Sybil reached into her snakeskin bag and pulled out a Nikon camera so huge it may have been a gift from the Greenwich Observatory.

'Oh, hun, before you go, would you mind taking a photograph of us both? I want to get these mountains in the background. They're nothing like the Rockies, of course, but they're just sooo cute!'

Carl was turning a frightening reddish-green colour, halfway between seasickness and rage. We locked eyes briefly, both thinking: A fucking photo? *Now*? Are you insane, woman?

'Now, stand up straight, Carl. I want this photograph to be just perfect.'

'You're insane, woman.'

'Don't talk to me like that! Now, come on. Smile!'

I clutched the camera with two hands, playing the

role of photographer. 'That's right, Carl, smile.'

I widened my legs, producing a steady tripod effect. 'Now, if you could just move a bit to the left... that's good... okay, if you're both ready... no wait, you've gone too far... to the right... that's perfect... now, on three... ready? Okay. One, two, three - say cheese... burger!'

The camera flashed in perfect rhythm with a freak wave. Unfortunately, much to Sybil's displeasure, the mountains were accompanied by a stream of thick yellowish puke that projected in random directions all over her poncho. I jumped back and lobbed the camera to Sybil, marvelling at her catching skills.

'Thanks, hun,' she winced, wiping pools of burger-vomit from her lovely poncho and Joan Collins sunglasses. I assured her it was my pleasure. I left the two lovebirds to their clean-up operation and walked to the other side of the ferry, the mountains very much in the background.

The travel media describes the Interislander ferry experience as 'stunning,' 'magical' and 'a joy', but dense clouds and chilly winds were rejecting such claims. I imagined the trip in better conditions and it served me well. The water was deep aquamarine and the occasional crests of foamy spray lashed the ferry with malice. On both sides of the ferry the scenery was semi-mountainous, with thriving vegetation growing densely on small, isolated islands. It was another world.

The sky turned deathly black, the wind a savage howl. South Island was nearing. The lazy cruise into Picton's harbour was a real tonic. This was unchartered territory; hazy mountains towered above the pretty little port, and I wished I could've shaken the Captain's hand and taken his plaudits. I was making progress. I was becoming a proper traveller.

Picton changed its name from Newton in 1859 to honour Sir Thomas Picton - a hard-nosed general in the Battle of Waterloo. I sat on a bench overlooking a mini golf course, smoking a Lucky and reminiscing over the past few months. They'd not been without scrapes, but they'd been good - every single one of them - but I felt I should be travelling *with* someone. Smoking cigarettes and taking photos of nauseous Americans just wasn't as much fun on your own. What was Jess doing? Where were my boys?

Picton was reminiscent of the Coromandel settlements and the small towns dotting Northland. It was a semi-tropical haven, with palm trees contrasting with lush mountains so typical of South Island. New Zealand is indeed a land of variety, and Picton served as a gateway to this new island's diversity.

The Marlborough area, in particular west towards Nelson, boasts the most amount of sunshine in New Zealand - about 2,500 hours a year, which is roughly seven hours a day. This optimal climate makes Marlborough the wine-growing capital of New Zealand, boasting 9,000 hectares of vineyards. Undoubtedly the jewel in the crown are the delectable sauvignon blanc wines, critically acclaimed to be among the world's best. I'm almost always in the mood for a drink, but my train to Christchurch was leaving in an hour, so I spent my time smoking Luckies, eating pizza from the delightful Picton Bakery, and losing my sodding train ticket.

Chapter scorecard: The lovelorn boy Varley successfully makes it down south on limited funds. True, the Captain discovered the place, but he had the whole British Empire behind him. Varley just edges this one.

Chapter 20

Scrambling on board the Coastal Pacific Express I searched for my ticket with obsessive urgency. Frequently when I lose things I'm content to sit back and relax, knowing that sooner or later they'll turn up in the most bizarre places - how did my cigarette lighter end up in my Spaghetti Bolognese? - but now I was overwrought with profound hysteria. How could I have been so blasé? Had the great Captain been so careless?

I sat alone, as eager to see the ticket inspector as I would pogo on a minefield. To my delight, the train was the only one in New Zealand with no one aboard. It was a ghost train, something I hadn't noticed due to my delirium. My compartment was deserted, and I hadn't seen a single soul on the Picton platform. Not entirely comforted with the suspicion there might be no driver, I sunk into my seat and decided that if a ticket inspector did make an appearance, I'd present myself as a deaf foreigner with no money, recently released from prison for violent assaults on train staff.

The 200 mile rail journey from Picton to Christchurch is considered by many to be one of the best itineraries in the world, proudly featuring in the compelling *The*

World's Great Railway Journeys. I'm no rail fanatic, but as my most memorable train experience was finding a Happy Meal on the 10.12 Leeds to Kings Cross, I had high expectations.

We approached Blenheim across a low slung bridge passing over coarse gravel banks and the glossy blue waters of the Wairau River; a time for reflection and tranquillity. But when the train rolled into the open area between Wharanui and Kaikoura, the journey took on a wickedly savage twist. The sense of importance being the only traveller on this scenic journey into the core of rural New Zealand was soon snuffed out by a young girl called Adele. She was wearing a frilly pink dress and black-buckled shoes. A copy of the *Independent Traveller's New Zealand* was tucked under her arm, and she was fast approaching. I had no time to dive under my seat. I'd been targeted.

'Hi,' she said.

'Hello.'

'Can I sit down?'

'Knock yourself out.' I ushered her with a flick of the hand to the opposite seat. She jumped into the seat right next to me, thrusting her travel book into my face. It was precisely then that I wished she *had* knocked herself out.

'I'm travelling,' said Adele.

'That's nice.'

'You travelling, too?'

'Sort of.' My enthusiasm wavered.

We sat in silence for a few moments, and then she said, 'So, I'm Adele.'

I forced a smile. 'Joe.'

'On your own, Joe?'

'Evidently.'

'So am I.'

I regarded her with suspicion, wondering if I had selected the only two trains in the whole country which harboured dangerous weirdoes. 'How old are you?'

'Twenty.'

'Pfff. And I'm the Pope.'

'Excuse me?'

'I said how do you *cope*? You know, travelling on your own.'

Adele shrugged. 'Just do, I guess. We travellers have our means.'

More silence. Adele slid closer. 'So, Joe, what-do-you-know?

I know that if you don't shut the fuck up very soon I will throw you from this train into the nearest river.

Adele ignored me ignoring her and ploughed on. 'Where you going?'

'Christchurch. Then onto Queenstown.'

'Cool. What for?'

'To work.'

'Choice.'

'Yeah, it should be... *choice*. Listen, you're not really twenty, are you?'

'What makes you say that?'

I pulled out a travel pass from her book. It'd been stamped with an 'Under 16 Discount'. I held it aloft victoriously. '*This*.'

Adele remained unruffled. 'Oh, that. That's my younger sisters'. She's in the other carriage.'

'You said you were on your own.'

'I... I meant in *this* carriage.'

'Right.'

Adele pursed her lips. 'You don't believe me?'

I sincerely didn't give one fifth of a flying fuck, but played along with this charade more to amuse myself than anything. 'Okay. I'd like to meet her.'

Adele shot up. 'Fine. Follow me.'

My bluff was called. We clambered through two carriages, both completely empty.

'She's in the next one,' Adele beckoned me with a head flick. 'You can meet my parents as well.'

I should have known. A young girl wouldn't be travelling alone. The last thing I wanted was to meet her bloody parents; I'd have preferred instead to have Adele sit on my lap and talk about Take That for the whole journey.

We stopped halfway through the next carriage. Two adults and a small girl were sitting together, hands in their laps. Adele smiled at them in turn. 'Mother, Father, Louisa. This is Joe. He's travelling to Queenstown.'

I smiled uneasily. Adele's parents were dressed neatly and solemnly, all in black. Large brown briefcases sat by their feet. The dad was quite young-looking with greasy black hair and thick-rimmed glasses. He looked like Clark Kent. Adele's mum was equally young-looking with greasy black hair and thick-rimmed glasses. She looked more like Clark Kent. Louisa appeared to be about 12-years-old and was dressed identically as her older sister: same pink dress and buckled shoes.

'Two for one?'

I shuffled into a seat and stared longingly outside. Lush green pastures spread out for miles ahead of velvety hills. Inside the carriage, the atmosphere was chilly. Finally - happily - Adele's father broke the silence.

'Well, it's nice to meet you, Joe.'

'You too.'

'Nice to meet you, Joe,' Adele's mother said.

'Yes, you too.'

'Nice to meet you, Joe,' Adele's younger sister said.

'You too, Louise.'

'It's Louis*a*,' she scowled.

'Sorry.'

She gave me a stare that translated, 'I'll let you have that one, *boy*, but call me Louise again and I'll skewer your testicles over a barbecue.'

'So,' the father said, 'what takes you to Queenstown?'

'To tell you the truth, I don't really know. I'm hoping to work in a hotel - maybe a waiter, or kitchen work.'

'Admirable work, I'm sure, but how do you fancy doing something a little more... fulfilling?'

'Sounds good. Like what?'

Adele's mother's hand was quickly on my knee. It was a cold, skeleton-like grasp. 'My husband means spreading the word.'

'Spreading the word? What's that? A magazine?'

She emitted a low chuckle, but it was a forced, fake snigger that told me she was annoyed. The two girls glowered with combined intensity. Where was the next stop?

'A magazine? That's a good one. I haven't heard that one before. No, Joe, what I'm talking about is the Good Book.'

'*A Farewell To Arms*? That's a good book.'

'No!' snapped the mother. 'I mean the Bible.'

Adele and Louisa nodded approvingly. Both parents took off their glasses and opened respective briefcases. Crammed inside were copies of the Bible, every single one bound in brown leather. I'd been reeled in.

'Listen,' I said, holding up both hands. 'I think you've got the wrong man.'

'But God believes no man is wrong,' urged the mother.

I backed away. 'No, what I mean is I'm not very good at selling things. I worked for a company in Auckland and I lasted one day. Really - I couldn't sell a pisspot in an old folk's home. Excuse my language.'

'We don't want you to sell it, m'boy,' exclaimed the father. 'We want you to *broadcast* it all around the country!'

'Yes,' said the mother. 'Spread the word of our Lord!'

'Spread the word of God,' chanted the girls.

'Jesus Christ our Lord,' muttered the father.

Adele and Louisa stood up and held hands, like the twins in *The Shining*. What next would come? A wave of blood gushing throughout the carriage? Was there an axe in the suitcases? I was sweating profusely, then delivered a crushing blow to the deranged family.

'Yeah, well, if we're all God's children, what's so special about Jesus?'

I still heard the chants when I made a desperate dash back to my carriage. Outside fluffy white sheep chewed on fresh cud. Would they be next to the slaughter?

The relief when Adele and her crackpot clan hadn't followed me was nothing short of indefinable. If the boys had been with me they'd have said, 'Sorry, pal, not interested', and walked away. I felt inadequate and a little embarrassed, and it put a damper on an otherwise splendid journey. Wishing to be in Christchurch at that very moment, I made a note to avoid obsessive

Europeans, Bible bashers and nauseous American tourists for the rest of my stay in New Zealand. My trip to Christchurch could only improve.

The small coastal town of Hapuku is a few kilometres up the coast from the famous whale-watching spot of Kaikoura. Selecting a suitable bush to hide from the Addams Family, I sat on the beach overlooking the Pacific Ocean and lit up a calming cigarette. A thin film of fog hung in the air. In an instant I forgot about the train journey, and I was overcome with a sudden feeling of immortality: I was still alive. I was still *surviving*. Nothing could touch me. Adele's parents were not Clarke Kent - *I* was Clarke Kent. I was Superman!

I arrived at the train station in the Christchurch suburb of Addington early evening, a bit dog-tired.

I found a room at *Charlie B's*, a spacious, friendly hostel with a pleasant lounge and a handful of sports videos - but no VCR. Feeling exhausted, I dumped my bag at the reception ('You can't leave it there, eh.'), ate a bowl of chicken Magi noodles, checked my e-mails and then crashed out on a medieval torture device shrewdly disguised as a bed.

In the morning, I explored the city. It was agreeable, if a little lacklustre. Christchurch is known as the 'Garden City' and is often described *ad nauseam* as the most English city outside England. I've never been to every city outside England, although Christchurch can certainly be dubbed, 'The City Most Like An English City That Happens To Be The Farthest From Any City Outside England'.

When viewed from Port Hills, Christchurch is spectacular: snow-tipped peaks watch over smooth green and brown pastures. The bulk of the city centre's buildings ease off horizontally into charming suburbs. But scratch the surface - up close and personal - and it rather disappoints.

Christchurch's layout is like Milton Keynes with a big green park. Sure, you can dress up like a Cambridge toff and go punting on the Avon River in a straw hat and sequined boating jacket - and there are some fine trees to be found in Hagley Park - but to me it seemed Christchurch was a nondescript grid of English-sounding streets: Salisbury Street, Oxford Terrace, Gloucester Street, Manchester Street, Worcester Boulevard. Even way back in 1897, Mark Twain had it nailed down when he wrote in *More Tramps Abroad*: 'It was Junior England all the way to Christchurch - in fact, just a garden... '

On the crossroads at Colombo Street and Worcester Street lies Cathedral Square, largely deserted except for a small cluster of people gathering around a giant chessboard. I smoked a cigarette and walked on.

I took a photo of Christchurch Cathedral. Built in 1904 from Canterbury stone and Australian wood, it possessed a certain English charm, but grasped my attention for precisely two and a half minutes. I moved on to the Bridge of Remembrance, built to commemorate the soldiers who crossed the River Avon on their way to Europe during World War I. A few hundred yards down the road was the City Mall. It suggested an awful juxtaposition; you pay your respects to the soldiers who died at war, then wandered off to buy a matching purse and handbag.

Riccarton Avenue splits North and South Hagley Park. The landscape was splendid - lush wide open spaces and subtropical trees - but flabby accountants sweating off an early lunch spoilt the mood. By now I was growing tired of Christchurch. Perhaps it was too flat, too boring... too English. It didn't feel like New Zealand at all, as though I'd spent a lot of money on an airline ticket and then travelled down North Island, across the Cook Strait and down farther along South Island... only to find myself in Surrey.

I opted for a few drinks in a bar on Gloucester Street, a bit fed up with Christchurch. Maybe I'd caught it on a bad day. Maybe I was itching to reach Queenstown to see a bit more action. I hadn't come all this way to marvel at a chess match and see businessmen jogging in a park.

Chapter scorecard: Varley makes it down to Christchurch, but finds the place dull. The Captain's travels were laden with non-stop excitement - or were they? Cook may have been bored stiff with endless months at sea. A nil-nil draw here for Varley seems fair.

VARLEY 5   COOK 6

Chapter 21

I turned the volume on the radio up a notch.

'Okay, Shane, you ready? For one thousand dollars, what was the first name of the English explorer who brought back tobacco and potatoes to Europe?'

A long pause. 'Sir?'

While it's quite evident some South Islanders are very literal folk, a local radio quiz isn't the place to display such attributes. South Islanders seem to have a bit more 'freshness' than their northern friends. Some may say 'stupidity', which is unfair. I prefer 'naive' - 'gullible' even. But I admired Shane's answer, considering he'd broadcast it to a few thousand people. I would have given him the cash just for his ineptness, having been reminded of similar answers I'd heard on the UK TV quiz show *Family Fortunes*:

'We asked a hundred people to name a bird with a long neck.' Answer: 'Naomi Campbell.'

'We asked a hundred people to name something you'd hate to find on your car windscreen.' Answer: 'A pedestrian.'

'Other than a Grand Prix, we asked a hundred people to name a dangerous race.' Answer: 'The Arabs.'

And, perhaps the best, was an answer from a local UK radio phone-in:

Host: 'Who had a 1967 hit with the song *What A Wonderful World*?'

Caller: 'I'm not sure.'

Host: 'I'll give you some clues. Name a famous French king.'

Caller: 'Umm... Louis?'

Host: 'And which body part contains the elbow and wrist?'

Caller: 'Arm?'

Host: 'Yes... and what is the opposite of weak?'

Caller: 'Strong.'

Host: 'So... who had a 1967 hit with *What A Wonderful World*?'

Caller: 'Frank Sinatra?'

I couldn't listen to the radio all day so I curbed the boredom by drinking in Christchurch with an English lad named Stuart, who was also staying at *Charlie B's*. We pounded the quiet streets and drank from bar to bar, until settling in a sports bar that served vicious cocktails and lukewarm beer. It was jam-packed with young people (roughly a third of the city's population) and I drank and listened to backpackers talking about Queenstown. The resort was described in gasping sentences as a mythical enigma, like the land of Narnia. Queenstown is world famous - often talked and written about - but still maintained that certain charm and magical presence that explained its cult status. This was all very well, but if it turned out to be anything less I'd be far from happy.

Next morning: intense sunshine. Just splendid for spending most of the day cramped in an eight by three-metre tin can on wheels called an Atomic Shuttle. I clambered on board, clipping a passenger's head with my luggage. The driver seemed a little inexperienced. He was about six feet all, kind of dopey looking, sported ginger wisps on his chin and appeared in the first stages of puberty. He was Shaggy from *Scooby Doo*.

The Atomic Shuttle was near full with rosy-cheeked travellers in Puffa jackets and woolly hats. I took a seat towards the back and immediately found myself sandwiched between a rotund gentleman in a baggy *Oz Experience* T-shirt and a plump lady in an even baggier *Oz Experience* T-shirt. I should have thought more about my seating arrangements but I was so excited about getting 'on the road' I selected the first seat I could find. These two people were huge. What exactly had they experienced in Oz - food? The man's pants must be a Mark F - one size up from a Marquee. How ironic to find myself uncomfortably hampered in one of the least dense areas in the world.

By 8.30 AM we left the leafy Christchurch suburbs

and soon cruised along the Canterbury Plains, a rich, sweeping flatland primarily devoted to farming and agriculture. As I understood it, South Island's topography is all over the shop. The contrasts down here are super-varied. The north is blessed with sunshine, which accounts for all the abundant aforesaid wine-growing. The west is largely wet and barren. (Some of the West Coast areas have the highest rainfall figures anywhere in the world). The extreme south is weather-beaten landscape, craggy mountains and pig-hunting rednecks brandishing knives, whilst the central and east areas are, to quote a recently-scanned guidebook, 'wide and open'. Fields of ochre and yellow and golden brown enveloped broad, straight roads. Farms scattered the landscape like peppercorns in a bowl of pea soup. Sheep were crapping on lush, litter-free greenery. This was *proper* countryside - The Big Escape - and I was revelling in it.

The apparent lack of other human life-form further demonstrated New Zealand's skimpy population density. Although the country's demography would suggest density is homogeneously low throughout, here in South Island the figures sink to an all-time low. The area of South Island is greater than that of England (and is the twelfth largest island in the world), but its population is merely half that of Greater Manchester. The dialling code '03' covers the whole island, though it's really only required if your 'utility truck' breaks down or you need to call your mates because someone's stolen your prize pet boar. To say South Island is sparse is like saying Oliver Reed enjoyed an occasional tipple.

'Hey,' said Plump Lady. 'Wanna Moro bar?'

'No, thanks,' I replied politely.

'I wasn't talking to *you*,' she scowled, and leant over my lap to offer the confectionery to Rotund Gentleman.

'Ah, choice!' he exclaimed, guzzling the whole lot as though he'd never eat again. Christ, I craved a cigarette.

But then, by divine intervention, Shaggy the Driver announced we were taking a comfort break at the superbly-named Twizel. My heart skipped with joy.

'How long will that take?' shouted Rotund Gentleman.

''Bout three hours, ay!' yelled Shaggy.

We drove through a landscape of billowy hills and flat pastures, through the towns of Ashburton, Geraldine, Fairlie and Lake Tekapo, slap-bang in the middle of South Island, or 'Mainland' as the locals call it. Regrettably we didn't stop at Lake Tekapo - all the photos indicated an eerie, romantic oasis with pale turquoise waters and an air of serenity, its milky appearance due to glacial rock dust suspended in crystal waters. If that didn't sound idyllic enough, Lake Tekapo is reputed to have the clearest air in the Southern Hemisphere. It sounded an ideal place to write to Jess, and I was disheartened I'd miss out.

It was late morning when we arrived in Twizel.

Plump Lady squeezed out from her seat with a loud *pop*. Joyfully I followed suit and lumbered to the front of the minibus. Twizel was a fine place to relieve an aching bladder after three hours of travelling - it had a tree, and gravity. Once my business was complete I lit a cigarette and offered one to Shaggy. He grunted, took one and trudged off to the nearest café - stealing my lighter in the process. What an Atomic Bastard.

I'd read about Twizel. It is known as the 'Town of Trees' and was currently (i.e. apparently) enjoying a 'mini boom'. How 'mini' this 'boom' was appeared to be a moot point. 'Boomless boom' was more accurate. More people had good things to say about *Highlander II*. Twizel was built in 1968 for the construction workers on the nearby hydro dams. Lucky them. The main reason for all this apparent booming was that Twizel is the nearest accessible town to Mt Cook and is a centre for fishing, mountaineering and hot-air ballooning. Fair enough, but I couldn't get animated about a town with more rubbish bins than its 1,200 population, so I just bought a newspaper to catch up on the local news (Headline: "Boy Buys Newspaper.")

Back onboard I asked Shaggy for a Biro (which I stole to make up for the lighter) and wrote a postcard.

Hi Jess,
Hope you're well and that things are working out with

Suzie. I'm writing this in Twizel - we have a 20-minute break until the minibus sets off for Queenstown in deepest Otago. The air is so clean but Twizel is like a ghost town. Has Chris, G-Man or Crispin been in touch yet? I'm sure they'd want to go out for a few drinks. Phone Crispin if you haven't already. Anyway, I'll write to you properly when I get to Queenstown. I'll give you my address when I know where I'm staying. Take care. Love you
Joe xxxxxxxxxXXXXXxxxxxxxxxx

Oh yes, this was more like it. Peace at last: open roads, rhythmic hills, flat plains and clear skies.

I'd changed seats to be able to stretch my elbows. My two corpulent friends had fallen asleep together on the back seat, no doubt exhausted from all that eating. We had reached central Otago - a mountainous area famous for its tramping tracks, precious stones, rugby, pig-hunting, *Lord of the Rings,* gushing rivers and people making lots of money by tying folks to large elastic bands and chucking them off bridges.

Some background history on the area:

Central Otago was once moa country, but it was also better moa-hunter country and, coupled with vast bush fires, the moa didn't hang around for long. The region was famed for its New Zealand greenstone and, in the mid 1850s, for its rivers bearing precious metal - mainly gold. The Shotover River quickly became the best known of these rivers and was dubbed 'the richest river in the world'. It is now dubbed, with rather less charisma, as 'one of the world's best rivers to go white-water rafting'.

By 1900 the villages around Queenstown enjoyed a universal local interest. Mountaineers and 'trampers' came from far and wide to indulge in their hobbies of walking up mountains and getting hopelessly lost. Pony treks were advertised. Nearby Mt Aspiring was made into a national park. Hotels and grog shops prospered. Things were on the up.

So it came as no surprise, as the evidence would suggest, when Queenstown inched ahead of its rivals in the tourism stakes. But what makes Queenstown the number one tourist spot in South Island? Probably its location, or its "location, location, location" if you're a smart-arse, sycophantic estate agent. And Queenstown really couldn't be better situated for tourists. Observe the following:

1) Queenstown is surrounded by The Remarkables - a mountain range ideal for skiing and snowboarding. People with too much money come from all over the world to do just that.

2) Queenstown has the second largest of the Southern Lakes - Lake Wakatipu - on its doorstep.

3) New Zealand is arguably the finest place in the world to go for a stroll, and some of the finest walks are

to be found in and around Queenstown.

4) Raging rivers provide 'thrilling' water sports in a 'safe' environment, i.e. the death-to-participant ratio is acceptably low.

5) Any activity that pumps adrenaline around your body can be found in Queenstown.

6) For the more sedate (i.e. sane) visitor, there is plenty to choose from including golf, fishing and bird watching.

7) There is a 'happening' club scene (actually, nothing much 'happens' after 1 PM).

8) Queenstown makes for a perfect base to explore such gems as Wanaka, Glenorchy and Arrowtown.

9) The town boasts a bevy of hotels, motels, guesthouses, lodges, and backpackers - most of them crammed all year round.

10) There are over 100 places to eat in Queenstown, including at least one Indian takeaway.

11) The view from the top of the Skyline gondolas is often described as one of the best in the world.

12) Queenstown has the only shopping mall for miles around.

13) And, yes, a few scenes from Lord of the Rings were filmed around Queenstown.

So in the space of a few years Queenstown had grown from humble settlement to modern-day phenomenon, from meek lamb to roaring lion. It's nothing short of staggering - the tourist board's very own whiz kid. *Conde Nast Traveler* ranked it third as a world destination. A survey of Concorde passengers tanked-up on free champagne once voted Queenstown their all-time favourite destination. In 1999, Bill Clinton was the first US president to make the trip to Queenstown to stock up on cigars and a fresh supply of gaffes. Queenstown is so successful it doesn't need a nickname, its reputation leading to dizzy comparisons with Saint Moritz and Val-d'Isere. It's a fair contrast. Even the French come here.

The immediate ride into Queenstown was less scenic, but it proved more exciting. In fact it was so exciting I put down my newspaper and secured a better viewing position. This place reeked of outdoor goodness - tourist slogan: '50% more outdoor goodness than most supermarket towns'.

The first testimony to Queenstown's tag of 'adventure sport capital of the world' was a red-and-white jet boat careering through a jagged valley on some of the greenest waters I'd seen. The thrill seekers onboard waved their arms as the jet boat zig-zagged across the surf amidst the deep chocolate canyon. All around, rich verdant water splashed and sprayed. Dazzling, for sure, but it begged the question: where did the hotels pour their bleach?

Another sight to the right filled me with both fascination and dread: a narrow, rickety bridge spanning a jaw-dropping canyon. It must be used for bungy jumping as no one in their right mind would *walk* across it; bridges in Queenstown are not used for this most basic of activities.

It was just after lunchtime when the Atomic Shuttle made its way back up Frankton Road, leaving me alone in the most famous small town in New Zealand. Queenstown is a healthy close-knit community held hostage by tawny mountains and steep forests. Though it was subdued now, I sensed that at any moment Queenstown could explode with blonde Norwegian skiers or bungy jumpers or drunken revellers and that I'd be swept along with the party and into a bar where I'd make friends with foreign people called Thom or Petra.

I bought a sausage roll. It was nice.

Second on my list of priorities was finding a cheap bed for the night. Though Queenstown is a dinky town with a population of around 10,000 it does have plenty of beds - about 20,000. With more than two beds to one person, finding accommodation should be a breeze.

An hour and seven hostels later I was still looking. Where the hell was everyone who'd booked their accommodation?

'On the slopes,' said one manager.

'On the mountains,' said another.

'In the mall,' shrugged a receptionist.

'In Wanaka,' said another.

'On the golf course, ay, mate,' said a glassy-eyed Aussie.

'Search me, bro. Looking for hobbits?'

Ah, the hobbits. The overwhelming success of the much-hyped *Lord of the Rings* trilogy had secured New Zealand's reputation as the fantasy film-maker's destination Numero Uno. Everyone was talking about how 'awesome' the Kiwi countryside was. Cinema-goers flocking *en masse* to see the films had come away wholly inspired by the legendary scenery. NZ tourism was raking it in, and all it'd taken was a whopping $NZ 650 million budget, 15,000 film extras, 1,600 pairs of rubber ears and feet, 1,460 eggs served to the cast and crew for breakfast on each day of shooting, 250 horses, 18 months filming and coach-loads of loopy foreigners tramping all over the country re-enacting sword-fight scenes and speculating whether Gandalf used conditioner in his beard. During the height of filming, 500 fans a day queued outside the casting rooms in Queenstown just to try their luck, and to catch a glimpse of the actors. Each to their own, but if you're thinking of joining in the hullabaloo, remember this: it's all fiction. The characters *don't exist*. And if that doesn't put you off, heed *The Guardian's* cautionary review: 'Warning! Film contains intense combat and fantasy horror scenes, long-haired men smoking unfeasibly long pipes, women with pointy ears, and lots and lots of interminable nerdish nonsense.'

I eventually found a bed at Backpackers Downtown on Shotover Street. Why it was called that and not Downtown Backpackers is anyone's guess. 'Downtown' in a place this size meant anywhere within 100 yards of *Pizza Hut*. Downtown charged about $NZ 20 a night - pretty decent for a place with clean bed linen - and it'd do nicely until I secured permanent accommodation.

It was time for a drink; the saltiness of my sausage roll had given me a thirst. What would Captain Cook have done in such unfamiliar territory? I hoped he'd venture into an exotic watering hole and order the most unusual local brew on offer. But I was not Captain Cook, so I stumbled around trying to find a pub that sold Guinness. I settled for an unashamedly English-looking pub close to the town square. Outside a sparkling stream flowed under a tiny stone bridge, quite possibly the only bridge in town not used for bungy jumping - but I bet a few had tried.

I asked the barmaid where I could find some cheap hostels.

'Dunno, love,' she snorted. 'I'm from Bolton.'

I drank deeply. The stout tasted wonderful. The fact that I was drinking Guinness in this most healthy of atmospheres (Queenstown, that is, not the pub) was as refreshing as it was odd. I downed my pint, ordered another, sunk it in one, slammed the glass down and ordered another. Miss Bolton raised an eyebrow - an eyebrow that said more than a frown ever could. You had to be careful with eyebrows - they're too often underestimated.

I left the pub and took in 360 degree views. Wispy white clouds floated over The Remarkables. Salmon pink skies hung above looming hills. Paragliders drifted gracefully through the air. Blonde-haired Germans in fluorescent ski jackets wandered about carrying snowboards and high-fiving each other. Life here was so different from North Island, and I was proud of my progress. Now all I needed to do was find a place to live, get a job, and save a little money. It should be easy.

Chapter scorecard: Putting Christchurch firmly behind him, Varley imaginatively settles down to a new life in the heart of Otago (sorry, Middle Earth). Cook was probably incapable of 'settling down'. For achieving a balanced life including adventure and a canny sense of when to hunker down and regroup, Varley scores here for a welcome come-from-behind draw.

VARLEY 6   COOK 6

Chapter 22

Bank balance: –$NZ 287.

I stayed at Backpackers Downtown for three nights. I liked the place but I'd set myself a target of finding permanent residence by the end of the week. This goal may have been unrealistic in such a popular town but all this newfound fresh air gave me an unpolluted lease of life. Money was running low but morale was definitely on the up.

Well, morale *was* on the up. That was before I trudged around most of Queenstown's hotels to check on the progress of my CV; or even if they'd received it. Not that it helped for one piddling minute. Talk about time wasting - which multinational hotel chain gave two shits if someone looking for menial work had faxed their CV to them *weeks in advance*? It would only be left on reception under a bundle of newspapers, or pissed on by the general manager. I had to start my job search from scratch.

The first on my hotel hit list was the Copthorne, a 3 star chain establishment on Frankton Road with waxed floors and a reception garnished with native plants. It was a run-of-the-mill hotel described as a 'Lakefront

Resort', but enough corporate bullshit - it was a hotel.

The lovely Natalie was the receptionist. I knew this because she was sitting at the reception displaying a name tag bearing her name. Natalie was beautifully manicured and adorned with sparkling jewellery, her pristine uniform relaying the utmost professionalism. I cleared my throat.

'Good afternoon, Natalie. I faxed my CV a couple of weeks ago and I was just wondering if - '

'Excuse me, Sir... ' She picked up the phone. 'Good afternoon, Copthorne Hotel, Natalie speaking. How can I help you?'

Natalie had got better things to do than talk to me, and she wasn't even talking to a guest because she was rabbiting on about what time she clocked off and when she would meet up with 'Steve and the gang in Lone Star'.

I sloped off, feeling a lone star myself. Hopefully when I returned Natalie might recognise me and apologise for putting her no doubt *marvellous* social life with 'Steve and the gang' ahead of her hospitality duties.

Next up was the 4 star Millennium - a 'grand' (pompous) hotel noted in the brochure for its 'luxurious' (overpriced) facilities and 'charming courtyard' (a patch of tarmac). Natalie had depleted any faith I had in the hospitality industry, and my cynicism towards hotels had skyrocketed. However, after speaking to Deborah the receptionist (who thankfully wasn't booking any marvellous social evening), a young bellboy asked me to take a seat.

Ten minutes passed. Nothing. 15 minutes, 20. Half an hour. Nothing. I went outside for a cigarette. An hour passed. Eventually the bellboy walked past me, nose in the air. 'You still here?'

I looked around, flabbergasted. 'Well, yes. I'm still waiting to see the manager.'

'No one told you, mate? The manager's not in.'

'How about the deputy manager?'

'The what manager?'

Christ. 'The head chef? Is the head chef free by any chance?'

The bellboy regarded me as though I'd pulled his nose hair with tweezers. 'He's in the kitchen - cooking. What else would he be doing?'

'How about... ah, forget it.'

I was pretty dejected. Where was my darling Jess to comfort me with cold beer and heartfelt reassurance? 1,500 kilometres away, that's where.

I stomped off in a huff. Those two hotels taught me a valuable lesson in job hunting: don't expect too much just because you've made the effort sending in your CV. They really couldn't have given a flying piss.

So I'd had it with hotels. I decided to ditch them for a few days whilst I looked elsewhere. I'd had it with their fake-tanned receptionists arranging their dinner dates with 'Steve and the gang'. I'd had it with their arrogant bellboys in pressed suits who treated you like something they'd found under their toenail. I knew my place in the Queenstown hierarchy, and it was at the bottom. I was going to get work where appearance didn't matter, where hard graft and integrity were rewarded, and where I returned home with rosy cheeks knowing I'd put in a hard day's slog. Hard yakka was what it was all about: blisters, skin sores, chapped lips, blood, sweat and tears, cups of weak tea and meat pies, thick boots, crude language and wolf whistles. In short, man's work. I'd made up my mind - I was going to be a labourer.

On Gorge Road - the main access route to the skiing areas of Coronet Peak, Arthur's Point and Arrowtown - lied a gem of a hostel called Alpine Lodge. It was opposite the town library and had great views to the Skyline Gondolas and out towards the Remarkables. The Lodge was compact and friendly and usually busy throughout the year - more by word of mouth than anything - but it had one available bed in a small room upstairs.

Taff was the curly-mopped Welsh proprietor and I paid him $NZ 100 up front for one week's accommodation, then took my key and pretended I'd understood what he'd said in his bizarre Welsh/Kiwi accent (most of his spiel was unfathomable but he made damn sure I grasped the 'One hundred dollars a week' bit).

Bank balance: –$NZ 398.

My co-inhabitant was a lovely Londoner called Lina. At first she exercised caution (quite rightly in my opinion), and I could speculate her thoughts: Who is he? Where is he from? What are his credentials? And will he leave the goddamn toilet seat up?

Fortunately, Lina broke the silence by offering me a bottle of Carlton Cold and some cheese. Not a cheese sandwich or cheese on toast - just a block of cheese. I stared at it politely.

'Go on,' Lina insisted, edging the chunk towards me. 'It's Colby cheese. You'll like it.'

I didn't want to offend the 'village chief' so I took the cheese and swallowed it whole. Lina beamed at me. I'd passed the test. And with that, she switched on the TV and patted an empty space on the small sofa.

'Do you like *Neighbours*, Joe?'

'Not really, Lina'

'Neither do I. Fancy another beer?'

Our friendship was cemented.

Alpine Lodge proved handy in finding labouring work. The wage was of no concern; I simply needed the work. This was a matter of survival.

Along Gorge Road, towards the Fresh Choice supermarket (as opposed to what, Rancid Uniformity?)

lied a building site, and I made this my first port of call. I didn't bring my CV, and put faith in my thundering enthusiasm and willingness to be bossed around by a Nazi in steel toe-capped boots to gain instant employment. The pleasant walk took me past the gondolas and forested mountains and provided an invigorating boost. I had a spring in my step. Once again I felt like Superman. I *would* get a job today.

Unfortunately the boss at the building site didn't think I was Superman. He thought I was Mr. Sheen. Once I'd laid my cards on the table and played my 'give-me-a-job- otherwise-I'll-starve' hand, he considered me a delinquent simpleton. My misery was completed when he informed me there was no work because:

1) I didn't own work boots.

2) I wasn't a suntanned, muscular beefcake who could lift 50kg loads all day long using only my little finger (I reckoned I *could* lift 50kg loads all day long - but not with my little finger - and I was neither suntanned, muscular, nor a beefcake, so he had a point).

3) He thought I was an idiot.

Though coming across as a Pommie-bashing twerp, he gave me the name and address of another building company around the corner. Ah-ha, I knew his game: he wanted all the weedy applicants to try their luck at the rival HQ's so if they were taken on, the work wouldn't be up to scratch and his company could claim to be the quickest, most reliable builder's company in Queenstown. Fair play to him, it wasn't a bad plan.

The rival company was Amalgamated Builders Ltd (ABL). The boss took a shine to me (I was Mr. Sheen, after all). He made me a cup of coffee and asked if I was fit ('But of course'), if I had experience ('I have *life* experience, Sir'), if I had suitable clothes ('A pair of Canterbury shorts I call my own'), and if I could stand 45 hours' hard yakka a week ('Certainly... *how* many hours?')

I was offered a second coffee; I had cracked it. Potential employers don't offer you more than one coffee if they're not going to take you on. The job was in the bag. I'd broken through the working barrier in New Zealand's premier resort town. I was instructed to be at the airport in the morning, 8 AM on the dot.

'We're transforming Queenstown airport from domestic to international status,' he explained. 'There's a minibus that leaves the town centre. Just go to the Tourist Information place and they'll sort you out, eh.' He extended a chubby hand. 'Glad to have you on board, Joe.'

In a couple of weeks - when I'd settled down into a routine of working like a mule and drinking like an Essex blonde in Blackpool - I should be in credit with the bank. I was back on track. Miss Bentley at ANZ in Auckland would've been proud of me.

I drained my coffee.

'Any questions, Joe?'

'Yes, Sir. What does *amalgamated* mean?'

Lina was purring in her sleep when I woke. It was cold and dark.

I made my way to the bus stop. It was pitch black. My fingers were blue. The wind had picked up, the Antarctic the chief culprit. The wind chill factor doubled my discomfort, but no one was around to share my pain. The whole of Queenstown was deserted. Finally the bus arrived, late.

'Wasn't there a bus at 7.40?' I asked the driver. 'The tourist centre said they'd be one at 7.40.'

'The tourist centre says a lot of things, fella.'

The bus was frigid but the ride to the airport along Frankton Road was superb. It was my personal taxi service. No one was up at this hour, probably sleeping off hangovers or stiff from skier's rash. Light was breaking; Lake Wakatipu was mesmerizing and a weird mist lingered in the air.

My labourer's attire: ripped black jeans (if they asked me about them I'd say I couldn't afford new ones), black trainers (if they asked me about them I'd say they'd got steel-toe caps but weakened by all the labouring I'd done in my time), and my old yellow Kings Plant Barn jumper (if they asked me about it I'd tell them, okay, you got me

- yellow's my colour).

I was at the airport car park at 8.30 AM - a bad start since I was already 30 minutes late and wearing a canary yellow jumper. Suddenly I was lost. The ABL boss hadn't given me a specific location. The bus driver hoped I'd catch my plane in time, but before I told him he'd got the wrong end of the stick and that I was here to work, he was already heading back to town.

I spotted a corrugated iron retreat bearing the ABL logo. It was like an air-raid shelter for builders, only less sturdy and more of an eyesore. Bingo.

I bounded over frozen gravel, trying to forget it was −15°C and that the next landmass of any size south of here was Antarctica. Scotland in winter is cold; early morning in a South Island winter is plain hostile. I wasn't wearing thermals or a woolly hat, or even gloves. Never before had I attempted anything - work-related or otherwise - in conditions so fierce. Slabs of blue-tinted ice - inches thick - covered huge potholes. What were once large puddles were now skating rinks. Across the wasteland a small bird carried a thermos flask. This was extreme weather: people *died* out here.

I peered inside the shelter, took in the aroma of rust, engine oil and damp frost. A calendar hung on the wall, on the wrong month. A blonde model with large tits smiled back at me. That'd been my problem recently: I'd been thinking too much about Jess, lovesick, the reason

I noticed the topless calendar was out-of-date before I noticed what made a topless calendar topless in the first place.

'If you look at them long enough you'll go blind, ay.'

Jesus Christ! I swung round, knocking over a sledgehammer and sending a nail gun skimming across the floor. A squat, heavily-bearded man stood in the doorway, screwdrivers and a tool belt hanging by his side. He was wearing a paint-splashed orange hardhat, a red chequered lumberjack's shirt and a pair of grubby jeans. The sledgehammer smashed to the ground six inches from his freakishly small feet.

'Good job you're wearing steel toe caps,' I observed nervously. 'That could have been nasty.'

The bearded dwarf grunted. 'And you are?'

I peered at him trying to make out where the words came from but his facial hair was so dense I had trouble locating his mouth.

'I'm sorry, my name's Joe.'

'That supposed to mean somethin' to me?'

'ABL didn't tell you? I'm starting work today.'

The hobbit looked at his watch. 'Well, *we* started work today at eight.'

'Oh yeah, the bus was... I mean I think my watch has frozen, ha ha ha!'

'No excuse, mate. I'll dock you half an hour's wages. Pick up that sledgehammer and follow me.'

This guy was hard work: a real southern Kiwi hard-case.

'Excuse me.' I tapped him on the shoulder, tripping over the sledgehammer. 'What's your name?'

He looked at me like I'd just gobbed on his boots. 'Gary. I'm the foreman. You got a problem, you come to me. You got an injury, you go to the fackin' hospital, ay.'

Charming. Short folk generally have nasty tempers - probably because they get sick of people talking down to them. Maybe he had a problem with Brits, or maybe my yellow jumper offended him. Either way I'd rubbed him up the wrong way. And Gary clearly wasn't a man to be trifled with, even if he was about four-and-a-half feet tall on stilts.

I followed my new boss out in the cold. The building site was connected to the front of the main airport complex. Two scaffolding columns rose into the early morning air. Wood shavings peppered the asphalt. An odd mixture of sweat, airplane fumes and rusty metal invaded the senses, coupled with a constant whirring from electrical tools and brusque shouting from the easily excitable builders.

Gary introduced me to my co-workers with all the passion of a man on Death Row - he just kind of grunted. Andy, Mike and Al were experienced builders from Cromwell, a small town 30 miles east of Queenstown, and clearly too good and experienced to shake my hand.

Christopher made the effort of climbing down his ladder to greet me. There was an English builder called Joff, his trademark a scruffy ginger beard and fingerless tramp gloves: Fagin from *Oliver Twist*. Phil was a hardcore builder and scary-looking pig hunter with dried blood on his hands. He was originally from a town in Gore - Southland's second largest town and the 'Brown Trout Capital of the World'. Phil had surely killed more than fish: pigs, sheep... humans? Gore - never a place more aptly named. The young shaven-headed electrician from Invercargill was Craig, nicknamed Sparkie. He was Phil's mate and wanted to be a pig hunter when his contract expired. I smiled politely, then walked away quickly.

Gary told me to move thin pieces of wood from one end of the airport to the other. All the pieces were 30 feet long, so when picked up, they sagged in the middle like liquorice ribbons. Turning corners carrying the wood was out of the question. I needed advice but Gary was happy wearing black goggles, shredding bits of metal piping with an angle-grinder and generally acting like a tough, bearded bloke from South Island.

By lunchtime I'd moved precisely 26 pieces of wood from point A to point B. My muscles ached. The job didn't require a Diploma, but it was laborious. I ate a Mrs Mac's steak pie washed down with a cup of tea, grateful for the rest.

'How do you get on with power drills?' Gary breathed tuna fumes over me. He'd had tuna for lunch.

'I've always had a steady relationship with them. Course, they can't hold a decent conversation, and their bedside manners are appalling.'

'Don't get smart, Pommie. Just get the drill from Phil and start on that wall over there.'

Gary pointed to a white wall along the corridor past an Avis car hire kiosk. It was about two feet thick.

'What would you like me to do to it?'

'I *want* you to drill the fackin' thing down, mate.'

Phil was reluctant to hand over the pneumatic drill, like it was his baby. His eyes were bright red. Phil scared me. Grizzly Southlanders scared me. Anyone who hunts pigs for fun are scary.

'Now listen, Philip,' I should've said. 'Stop being so childish and let me get on with my job. There, there, there's no need to get all protective over your little drill. I'm not going to steal it. You can have it back at five-thirty.' Then he'd strangle me with those big, hairy, bloodstained hands...

After a little cajoling on my part ('My, what big, hairy, bloodstained hands you've got... '), Phil handed over the drill. 'If you break it, I break *you*.'

'Well the hospital is near enough!'

'Go now.'

'Farewell, Philip.'

Studying the wall, the drill looked a little inadequate. The wall was hard. Not chalky, Mediterranean stucco hard; rock-hard granite hard. *Hard* hard. It was the Chuck Norris of walls, endorsed with the quote, 'Chuck Norris is so hard when he crosses the street, cars need to look both ways.'

I turned the drill on. At once a whirring, buzzing sound cut right across the corridor, startling at least one of the Avis girls. I stared at the wall with narrow eyes; it stared back. It was a Wild West showdown. This was a two-handed operation but my fingers were so stiff I couldn't hold the drill at eye level. On first contact the drill tip didn't grip at all, and skewered right across the wall's surface. I began sweating - surely unnatural in sub-zero temperatures.

A second attempt proved equally fruitless. The drill hadn't yet made a single dent. Changing tactics for round three, I leaned against the drill, *willing* it into the wall. The wall didn't yield. I didn't want Gary and Phil to think I wasn't cut out for this type of work, as I'd been lucky to score the job - I simply couldn't afford to do shoddy work.

At the end of four long hours I stepped back to admire my work. A small mound of white dust had collected at my feet. The wall itself was still standing proud. If anything, it looked stronger. I wiped a thick glob of sweat from my forehead before saying out aloud,

'Wouldn't the fucking sledgehammer have been easier?' but no one was around to hear my cry for help.

5.30 PM. A two-man aircraft glided above the snow-tipped Remarkables.

It was knocking-off time. I was exhausted. Joff offered me a lift back to town in his 'piece of shit on wheels', as well as the return journey in the morning. I hoped Lina was home so she could run me a hot bath with lavender oils and pamper me with cold beer and cheese toasties.

I'd been working too hard. I was dreaming. And the worst thing was, I knew it.

Chapter scorecard: A new bed and a new job in the bag for the boy Varley, but once again his boss proves an obstacle, and the future is uncertain. By late 1774, Cook arrived in New Zealand for the second time. Both have made solid progress: another score draw.

VARLEY 6   COOK 6

Chapter 23

The next morning I woke even earlier. Frequently in Auckland I didn't sleep because of the steaming mugginess of the subtropical suburbs. Now the crisp southern air suited me better. And, to my credit, I'd mastered the art of walking in the dark without bumping into a bedpost, kneeing Lina in the head or stepping onto a girly electrical appliance.

I took a cold shower and changed into my work gear, which comprised of yesterday's clothes, simply because the mechanics of our washing machine remained inexplicable. Lina had shown me the basics on the first day, but they went straight over my head - the concept as well as the washing powder.

I watched a rerun of *Home and Away.* It reminded me of teenage days lusting over young Aussie actresses, longing to frolic with them on sandy beaches. Alf Stewart was still wearing that same old straw hat and throwing his weight around like he owned the place, saying 'stone the flamin' crows' and calling everyone 'flamin' yahoos'. Australians - very good at sport and insulting people.

Joff was true to his word and was waiting outside Alpine Lodge. He hadn't lied; his car was a piece of shit on wheels.

'Ready for another day in paradise, mate?'

'Yep.'

'You're a good liar!'

'You blokes are late.'

'Sorry?'

'You deaf? I said you're late.'

'It's eight o'clock.'

Gary put his watch to his face, shaking it as if on the blink. He tapped the watch-face. What a joker. 'Nope, mine says five past.'

'Aw, come on!'

'I'll let you off - this time.'

'Sir, you're too kind.'

Gary pursed his lips. 'You've got that wall to finish off, ay.'

'Can I use one of the sledgehammers?'

'Nope. Mike an' Al are using 'em.'

'But it's going to take forever.'

Gary nodded happily. 'Yes it is.'

Then the bearded oaf jerked his thumb in the wall's direction that could've been translated as, 'Now, there's a good chap, if you don't mind having another crack at it, that would be *most* kind', but really it meant, 'Stop being such a fackin' whinging Pom and don't you fackin' dare talk to me again until that fackin' wall is destroyed.'

Some call it 'character building'. I called it sadistic slave labour.

The day dragged. It was depressing. Drilling the wall was as much fun as sniffing a tramp's jock strap. The drill simply didn't penetrate the wall with any force that resulted in it being reduced to a pile of rubble. It wasn't feasibly possible. The drill bit was too blunt. My hands were too cold. And the wall was *just too hard*.

A BRIEF WORK SUMMARY

Plus points:

1) I should be paid more than I did at Kings.

2) Sometimes I got to see some planes up close.

3) I didn't have to wear clean clothes everyday - even boxer shorts!

4) The reps at all the hire companies flirted with you.

5) The café sold Mrs Mac's peppered steak pies - the king of lunches.

6) The faces on the new arrivals made me happy.

7) There wasn't a bag of compost in sight.

Minus points:

1) Exhaustion. Back at Alpine Lodge I once had no energy to open a tin of corned beef.

2) Blisters. They hurt. A lot.

3) Gary - the fackin' soap-dodging, fackin' pig-

hunting, fackin' tuna-munching, fackin' chain-swearing idiot of a boss.

4) The cold. It was so... cold.

5) Phil - Gary's right-hand man. He had this stare...

6) Insulating glass fibre. It got in your eyes.

When I got home I wrote a long overdue e-mail.

Hi Jess,

I'm writing this in Queenstown - NZ's self-styled non-stop party town! I haven't actually seen a party yet but there's always time...

The scenery is fantastic. I can see the Remarkables from my window and in the evening the skies go pink. I can't believe you haven't been here and you only live 7 hours away! You'd love it.

I've started work as a labourer at the airport. It's hard but the lads are great - except Andy our foreman who's a complete bastard, and his best mate Phil who is really scary. I try not to make eye contact with him. I think he's a criminal on the run. My friend Joff gives me lifts every morning to the airport and says I should get about $400 a week, so that's way better than at Kings. I'll be in credit with the bank in no time so I'll take you out to dinner again when I fly back to Auckland.

I've also found somewhere to live. It's called Alpine Lodge. I share a room a girl called Lina. Okay, before

you say anything, yeah I know it's not ideal but at least the washing-up gets done. Lina's cool.
It's nearly 7.00 PM and I know it's early, but I'm really tired. I need my beauty sleep...
Hope you've seen Crispin, G-Man and Chris since I left Auckland. If not, PHONE THEM! Write soon.
Lots of love,
Joe xxxxxxxx

By the end of the week I felt like a proper labourer: I wore the same clothes for days in a row, smoked at regular intervals, cursed every other word, ate peppered steak pies for lunch, and leered at the holiday reps (but not properly - it was only half-hearted).

And today, Gary gave me my wage slip. Well, he just kind of threw it at my feet. He was a fool. I really disliked him.

I picked up the envelope from the sawdust. $NZ 454 for a week's work.

I was back in the money.

Chapter scorecard: Varley gets his first decent wage slip, but work is proving a struggle. Cook would smile knowingly. Life on the sea is rather like that: decent pay (for a captain, anyway), but a struggle. The Captain, credit to him, returned to Britain in one piece after his second NZ voyage. Neither quibble with a draw, and the score remains tied.

Chapter 24

Outgoings for the week:

$NZ 100 rent.

$NZ 27 food (mainly bread, dried pasta sachets, tomato soup, chocolate and Magi noodles).

$NZ 26 Absolut vodka.

$NZ 24 beer (a crate of Speights).

$NZ 27 cigarettes.

$NZ 5 second-hand gloves.

$NZ 5 second-hand hat.

$NZ 10 second-hand coat.

$NZ 5 Internet.

$NZ 10 laundry.

$NZ 30 deposit for a library card (I took out Jack Kerouac's *The Dharma Bums,* which I read on the grassy slopes of Queenstown Hill Recreation Reserve).

Bank balance: –$NZ 261.

The second-hand clothes were a mixed bag - an old plastic bag to be exact. My gloves were woolly black *Thinsulates* with more 'thin' than 'insulate'. The brown hat was like a tea cosy - which was nice - but the coat was grossly sub-standard: lime green with hideous blue streaks running down each flank. It was truly dreadful, although I'm not ashamed to confess I'm what they call in America a 'thrift shop junkie'. I'll buy anything if it is cheap. As Gore Vidal once stated, 'Style is knowing who you are, what you want to say, and not giving a damn.'

Life at Alpine Lodge clicked into place. It was all about routine. I woke up ridiculously early, watched *Home and Away*, smoked cigarettes and waited for Joff's lift to the airport where Gary barked at me for being the only worker wearing a canary yellow jumper.

My favourite times were payday and coming home. Frequently the Lodge was bustling with activity when I returned, so it felt like home as opposed to just a place to live. And the people downstairs were great. Though Lina and I were upstairs, we frequently mingled with other lodgers watching TV and having drinks in the lounge.

Lina was my best friend at the Lodge. She had a quirky, almost zany demeanour which was endearing, and her style was chic bohemian - flared denim trousers, beanie hats and floral shirts. She had a wry sense of humour and we often had long, drunken conversations about films and books. She knew all the town's bars, and relished playing chess. A tad conservative considering Queenstown is the adventure sport capital of the world; no one would jet set into deepest Otago just to play a strategic board game. But Lina's enthusiasm proved irresistible and our creative minds were soon locked in a mental battle.

A couple of minutes into the game Lina's eyes lit up.

'My horsey is now going to take your prawn. Prepare to die! Giddy-up, horsey!'

And that was the sum of Lina's chess know-how. I beat her 5-0 in half an hour.

'We must go to Pogs, Joe,' she insisted, grabbing my sleeve. 'It is absolutely imperative that you try the one hundred pint Guinness challenge!'

And so, walking around Rees Street an hour later, we were in Pog Mahones, reputedly the most southern proper Irish pub in the world.

'Drink one hundred pints of Guinness in less than six months,' said barman Luke, 'and you'll get a certificate, a T-shirt and your name on the wall.'

'You English poof,' goaded another barman, Grumpy Jack. 'I bet you can't do it.'

100 pints in six months is a doddle. Hell, one hundred pints in a week is achievable. I handed over $70 to Grumpy Jack and settled into my first of 11 pints of vitamin G. I never looked back.

Point 6 in the "Working at the Airport: Minus points" list referred to one of the most loathed products a labourer will have the displeasure of working with. The words themselves were nauseating: glass fibre - great big pink slabs of itching, glass-laden cotton wool-like material inserted between wooden slats to aid insulation. Gary refused hire of proper work gloves, claiming there were no spare pairs, even though I'd seen some in his rusty 'ute'. My second-hand gloves were inadequate; what I needed were thick leather gloves - the sort Phil used to wrestle wild pigs.

Gary wasn't a complete bastard of a boss. Sometimes he didn't bother me for whole afternoons, preferring instead to show how macho he was in his hardhat and work boots by grappling with lengths of metal piping or taking over the drill and ploughing chest-first into concrete walls. I could cope with all that palaver. What really bothered me was that Gary knew *for a fact* that whoever was working with glass fibre required extra protection. It was probably statutory law, especially up a ladder. When inserted above your head, a barrage of glass arrowed into my hair and into my eyes - I actually got pieces of glass *in my eyes*. The safest place with glass in your eyes really isn't up a ladder.

On one day, sufficiently hungover from Guinness to have the courage to face Gary, I asked to borrow his goggles.

'Eh? What for?'

I told him about the glass and showed the inflamed and bloodshot corner of my eye - I'd gone to the airport toilets to investigate and my eye was red raw. Gary stared into my eyes, fishy breath invading my nasal area. He'd had tuna again for his lunch.

'What am I suppose to be looking at?' he said.

'The corner of my eye. There's glass in it.'

'Can't see anything,' he snapped.

'But it's there. See? Please, if you would just - '

'Nah, mate, can't see anything,' he said again, as though repeating himself made him right. 'Now get back to fackin' work.'

Labouring at Queenstown Airport continued in similar vein for the next few weeks. It revolved around a strict routine of early starts, hard graft and wobbling on ladders getting glass in my eyes. Transforming the airport to one with international status meant the town would be more accessible from Australia, but it was a strange concept. Queenstown is smaller than most small English towns, with a population of around 10,000. It'd be like flying from Paris to Truro.

Even so, with the deadline ever nearing, I was part of a team. I was the lowest paid ABL employee (and was so reminded constantly by my workmates), but I couldn't complain. I'd travelled down to this famous town alone, found accommodation, made a new set of friends, scored a job and, more importantly, had a local pub where my pint was poured before asking for it. I was doing alright. Cook would've shook my hand and bought me a drink, that I had no doubts about.

My weekly wage of $NZ 450 came in handy (and kept Taff happy). But as much as it helped, money wasn't central to my apparent success. I was *surviving*. Simply living in Queenstown was a real tonic. Pulling back the curtains to reveal a backdrop of pink clouds melting above The Remarkables was hard to beat. I learned to appreciate the beauty, rather than take it for granted. Indeed, it became a ritual to stare outside the window across the town and picture old friends above the mountains.

Earning extra money meant I splashed out on some extravagant purchases, like CD's, bottled beer and round tea bags. When I felt reckless I paid Taff in advance (and in fact, on one giddy day, I went wild and bought a loaf of *premium* bread). And I still had the Guinness challenge to be cracking on with, but I only gave it a good go on the weekends. Labouring in subzero conditions at 8 AM with a cracking hangover is supremely idiotic and highly ill-advised.

One of my drinking partners at the Lodge was a heavily bearded lad from Brighton called Dangerous Dave, so-called because he was a madman on the snowboard slopes. He hadn't killed anybody yet, but it was only a matter of time. Dave had been at the Lodge for a month, sharing a room downstairs with a feisty Irish girl called

Amanda.

Dave was looking for work, so I suggested ABL at the airport.

'What's the boss like?' he asked.

'You like tuna?'

So when Dave secured a job as a labourer three days later I was instantly jealous because he owned proper work boots and a chunky red body warmer. He actually *looked* like a labourer, whilst I was still making do in black jeans and yellow sweater. We double-teamed on walls with sledgehammers and drills, installed glass fibre sheets and shared our lunch breaks at the airport café instead of the fishy ABL hut.

'Right, you Pommies, listen up. There's a pile of asphalt by the tool shed. I want it moved by the end of the day.'

Dave looked at me, thinking, 'I've left my magic wand at home, now what?'

'Where should we dump it?'

'Wherever the fack you want, mate. Just make sure by half-five it's not there.'

Our bristly foreman left us under a tuna haze. We needed a strategy and some equipment with which to enforce it. It was strange Gary hadn't told us what we should use to complete the task, but maybe this was a test in itself, like the mental agility round in the *Krypton*

Factor. Or more likely Gary wanted to make our work as difficult as possible. Either way the task wouldn't defeat us. We were two young, intelligent English lads. We would rise to the occasion. Nothing would stand in our way. Nothing.

'Jesus, that's *massive!*'

On first sight Dave's description was a little understated. The asphalt spread across the airport tarmac, peaking in the middle like the Matterhorn. The outer crust was rock hard, jet black and tinged with ice. The dimension of the pile was difficult to assess accurately, although a width of 30 feet and a height of half that didn't seem imprecise. This was a gargantuan chore, even for two young, intelligent English lads. I let out a small squeak. Dave glanced at his watch.

'Right then, me old mucker. We've got four hours to move all this. What do you reckon?'

I studied the asphalt mound carefully. 'Cigarette?'

'Good idea.'

Ten minutes later, smoke break over, we assessed the situation. Dave concluded the pile was an eyesore and it blocked the direct route from the tool shed to the large builder's skip ten yards behind it. This seemed reasonable but not altogether justified; we're only going to move the eyesore from one place to another, so why bother? And why couldn't the builders simply skirt around the asphalt to dump their waste into the skip?

They'd only increase their journey time by a meagre ten seconds or so. It wasn't a difficult concept to understand, even for South Islanders. No, Gary had run out of jobs and wanted to derive pleasure by making us Pommies suffer.

'Let's try the tool shed,' Dave said. 'Maybe we can find a wheelbarrow or something in there.'

'And if not, maybe the calendar girl will give us inspiration.'

We rummaged around the shed for a quarter of an hour, picking up potential useful devices. A large pick or a solid gardening fork would've been useful to penetrate the mound, then a spade would do the donkey work.

I pondered the task ahead. I reminisced about working at Kings Plant Barn - and for that crazy hag, Mrs Brewer - and reflected that a lot of labouring work, when you got down to the essentials, boiled down to 'moving stuff'. People wanted things moving all time, whether it be bags of compost, plants, stones or piles of rubble. The objective of all this moving was often debatable, and for job satisfaction it's pretty lame, but as employees we're not in a position to question the rationality of these jobs - we just had to get on and do it. How depressing.

'Bingo!' said Dave triumphantly, pulling out two rusty spades from under a wooden shelf. 'We can use these.'

'Good work. Let's get cracking.'

'Listen, Joe, you think Gary really expects us to move it all before half five?'

'I've never been more certain of anything in my whole life.'

'And if we don't?'

'You know Phil, the scary-looking guy? Best mates with Gary?'

'Looks like a pig hunter?'

'That's the one. You seen the size of his hands?'

'Massive, aren't they?'

'Yup. And blood-stained.'

The penny dropped. 'No time to waste, then.'

Dave lumbered towards to the asphalt pile, hitched up his loose jeans, pulled on leather gloves, raised a spade high above his head, and brought it down firmly on the asphalt. *Bosh!* The sound of impact was thunderous, but the effect minimal. The spade juddered comically like a tuning fork, and for a second Dave vibrated like he'd been electrocuted.

'This is rock-hard, mate. We're going to need something else.'

'I'll check the tool shed again.'

'Cigarette first?'

'Good idea.'

Second smoke break over, Dave located a pair of wooden-handled picks. This was more like it. Dave slung his pick over his shoulder, breaking out into a melodic rendition of:

'Hi-ho, hi-ho, it's off to work we go... we've each got a pick and our boss is a prick, hi-ho, hi-ho-hi-ho-hi-ho...'

'Let's prove Gary wrong,' I said. 'He reckons we're not up to this.'

'Yeah, let's show that Kiwi fuck-wit what we can do.'

We attacked the pile with gusto. The picks proved a revelation. Sharp fragments of asphalt whizzed over our heads in a whirl of cold steel. Wearing goggles would have been advisable but Dave didn't acquire his nickname on a whim; we were men possessed. We had neither time nor regard for health and safety. Working to a strict deadline had never been so critical. Our jobs were on the line, and we didn't want Phil to be let loose on us. I could picture the scene: Gary would give us a brief head start, before allowing Phil to pick us off with a rifle as if we were wild boar.

'Three-thirty,' said Dave.

'Christ. I thought time was supposed to fly when you're having *fun*.'

'Tell me about, Joe. Fancy another cigarette?'

'Lovely.'

Dave collapsed on the asphalt, rolled a cigarette. I lit up a Lucky, threw my friend some matches.

'You know what, Dave? We've actually made good progress. I reckon we can start to put all this shit in the wheelbarrows now.'

'Where should we put it?'

'Gary said wherever.'

Dave grinned. 'Let's dump all of it in his ute.'

'I'd love to, pal, but I quite enjoy breathing.'

'How about behind the car park? It's a fair trek - maybe fifty yards - but it's out of the way.'

'Okay.' I stubbed out my half-smoked cigarette. 'You finished yours, Dave?'

'Yeah.'

'Fancy another?'

'Sir, what a splendid idea.'

We filled our wheelbarrows and toddled to the car park where we dumped the loads onto a patch of wasteland. High above, under a cloudless sky, paragliders swooped and soared like vultures looking for scraps.

After an hour or so we had moved half of the asphalt.

'Quarter to five, Joe. What do you reckon?'

'Forty-five minutes left. Piece of piss.'

'How are your arms?'

'Aching. Yours?'

'No idea, pal. Can't feel them.'

By half-past five the job was complete. We were knackered.

'I'm ready for a beer.'

'Too right. Watch it, Dave - here comes Gary.'

An orange hardhat loomed. Hammers and screwdrivers swung from a leather tool belt. Gary scratched his beard, grunted, spat out tuna flakes.

'Right, you two. All done?'

Dave was triumphant. 'All done, boss.'

'Where've you dumped it?'

'Near the car park.'

'What?'

'Near the car park. Over there.' Dave jerked his thumb towards the wasteland, smiled contently.

'Jesus - anywhere but there,' spat Gary. A flake of tuna torpedoed straight into Dave's beard. I stifled a guffaw. 'That's a health and safety issue,' our foreman growled. 'Jesus, don't you fackin' Pommies know fackin' *anything?* Fack.'

'But you said - '

'Too late for excuses, mate. Move it first thing tomorrow. Be here early - and don't take so much fackin' time over it.'

Gary marched back to the main airport entrance, leaving Dave and me dumbfounded. Fortunately Gary didn't have eyes in the back of his head. If he had, he would have seen Dave's hairy arse mooning him.

On a Saturday I ambled into town to buy postcards. The day was turning into a humdinger. I sent four back to Auckland: one to the boys, one to our neighbour Griff, one to Kings Plant Barn, and one to Jess. I remembered writing the last one because I used a red pen to draw the heart.

Chapter scorecard: Varley gains a new drinking challenge, as well as a new work companion. Cook probably didn't have fun drinking buddies. The Captain climbs to the crows-nest and waves the white flag on this one. The tie is broken.

Chapter 25

For the next two weeks Dangerous Dave and I continued working for ABL at Queenstown Airport. Completion was imminent. My bank balance was healthier; once an anaemic bag of bones, it was now rosy-cheeked and vibrant. I'd been a labourer for seven weeks, and it had been a success.

Dave bagged a job as a snowboard instructor at the Coronet Peak resort. I didn't envy him because... I didn't like snowboarding. But I still needed work. My plan was to remain in Queenstown for two months before flying back to Auckland, then back to the UK. My skills still needed to pay the bills.

I walked around town with no incentive or ambition. Whilst people scrambled to book skiing sessions or horse riding lessons or white-water rafting or whatever it was they were risking their lives for, smoking Luckies and watching the 'adventure capital of the world' drift by was my tonic. Snowboarders ambled, discussing 'half pipes' and 'gnarly rides, dude.' I smiled; Queenstown is a place where just about any activity can be enjoyed, and all I'd done was work my socks off and drank Guinness.

I didn't care. I genuinely had no desire - absolutely none at all - to engage in any of the sports on offer. Bungy jumping to me had the appeal of a slap in the face. I remember reading about its dangers in a NZ sports book. Bungy jumping, it warned, possesses 'inherent dangers'. Well who would have thought? The book then explained 'a relatively common mistake in fatality cases is to use cord that is too long. The cord should be substantially shorter than the height of the jumping platform to allow it room to stretch'. Well I never! Imagine the scene: 'Ready? 1... 2... 3...*jump!*...Right, he should be coming back up in about... oh shit.'

I dislike skiing. It's pointless. Yes, it's globally enjoyed as a glamorous, high-octane winter sport, but to perfect it you have to shell out a small fortune on travel, equipment and tasteless clothing, only to dish out more money for lessons and ski passes.

Snowboarding? No thanks.

Heights scare me. Paragliders are serene soaring in the cloudless skies, but you can't hear their screams because a strap has come loose and the poor sod fears he'll hurtle to earth in an ungainly mess of synthetic fibre, cheap plastic and human flesh.

And what is the point of 'river surfing', 'fly by wire' or 'zorbing'. What are they? Though walking wasn't high on my list of pastimes, several times Lina and I took lazy strolls along the shores of Lake Wakatipu. We connected in a way that was sometimes spooky: no subject for conversation was off limits. The walks were times for deliberation and friendship. In between jobs, and with no Jess or my boys in town, our walks formed an important routine in my life down south. Lina was a true soul mate, the lake an irreplaceable setting.

I didn't want to be chucked off a bridge. First-rate views could be found without aerial pursuits - you could climb a hill. The mountains were staggering. Lake Wakatipu was on my doorstep. I could hitch a ride to nearby Wanaka or Glenorchy - undoubtedly two of the most beautiful places in New Zealand, possibly in the world. With such splendid scenery on offer, what more do you need? I didn't feel the need to try everything Queenstown had to offer just so I could get sozzled in a bar afterwards and boast that, 'Wow, dude, it was like flying... only it wasn't.'

That said, a lot of my friends at the Lodge got a buzz from these things. Lina enjoyed white-water rafting, Amanda paragliding, my Yorkshire friend Dan swore by 'night bungying', and another friend Rod was fond of rolling down hills in a gigantic plastic ball. This was the mysterious zorbing, although I had no idea why anyone would want to do it.

In conclusion: Queenstown, like the rest of New

Zealand, is a place of contrasts. For every adrenaline sport you had a quiet pub; for every penniless worker you had a millionaire playboy; for every run-down hostel you have a gleaming five star hotel. And for every dream job you have a stupendously crap one.

One evening, in the middle of July, I swallowed my pride and returned to the Copthorne Hotel. Natalie was still on reception.

'Can I help you, sir?'

I pulled back my shoulders, puffed out my chest, and told her I'd faxed my CV weeks ago and I now needed employment.

Well, I couldn't really believe it when Andy, the head chef from Wellington, offered me a job in the kitchen there and then. It was a joke, surely. I waited for the punch line, but it didn't come.

'We're looking for a Crockery Hygiene Operative,' said Andy.

'Excellent... that means washing-up, right?'

'Got it in one.'

'I think they're desperate,' said Natalie.

'We are,' confirmed Andy.

So, job-wise, I was on another roll. Gone were the days wandering around Auckland in the summer heat trying to score the ideal temporary graduate job. Queenstown was brimming with tourists and job-hunters alike, competition weaning out the ugly, the stupid and the inept. I'd been lucky. Kitchen work wouldn't be glamorous, but that was irrelevant.

'I'll take it!' I told Andy.

'Oh, I know you will,' he said. 'Come in tomorrow morning at six and go through the back to the kitchen. Ask for Joy. She'll show you around. I'll be in at noon.'

That night I retired to bed early. I dreamt of glitzy hotel guests tipping their top hats and handing over coins of gold. I dreamt of taking cigarette breaks in a comfy armchair next to roaring log fires in the marble-floored foyer, and of waitresses serving free staff lunches of smoked salmon and pink champagne. I dreamt of success.

'Jesus, what time do you call *this?*'

I'd slept in.

Joy was silver-haired, eyes as black as coal, and she had a pockmarked face. She looked like she'd been set on fire, then extinguished with a golf shoe. She wore a white apron and a blue-and-white baker's cap. Already I'd made up my mind: she was the female equivalent of Gary. She held an eight-inch chopping knife in a manner that suggested she wouldn't hesitate about using it on items other than fruit and veg.

'Sorry,' I replied, fidgeting in the doorway. 'I guess I'm not used to getting up this early. You see, I used to work at the airport and haven't been working for a few - '

'Never mind all that,' she barked, shooing me inside. 'Fetch yourself an apron. There's washing-up to be done, ay.'

The kitchen was a simple affair, consisting of two large stainless steel 'prep tables', a set of wide double doors leading to a walk-in fridge, metal shelves holding copper pots and pans, and three industrial-sized ovens. The smell was an odd mix of burnt metal and wet vegetables.

The sink was massive, and crammed with dirty cutlery and plates.

Joy nodded at the grime. 'That's why we need someone in at this hour. Lazy bastards don't wash-up in the evening.' She paused, then said, 'Sometime today would be *really* helpful.'

That morning, time stopped. Or I thought it did. Staring into the soapy abyss was disheartening. Congealed food stuck to the silver as grimly as limpets to rocks.

'Yep, that looks like ketchup,' I said out loud. Joy shook her head.

Plates and saucers were easier to clean because they had flat surfaces and you could aim the hose at an angle; dried food flew off under the sheer force of the water. Hot water was key, although rubber gloves were futile as they had no grip and were so thin they melted under the heat.

Joy, naturally, kept a close eye on the operation. In fact, her eye was so close I heard it blinking. She stood over me, pointing into the soap suds.

'Get that plate... yep, that one right there. Don't skip on the cutlery... '

Joy was a witch. Never had a first name been so erroneously accredited to someone: my new boss had about as much joy as a nuclear disaster.

The rest of my kitchen colleagues arrived; a real motley crew, but not without their charm. Randall was a lively sous chef from San Diego who wore a Stars & Stripes bandana over matted, black hair. A handlebar moustache hung from his chin in a way that would entertain a small monkey for hours. His interesting tattoo collection consisted of a snake wrapped around a dagger, and a naked woman smoking an enormous spliff. Clearly Randall wished he was a Hell's Angel instead of chopping asparagus for a living.

Hinton was a Billy Bunter type with a crew cut - a real Otago lad who took no shit, especially from Andy, whom he despised. Although a junior sous chef, Hinton and authority went together like Winona Ryder and security tags. I kind of liked him, especially when he revealed his feelings towards Andy ('He's a knob-jockey, eh.')

The commis chef was Georgina. She had a big heart, and assisted Joy with making pastries and breads, most of which she ate. I got on with her - except the first time

I called her Georgie.

'Don't call me that,' she warned, reaching for a bread knife.

The front of house staff were magnificent and we clicked instantly, maybe because we pitied each other in equal measure. The General Manager, Alan, was an officious prick. He arrived late, putting on his tie as he sauntered into the kitchen.

His first words were, 'Menus ready yet?' A 'good morning' would've been nice.

'I'm on to it,' said Hinton. 'Andy wants the lamb chops on the specials.'

'You prepped the starters?'

'They'll be ready in half an hour.'

'Then don't waste time talking to me.'

Alan combed his hair, patted down his eyebrows, and disappeared into the dining room to see the waiters.

'Prick,' said Hinton.

There was no doubt Andy was the head chef. It was his swagger: 'Look at me! My job title has the word 'head' in it - and it's not 'dickhead!''

Some head chefs appear preposterous with floppy white hats, chessboard trousers and 12 varieties of stainless steel Japanese searing knifes. Chefs - particularly head chefs - assume they can reprimand junior colleagues for minor offences because they command a higher salary.

Carrots Julienne not sliced equally? That deserves a prod in the ribs. Chicken consommé too hot? That surely merits a kick in the knackers, no? Duties of a head chef are laced with pressure and trauma - no argument there - but many people have similarly stressful jobs and you don't hear them growling and barking. Head chefs are an odd breed, but the type of breed is open to discussion.

Andy was no exception.

It was nearly 1 PM when he decided to grace his presence on us. Joy had bollocked me for my 10 minute over-indulgence; it seemed Andy could come and go as he pleased. I looked over from the sink and caught Randall's attention. He rolled his eyes. Randall was okay. He was a rebel.

'How's it been?' Andy asked Joy, who was slicing melon into crescents.

'Mad rush on at breakfast, ay, but all good.'

'What about Joe?'

Silence. Confusion.

'Who's Joe?' said Joy.

'The new guy. Pommie. On sink duty.'

Sink duty. One thing about Andy: he could make a shit job sound shitter. I preferred 'kitchen-hand', or 'skivvy'. Even 'washer-upper' would do. I took umbrage with 'sink duty'. It didn't even *sound* good.

'That his name?' asked Joy. 'Came in ten minutes late.'

'Really?'

'Aw yea.'

'So he came in at... ?'

'Ten past six.'

'Ten past six?'

'Ten past six.'

'Are you sure it was ten past and not five past?'

'Ten past, for sure. I looked at my watch.'

I was fishing out leftover spinach from the plughole when Andy was on me like a dose of pneumonia, and twice as unpleasant. He wasn't happy. I was getting used to the mannerisms of my New Zealand bosses: the flushed face, the flaring nostrils, and the steam coming from the ears.

'Joe!' he bellowed. 'You were *late*.'

'Sorry, I slept in.'

'It won't do. We run a tight ship here, yeah?'

'I really am sorry. It won't happen again.'

Once again I was a dogsbody in the doghouse.

To his credit, Hinton stopped preparing a duck terrine to make a rude gesture behind Andy's back. I didn't approve of Hinton's actions, but it was nice to have someone on my side. I won't explicitly detail Hinton's gesture, but it involved the combining of thumb and forefinger coupled with a lot of jerking up and down.

'Mop the floor,' said Andy. 'It's filthy.'

'Yes, Sir!'

At 2 PM a young girl named Anna took over. I was free. I felt like Tim Robbins in *The Shawshank Redemption*, when he'd crawled through 500 yards of crap and finally made it out into civilisation. The rest of the day belonged to me. I could indulge in some of Queenstown's finest leisure activities: a pony trek; a raft trip, maybe, or possibly a spot of zorbing. But instead I went to Pogs, drank seven pints of Guinness and headed home to bed. I slept like a baby.

Chapter scorecard: A new job in the bag might indicate another point for Varley, but the new boss comes from behind to steal the headlines: not exactly a 'command performance' by Varley. Cook is certainly a commander, if nothing else, and was even made a member of the Royal Society in 1775 and consequently promoted to "post-captain". And then, as if rubbing salt into the wound, the Captain wrote an account of his second NZ voyage. He pulls one back to level the score.

VARLEY 7   COOK 7

Chapter 26

At first the mornings were a drag because walking to the hotel was a cold, lonely experience. The parties had ended. With every howl of the chill winter wind I wished I was back in bed.

But by August I found the work steadily improving. On the few occasions I beat Joy into the kitchen, she allowed me a cup of tea and toast before I contemplated the washing-up. That's the thing with middle-aged female Kiwis - you had to earn their respect. I'd learnt that with Brenda. When I left Kings Plant Barn I was sure she thought I was a good worker. And towards the end of my employment there, even when she put on a grim face, I knew she really wasn't mad with me. Behind that hard stare was the hint of a smile.

Joy was a bit like that. After putting in the hours, she gradually relaxed. She allowed more perks: an extra cuppa here, a five-minute break there. Soon, the days didn't feel like a chore.

I tried to save weekend money because mid-week boozing plus a 5AM start equalled a sore head and scolding from Joy. For a long period I showed reasonable dedication that gained Andy's esteem. Not that he showed it, of course, but I knew. If he asked me to sweep the floor or help with the morning's food prep, he'd say a quick 'thanks' and that was good enough for me. He was human after all.

A kitchen is a curious environment in which to work. It is often crowded, hectic and intensely hot, where people on 'sink duty' and commis chefs are regarded as subhuman. In military terms, a kitchen-hand is the foot soldier risking his life by going 'over the top'. A sous chef is further up the rankings, second on the death-list. By contrast, head chefs are regarded as cigar-chomping generals, relaxing in plush leather chairs perusing maps and concocting complex strategies. Head chefs can get away with murder - and I suspect many have.

I considered this whilst holding a bin liner. Emptying bin liners was unquestionably the worst part of being a kitchen-hand. The Copthorne catered for many guests, so the kitchen bins soon piled up with cold baked beans and soggy bits of sausage. My task was to take these bulging bin liners and hurl them into huge steel containers out the back. It was a thoroughly wretched experience, particularly when the plastic split and the pungent mess spilled onto the kitchen floor. Not only did the foul stench of lukewarm meat and eggs hit the nostrils with the pungency of Rotorua in a heat wave, I had to kneel down to scoop the whole stinking lot up.

My relationship with these bin liners deteriorated rapidly. They simply weren't strong enough to cater for the bulk of the food. Andy vehemently refused the use of two bags per bin to 'double up' as it was a 'waste of resources'. After I'd shovelled the third bin liner of the morning I offered to buy the extra bin liners myself, but Andy shook his head.

'One's enough, mate.'

'But two bin liners really would help.'

Andy glared at me. Just as I thought he'd explode and yell, '*What is your major malfunction?!*' he threw a bin liner at me and told me to stop moaning. This wasn't Kiwi pigheadedness; this was about the pecking order. Andy was the prize rooster, and I was the disabled chicken foraging in the shit.

Chris eventually made his way down to see me three weeks before I was due to leave. He'd flown to Christchurch and hitchhiked all the way to Queenstown, using an incredible seven cars - one of which had picked him up twice. I'd e-mailed Chris to say he could stay with me and Lina the Lodge. Taff didn't need to know.

Whilst Chris's enthusiasm was welcome I was a little disappointed he would be here for just three weeks. Over the years at university I'd developed a strong bond with him. Chris was always haring about or drinking wildly or getting up to mischief, and I was looking forward to showing off his qualities to my new Kiwi friends. But three weeks just wasn't enough. He could have come down earlier but as he explained to me, 'Sorry, Joey, but I was enjoying myself too much in Auckland.'

Every afternoon, after my kitchen shift, I dashed home to show Chris around Queenstown. We hitchhiked with Lina to Glenorchy several times. Lina and I had acclimatised to our blissful environment; Chris was gobsmacked. Glenorchy was a whole world away from the tourism and gaudy fashion sense of Queenstown.

Another time we strolled on the pebbles of Lake Wakatipu when male ego took over and we decided to have a stone-skimming contest, simply because I knew my cricketing arm would fare better than Chris's amateur technique. However, much to our dismay, a large flock of aquatic birds had settled on the waters' surface. Whilst not technically an obstacle to our competition, the birds proved a source of temptation, and the contest was to skim a stone over them. The first pebble I chose was smooth, shiny and flat - a sure fire winner. Taking a step back, I wound my arm round and let fly. Pity the birds didn't. The stone hit the first bird dead straight in the beak, the resulting hideous squawk and cloud of feathers sending me into spasms of guilt. I felt awful.

'Get in there and help it out, man!' Chris yelled. The poor bird spiralled below the icy depths and met a quick, but unacceptable, watery grave. It wasn't a high point in my New Zealand adventure, and it brought a downer to the rest of our day.

That evening, though, brought a coincidence of the highest merit. The cloudless sky turned a gloomy grey, with Queenstown besieged by heavy blankets of rain. Chris was showering, ready for a night at Pogs. Lina was cheating at chess - her tactics were moving her 'horsey' in a series of illegal diagonal moves that rendered my resistance futile.

'Giddy-up, horsey! Come on, giddy-*up!* Let's eat all of Joe's prawns!'

Chris strolled into the living room, opened a beer, grimaced.

'Got an umbrella, Joey?'

'Afraid not, pal.'

'Christ, we're going to get soaked. It's wetter than an otter's eyelash.'

Lina suddenly jumped up from the chessboard. 'We need hats! Hats are the answer!'

'You got any, Linny?'

'I've got a plan. Joe, darling, throw me some tinfoil. It's in the second drawer down.'

Lina's idea was inspired. With ingenious dexterity Lina fashioned three makeshift hats from the tinfoil. She even moulded wide rims to act as a defence against the rain. She laid them neatly on the floor: three sparkling, silver cowboy hats.

'Genius!' said Chris. 'Let's go get 'em!'

Walking through Queenstown in the lashing rain wearing cowboy hats made from tinfoil turned a few heads. The hats were surprisingly substantial, too; Lina had used two layers to produce a rigid 'ribbed' effect. She had excelled herself.

Pogs was busy, the drinkers shoulder-to-shoulder. We struggled with the door, and fell inside.

Half the pub became silent, staring at three slightly inebriated, soaking-wet tosspots in homemade aluminium cowboy hats. We stood there, gormless, rain dripping from our hats.

The applause was deafening. Everyone in the pub started clapping. The whole place cheered wildly.

'What the fuck?' whispered Chris.

A broad man with a crumb-infested ginger beard waded through the crowd and thrust out a lardy hand. I shook it wholeheartedly - with no idea what was going on.

'Well done, young 'uns!' he said, grinning. 'Top show, top show!'

'What the fuck?' repeated Chris.

A banner above the bar read, 'Hat Wearing Competition'.

Chris, Lina and I were presented with second prize at the inaugural Pog Mahones contest for Original Headwear. Nine pints of Guinness later I concluded that tinfoil hats were the future.

'You need a hand, Georgie?'

'Don't call me that. And no, I don't need any help. I can prepare a salad all by myself, thank you very much.'

It was my fifth week at the hotel. Georgina was in a foul mood. She wasn't usually unfriendly - or *impolite* most times - but sometimes you knew when she wanted to be left alone.

I'd been at the sink for an hour and was wholeheartedly bored. I needed human interaction. There was only so much washing-up you could do before breaking up the routine to chat with other dogsbodies. Washing-up will drive anyone crazy. And to top it off, we were in dire straits: Hinton was creating a 'corporate cake' for a function tomorrow; Randall had called in sick, as had a few waiters; Joy hadn't been in all morning, and Andy was late.

We had a full-house of diners this afternoon, and few staff. Alan was getting desperate. He approached me at the sink, where I was rinsing cutlery. He looked liked a child.

'Excuse me, Joe.'

'Yes?'

'We're down on staff today.'

'So I see.'

'Yes, well. You done any waiting before?'

'Only for you when you're late.'

'Ha-ha, good one. No, I meant as a waiter. We've got a hundred diners today. We need you.'

The Great General Manager was essentially begging. I was enjoying it.

'You'd only need to take their orders,' Alan persisted. 'You wouldn't have to work the till.'

'But I don't know the menu.'

'Neither do half of the waiters. Please... you'd be doing me a... a favour.'

Alan was a grovelling piece of putty in my hands. The sycophantic turd was reduced to asking a Crockery Hygiene Operative to work front-of-house.

'I'll need a tie, a black shirt, and a copy of the menu.' I was a kidnapper giving my demands to the FBI.

'Coming up,' said Alan. Then: 'Make sure you've finished the washing-up before changing.'

'Would you like to order, madam?'

'No, I'd like you to stand there looking at me like a half-wit.'

The dining room was full, but hardly bustling. The average age of the customers was about 103. Most were tourists, probably. My first table was occupied by two ladies who reminded me of Mrs Slocombe in *Are You Being Served?* The answer to that question, evidently, was 'No.'

'What would you like?'

'Slow roast rare breed belly pork,' said the first lady. 'Buttered garden peas, roast fennel, grilled king prawns, crushed new potatoes, and pork sauce.'

On my pad I wrote, 'Pork.'

To the second lady, 'And for you, madam?'

'Slow roast shoulder of lamb, champ potatoes, tenderstem broccoli, mint pickled onions, and redcurrant jus.'

Next to 'Pork' I wrote 'Lamb'.

'Lovely. And to drink?'

'Water, twice.'

'Yes, I heard you the first time... sorry, a little joke, ladies. Umm... would you like lemon in your water?'

'We're not *that* posh, young man.'

'I didn't think you were!'

I scampered to Alan to give him the order before the ladies could think of a rebuke.

Alan was sweating, clearly stressed about the customer-to-staff ratio, though he still had time to check his hair in the mirror.

'Go to table twenty-six,' he bellowed. 'They've been waiting forever.'

'Which one's twenty-six?'

'In-between twenty-five and twenty-seven.'

'Thanks,' I said, then under my breath, 'Einstein.'

It was bedlam. The two other waiters, Jack and Elsa,

were dashing about, taking orders for several tables simultaneously. I was picking tables at random, because I had no clue regarding the table numbers.

'Twenty-six!' yelled Alan. 'Table twenty-six!'

Alan rushed towards me, grabbed my elbow. 'Twenty-six! Go to table twenty-six!' Then the hotel mobile phone buzzed in his pocket. Alan threw it to me. 'Answer it.'

'But table twenty-six? For the love of God, what about table twenty-six?'

'Just answer it.' Alan dragged a hand through his hair and drifted off to take an order. I noticed with annoyance he walked straight passed table 26.

'Hello, this is Joe speaking. How may I help you?'

'I want to speak to the manager. What's his name... Alan?'

'I'm sorry, Sir, Alan is busy. I may be able to help, though. I'm Joe, the pot-washer.'

The gentleman exploded, as if he had been connected to a joke line at a pirate radio station.

'The what? The bloody *pot-washer*? This is Mr. Nugent in Room eighteen. I specifically asked for a *twin* room, and... what's his name?... Alan said he'd arrange it. I need a bloody twin room, now!'

Mr Nugent's outburst took me off-guard. I was used to being spoken to by bosses and customers as if all inconvenience or mistakes laid solely on my shoulders, but Mr Nugent was an unidentified problem; I'd never met him and certainly knew nothing about hotel accommodation. I decided to wing it.

'Mr Nugent, please calm down.'

'Don't tell me to calm down! I told the manager I needed a twin room, and I don't have one! I want it fixed, now!'

'OK, Mr Nugent. Please bear with me. I'll have to put you on hol - '

'Don't you dare put me on hold! Put me on to the manager, now!'

'Just one second, Mr Nugent.'

I held the phone at arm's length, whispered 'Fuck' and proceeded to Alan, who was talking to a table of six about the merits of the house special ('Wonderful choice, Sir. The crab will indeed compliment the Te Mata Estate Chardonnay.').

'Alan, excuse me, I need you to speak to Mr Nugent in room eighteen.'

My manager rolled his eyes. He held up a finger and said to the party, 'My apologies, this our kitchen-hand. It's his first day front-of-house.'

I waved at the diners. 'My speciality is the cutlery.'

Alan glared, daring me to say something else equally hare-brained. The supercilious wanker was clearly embarrassed, so I gave myself a mental pat on the back.

'What is it?' Alan said, exasperated.

'Mr Nugent needs a twin bed. He's in room eighteen. He said you should have sorted it.'

'I'm busy. You sort it.' He then he shooed me away - he actually hissed the word 'shoo' - as would a homeowner to a stray cat. The last thing I heard before departing the dining hall was Alan bleating, 'I apologise again. He belongs in the kitchen. As I was saying, your choice of Chardonnay is exceptional. You must really know your wines... '

'Hello, pot-washer... ?' Mr Nugent wasn't going away.

'Mr Nugent, sorry for keeping you waiting. The manager was busy. I'm available to help though.'

'How can *you* help? Get me the fucking manager *now*! Don't make me come down there!'

'You're the boss, Mr Nugent.' I put the phone down on a table, turned up the volume, and walked away. I kept walking. Mr Nugent's voice was audible from ten yards: 'You there, pot washer, I want a bloody twin room... '

It was the last straw. I stomped into the kitchen. Alan had made an appearance, pausing only to check his hair.

'Where do think you're going, eh?'

'I don't *think* I'm going anywhere,' I said. 'I *know* I'm going out of this shit-hole.'

I passed Hinton - 'Nice icing, pal' - and patted Georgina on the back - 'See ya later, Georgie.' I dumped my tie in a bin outside.

My hotel career had ended.

By early September I was due to leave Queenstown. It was a shame Crispin and G hadn't made it down south. They'd e-mailed saying they had work commitments and couldn't get time off. Understandable, for sure, but I had to chuckle. Both my boys had regular jobs, earned more money and had a share of the Toyota, and yet I had seen more of New Zealand than both of them combined. I'd lived as a rich man in a beggar's world, and I was a better person for it.

Chapter scorecard: Life down south is coming to an end, but it has been a life-changing experience for the boy Varley. Even Cook's discoveries were probably not life-changing - for he had made many others - although by late 1776 he had raised the anchor for his third and final trip to New Zealand. Varley, however, takes a point for youthful accomplishment.

VARLEY 8   COOK 7

Chapter 27

I'm not keen on goodbyes. I find them unsettling. I'd offer an elderly relative a handshake and a simple 'see you later' upon hearing of their departure to a nursing home rather than risk crying in public or saying the wrong thing.

I'd intended to bid a customary farewell to everyone at the Lodge, knocking on doors and embracing each and every one of my friends in tear-inducing bear hugs, wishing them heartfelt regards in their long-term goals and aspirations. But after a moment's hesitation - and, I suspect, good sense - I decided it was too early for such sentiment. So it was with sadness and a twinge of guilt that I left $NZ 100 rent for Taff in an envelope, and then slunk from the Lodge into the crisp South Island air.

I smoked a Lucky with a heavy heart on the small gravelled car park. Across the road the thick-forested Bob's Peak towered above this famous town. High to my left, the now seemingly ubiquitous cotton wool cloud hovered tangibly ahead of The Remarkables.

Chris and Lina had woken early to see me off to the airport, red-eyed and puffy from the night before. I'd told them of my plans, but as they'd gone to bed only four hours ago, I hadn't expected their impromptu leaving party.

'Let's hitchhike!' squealed an over-zealous Lina.

'It's only fifteen minutes by bus.'

'Come on,' she said, tugging my arm. 'It'll be fun!'

Chris and Lina jumped out in front of the first car, demanding the startled driver perform an emergency stop.

'This man has a flight to catch!' yelled Chris.

'And step on it!'

The poor driver, too alarmed to argue, put foot to pedal and in no time we were whizzing past the magical Lake Wakatipu and out of Queenstown.

'And this thing is still standing after they let you work on it?' said Chris at the airport.

'Leave him alone,' snapped Lina, sensitive to the playful criticism. 'Joe's worked really hard, haven't you, darling?'

And it was precisely then that I appreciated what I'd achieved. Travelling the length of this terrific country without the guarantee of a regular job and with the funds of a pauper *was* quite an achievement. Looking back to the ridiculously early hours, the back-breaking work, the verbal tussles with tuna-breath Gary, the splinters, the glass fibre, the washing-up, the bin liners... all of it made sense. I *had* worked hard. I'd made it. And then I realised - perhaps for the first time in my life - that I was overcome with a feeling I'd never felt before: pride.

I thanked our driver ('No worries, mate.') and turned to my two friends.

Lina gave me a peck on the cheek. The fresh air had sobered her up. 'We'll definitely catch up back in the UK, darling.'

I returned her kiss. 'We definitely will, Linny. And Chrissie? You promise me you'll behave yourself.'

'I promise,' he said, his crossed fingers poking out from behind his back. 'See you back in the UK, too, Joey.'

The flight from Queenstown to Auckland took a couple of hours. The South Island experience had been exhilarating, taking in deep gorges and raging rivers and all the things described in travel guides. And on that minibus ride down to the heart of Otago, the sense of the unknown had never been more genuine. Rarely had I been so consumed by nervous excitement, travelling down south with nothing more to my name than a few dollars and a couple of work leads. Now, a few thousand feet in the air, I was retracing my journey in a cramped seat next to a Chinese woman with acne. And I couldn't even get a drink.

'Ahhh... you taking up too much room.' My new Chinese friend poked me in the ribs. 'Elbows! In!'

The plane dipped, and a pleasant calm restored my

belief that for the next hour I wouldn't clout my fellow passenger around the ears. The small window allowed prefect views of the land I was leaving behind. It was astonishing. The terrain was dense orange marble. Rivers meandered sloppily among white-tipped peaks. Precipitous valleys viciously cut through The Remarkables.

'You! Elbows in! Ahhh, you so rude!'

I wasn't listening. My mind was elsewhere - back in Queenstown; then to when I first saw Crispin at our Auckland flat; when we spent the day at Goat Island; our trip to the wonderful Coromandel beaches; and then to Jess... all these swirled in my head like a cerebral eddy. The old Chinese crone could've scored my temple with a screwdriver and I wouldn't have noticed.

A warm breeze hit me as it had done nearly 12 months previously. There was no Tamati, but the sight of a clapped-out taxi took me back to my first day in the City of Sails, and to the uncertainty of my working holiday. I asked the driver to take me home. *Home* - I hadn't used that word for months.

Auckland was heating up. The lazy sun lingered regally in intense skies; birds swooped amongst luscious pohutukawa trees; brown-skinned kids played cricket in open parks. Queenstown, for sure, felt like a different country. So when the Sky Tower emerged into view, it occurred to me the magnitude of variation New Zealand had to offer. Two hours ago I was leaving behind a tiny alpine town that was as famous as any town of its size in the world; now I imagined what Queenstown would look like if this huge concrete structure was ripped up and placed next to the gondolas or the mountains or Lake Wakatipu.

For the next few days I did as I pleased - mainly doing as little as possible and drinking cold lager. Crispin and G were still working at NIWA, but were both scheduled to conduct some research up the coast near Ninety Mile Beach, so they could only fit me in for one last evening before heading north.

Both the boys were a little shell-shocked. The year had nearly come to an end. My boys had both extended their visas, keen for another Auckland summer. I was heading back for the dismal British winter, and an uncertain future.

'So when exactly are you leaving, baby?' Crispin asked. His voice quivered.

'Tuesday, pal, two o'clock. Jesus, it's gone way too quickly.'

Crispin nodded thoughtfully. 'I know. Shame you can't stay longer...hey, I've got an idea. If I can get you another job, and if G-Man lends you some money - '

I cut off Crispin with a raised hand, although I didn't have anything to say. I knew they both wanted me to stay, but my visa had expired and I had some debts to pay back in the UK. I'd had a good innings, and I couldn't complain.

'So after tomorrow I guess we'll see you back in the UK in a few months,' Crispin conceded. He embraced me.

'We had a good time, didn't we?'

'The best.'

G followed his lead, hugging me, and as I caught a tang of sea-salt in his hair, for a moment I couldn't breathe.

'Easy, tiger. You're giving me a hard-on.'

'Tosser.'

Crispin handed out cold beer. 'So G and I are packed for tomorrow's trip up north,' he said, suddenly in happier mood. 'Tonight we can go anywhere you want, baby. The city is all yours. Any requests?'

I took a long pull on my beer. 'It's funny you mention that. I've wanted to go somewhere for ages, but we never got round to it.'

The boys smiled knowingly.

'Better get on the blower, G-Man. We need a taxi in thirty minutes.'

'Mermaids?'

'How did you guess?'

The waitress brought our Heinekens on a silver tray. She

had a shapely figure and luscious brown hair - twisted into plaits - and minimal make-up. White stilettos hugged delicate ankles. Soft, rose-tinted lights drew attention to her glowing eyes, which were jade green set behind brown skin. Her breasts - impeccable in every way - drew more attention to the hoards of lubricious customers drooling into their beers.

'Even the waitresses are topless,' whispered Crispin.

'Yes, I can see that.'

The atmosphere in Mermaids was that of a good-time shindig rather than that of a seedy strip joint. Sure, a lot of the clientele appeared insatiable in their cravings for naked flesh - Crispin and G included - but there were no crude gestures aimed towards the pole dancers or alcohol-fuelled oafs invading their stage space.

'There you go, boys. Give me a shout when you're ready for another round.' The waitress winked, then tottered off to serve champagne to a group of sunburnt businessmen.

I drank deeply. 'She's a cheeky one, all right.'

'Yeah,' said Crispin. 'Reckon she's been cocked more times than Elmer Fudd's shotgun, too.'

G giggled. 'Wow, this is awesome. And look at the girls over there! Are they...swimming? Christ!'

Situated near the back wall was a purposely built aquarium, approximately 5 x 2 metres, near full with clear, rippling water. Two naked girls spun and glided like eels, pirouetting gracefully through the water while being ogled at by both customers and staff. A pole dancer - a leggy blonde with blue ribbons in her hair - walked to the aquarium and watched, transfixed, as her colleagues displayed their sumptuous attributes.

'I've never seen anything like this. This alone is worth the air fare.' Whilst G's comment was undoubtedly a hyperbole, he made a fair point. I wouldn't have missed this - the last night out with my boys - for anything. And the addition of naked girls swimming in an over-sized fish tank made it all the more memorable.

A mermaid stopped her routine and swam to her colleague, then pulled herself up and onto the top step. She calmly walked down and was met by euphoric applause. Her friend wrapped a large white towel around her dripping torso. The second mermaid followed suit, and as a grand finale both girls whipped off their towels to reveal glistening bodies to a deafening ovation.

'That,' gasped Crispin, 'was pure class. Another beer?'

During the last few days my thoughts, inevitably, turned to Jess. I'd been in touch with her by e-mail once since my arrival and was eager to see her properly. In fact, Crispin had left me his mobile so she could ring me. The problem was, Crispin had used G's mobile to ring up shortly after they'd set off and explained that he'd forgotten to tell all this to Jess, and as I didn't have her number, his generosity proved more or less worthless. All this meant I had to e-mail Jess again and hoped she responded in time, which I hated. I wanted to *know* I'd see her again.

But after two unproductive days (during which I got drunk twice and chain-smoked and felt pretty dreadful), it occurred to me Jess may have returned to Christchurch. She didn't know I was leaving so soon and she had no reason to phone me on Crispin's mobile, but still... why hadn't she at least come round to the flat? With the boys away up north and Chris back in Queenstown, not being able to contact Jess was agony.

Chapter scorecard: Feelings of a year's accomplishment are tainted by feelings of the heart, and Varley penalizes himself for failing to properly keep in touch with his paramour. It's likely that Cook also suffered from missed romantic opportunities, but they didn't have mobile phones then, so he had a better excuse. Also, in 1777, Cook was living it up in Tonga and Tahiti, thus claiming a point to level the score.

VARLEY 8   COOK 8

Chapter 28

I returned to Kings Plant Barn to see the staff. It hadn't changed. The place was as mad as ever, what with all the discounts and the early opening hours and the crazy landscape gardeners careering around the place carrying wooden stakes and trying to find sheep pellets or bags of blood-and-bone or whatever was now in fashion.

James clocked me first, as eagle-eyed as ever. He skipped over the tarmac to say hello, his legs moving faster than his frail body could keep up with.

'Joe! Guess what? Baxter's a dad! He's got... let's see... six puppies! No, wait... *seven* puppies!'

'Wow, James, that's great! Are you still giving him two tins of food every morning?'

'No, he's up to three now! He needs to keep his strength up, ay.' And with that, he chased after a leggy redhead struggling with a bag of potting mix.

Sonya and Julie were working on the tills, and I blagged a free ice lolly from them.

'Don't tell the boss,' Julie winked. 'Speaking of which, Alexander's in the office. I think he's been trying to call you on his brother's phone or something. Says it's urgent.'

Alexander was writing up some paperwork. His tanned legs perched high up on his desk, and a pencil twirled between his fingers. It was reminiscent of my first day at Kings, only this time I didn't have 50 weeks of work to look forward to.

'Hello Joe, how's it going?'

I was slightly taken aback by Alexander's concern - not that he was a complete bastard or anything, just because I'd learned that as a boss, Alexander was generally a bit of a sod in his working environment.

'Anyway, glad you called in,' he said cheerfully, not waiting for my answer. 'I've got a message for you.'

'Go on.'

'Yes, a girl rang here and asked for your number. Said it was important.'

'Really?'

'Uh-huh. Crispin told me he'd left you his phone, so I suggested she call you on that.'

'But no one's called me for about three days,' I bleated.

'Couldn't have been that urgent, then.'

'But what exactly did she say?' I scrambled around in my pockets for the phone, desperate to find any clues to a miss-call.

'She just mentioned she wanted to get in touch. I gave her G's number, so she might have called him.'

I found Crispin's phone in a zip-up pocket and handed

it to Alexander. 'Well I can't do anything now. I have to get going. My flight's in about four hours.'

My ex-boss examined the phone. He tapped the screen and shook it around for a while. 'Might have helped if you had the phone switched on,' he said.

In the car park a soft tap rapped my shoulder. It was Brenda. In her podgy hand was her trusty pricing gun. I was glad to see her.

'I was working on the frangipanis round the back,' she said, 'and thought I saw you. Remember the frangipanis?' She laughed a little, as did I. 'Anyway, I guessed you'd be leaving soon and just wanted to catch you before you left.'

'Well I'm pleased you did, Brenda. Listen, I want to say that whatever you thought of me, I really didn't mean to - '

She glared at me, but a second later her frown broke into a smile. 'Thanks for all your hard work, Joe,' she said, and planted a *Special Offer* sticker on my forehead. 'I'll miss you. We all will.'

Auckland Airport wasn't spectacularly busy. I thought about Jess. I filed her under 'another missed opportunity' and vowed to get on with the rest of my life once home.

I walked towards the airport doors. It was the last few minutes of sunshine I'd treasure for maybe another seven months. In about 26 hours I'd be touching down in cold, damp, miserable Manchester - and no doubt working in a cold, damp, miserable office somewhere in Yorkshire. I now knew what it was to be an Innocent Abroad. I knew what I'd achieved was something to be savoured, cherished and to be appreciated. I regretted nothing.

As if to signal my final steps on NZ soil, I recreated what I thought the great Captain Cook would have done to cap off his adventures. I dropped my bag, spun round, and waved an earnest goodbye to the country I had well and truly fallen for. It didn't feel wrong waving to no one in particular. I was waving goodbye to everything I'd loved during my stay in this fabulous country.

'In a hurry?' said Jess. 'I've been here since early morning.'

My eyes widened in a freakishly cartoon way. 'Jesus! What are you doing here?'

'You idiot,' Jess laughed. 'Did you really think I'd let you leave without saying goodbye?'

'I... '

'I rang Crispin,' she explained, 'but his phone is always switched off, so I called G and he told me what time your flight was. I know you don't like technology, but not being able to turn on a phone?'

She giggled again. She wore beige knee length shorts and ankle socks over white trainers. Her wavy brown hair was pristine. A tight, pink vest completed the look, and completed her.

'So this is it,' she said, wrapping a warm arm around my neck.

I returned her embrace. 'I guess so.'

'Listen, babe, I've been thinking. You could extend your visa and get a job working in - '

But her voice trailed off as she realised this would never happen.

'Here,' she said, reaching into her bag. 'I want you to take this.'

I looked at the small white envelope, tearing the flap. Immediately Jess took my hand.

'Joe, please, no. I don't want you to read it now. Read it when I've gone.'

So as I slipped the envelope into my pocket Jess stepped back and we shared a soft kiss. She stepped away. She smiled and kissed me again. When Jess stepped back for the second time, her smile gave the game away. We both know she was about to leave for good.

I watched her float past a small clump of nikau palms. She disappeared behind a coach packed with tourists. And then, a painful minute later, Jess was out of view, and out of my life.

My angel had flown.

Inside the envelope was a small photo of Jess. She was

sitting cross-legged on a wide-open beach - Piha by the look of it - her hair flowing in the wind as the treacherous surf crashed behind her. It was cheesy as fuck, of course, but somehow I wouldn't have had it any other way.

On the back was a short message.

Dear Joe,
Have a safe trip.
I know you'll be back.
I love you,
Jess xxxxxxxxx

And Jess was right, as I knew she would be. I would be back, if only because, looking back, all the mistakes I'd made couldn't cancel the wild times and great memories that would stay with me forever, or the friends I'd made and all the terrific places I'd been to.

And when I return, which was something I'd already promised myself, maybe - just maybe - I'd have a go at zorbing. I bet Captain Cook never tried it.

Chapter scorecard: Varley leaves it in the trusted hands of Captain James Cook. The Captain's voice comes clearly to him across the long paths and endless ages of adventure they have both trodden in their own ways and own times.

'A closely fought battle,' declares the Captain, saluting.

'My respect and commendation in the form of the final point to my young protégé.'

Varley lights a cigarette and nods in mutual admiration. For perhaps it is fitting that the final spoils go to the underdog. The Captain senses that next time, with a bit more experience, the boy Varley will find the competition a little easier as a man.

FINAL SCORE:
DOGSBODY 9
COOK 8

The end